ro
ro
ro

rororo sprachen

Herausgegeben von Ludwig Moos

Master your Business Phrases ist ein umfassendes Kompendium für die Welt der Geschäfte. Sie finden darin die unentbehrlichen Redemittel und typischen Redewendungen zum treffsicheren Gebrauch nach Themen und Situationen des Geschäftsalltags geordnet. Dazu die passenden *jokes* und Übungen. Da unser Gedächtnis ein kurzes Satzmodul genauso behandelt wie ein isoliertes Wort, lohnt die Arbeit mit diesem *phrase book*. Das Behalten wird überdies durch die Verwendung im Kontext erleichtert. So können Sie sich zielsicher auf den Geschäftsverkehr mit Ihren ausländischen Partnern vorbereiten und erwerben ein Gespür für das rechte Wort zu rechten Zeit.

Dr. René Bosewitz ist Native Speaker und bereitet in einer deutschen Zweigstelle der London Chamber of Commerce Firmenangehörige auf einschlägige sprachliche Prüfungen vor. Er trainiert zudem seit vielen Jahren Manager aus Banken und Industrie in Business English. Mit Robert Kleinschroth hat er bei rororo sprachen *Joke Your Way Through English Grammar* (18527) und *Joke by Joke to Conversation* (18795) veröffentlicht.

Robert Kleinschroth unterrichtet Englisch am Gymnasium und an der Universität Heidelberg. Er hat zwanzig Jahre Praxis in der Erwachsenenbildung und leitete fünfzehn Jahre lang die Sprachabteilung eines Großunternehmens. Robert Kleinschroth hat zusammen mit Dieter Maupai *La Grammaire en s'amusant* (18714) verfaßt und außerdem *La Conversation en s'amusant* (18873), *Business by Jokes* (60721) sowie *Sprachen lernen* (19140) und *Neues Lernen mit dem Computer* (19841) geschrieben.

In der Reihe Business English sind von beiden Autoren außerdem erschienen: *Manage in English* (60137), *Better than the Boss* (60138), *How to Phone Effectively* (60139), *Drop Them a Line* (60261, mit Bryan Hemming), *Get Through at Meetings* (60262), *Check Your Language Level* (60268), *Business English from A to Z* (60269, mit Bryan Hemming), *The Way Things Work* (60369), *Small Talk for Big Business* (60439), *Get to Grips with Company English* (60845), *Spice up Your Speeches* (60804), *Better Your Business English* (60846), *Making Money on the Web* (60368), *How to Communicate Effectively* (61146) und *Idioms at Work* (61333).

RENÉ BOSEWITZ / ROBERT KLEINSCHROTH

MASTER YOUR BUSINESS PHRASES

SPRACHMODULE FÜR DEN GESCHÄFTSALLTAG

Rowohlt Taschenbuch Verlag

4. Auflage April 2002

Originalausgabe
Veröffentlicht im Rowohlt Taschenbuch Verlag
GmbH, Reinbek bei Hamburg, Juni 1999

Umschlaggestaltung Barbara Hanke
Grafik Zarina Sheriff
(Illustration Cathrin Günther)
Layout Anne Drude und Alexander Urban
Satz OCRA und Stone PostScript, QuarkXPress 3.32
Druck und Bindung Clausen & Bosse, Leck
Printed in Germany
ISBN 3 499 60725 5

Inhalt - Contents

Wegweiser 6

Vorwort 13

PART ONE:
Geschäftsleute unterwegs 15
Business people on the move

PART TWO:
Effektiv telefonieren 127
Telephoning effectively

PART THREE:
Perfekt präsentieren 165
Perfect presentations

PART FOUR:
Erfolgreich verkaufen 192
Selling successfully

PART FIVE:
Professionell verhandeln 233
Negotiating professionally

PART SIX:
Besprechungen meistern 248
Master your meetings

PART SEVEN:
Gekonnt diskutieren 274
Discussing the clever way

Anhang
Anregungen für Kursleiter 308
Schlüssel zu den Übungen 312

PART 1: Geschäftsleute unterwegs – Business people on the move 15

1. **Die Geschäftsreise vorbereiten – Preparing the business trip** 16
   Im Reisebüro – At the travel agency 16
   Den Flug buchen – Booking the flight 16
   Auf Nummer sicher gehen – Make sure you've got it right 17
   Reisepläne ändern – Changing the itinerary 18
   Ein Zimmer reservieren – Booking a room 19
   Einen Termin vereinbaren – Making an appointment 20
   Tag und Stunde – Day and hour 20
   Treffpunkt vereinbaren – Arranging the meeting point 21
   Termine verschieben – Rearranging appointments 22

2. **Unterwegs – On the way** 26
   Am Bahnhof – At the station 27
   Mit dem Flugzeug reisen – Going by air 29
   Einchecken – Checking in 29
   Durchsagen verstehen – Understanding announcements 31
   Bei der Sicherheitskontrolle – At security control 32
   An Bord des Flugzeugs – On board the plane 32
   Eine Seereise machen – Going on a voyage 35

3. **Ankunft im Ausland – Arrival in a foreign country** 38
   Ein fremdes Land betreten – Entering a foreign country 39
   Bei der Paßkontrolle – At the passport control 39
   Am Zoll – At the customs 40
   Erste-Hilfe-Kasten – Survival kit 40
   Mit dem Auto unterwegs – Going by car 43
   Einen Wagen mieten – Renting a car 43
   Unterwegs im Auto – On the road 45
   An der Tankstelle – At the petrol station 45
   Ärger mit dem Auto – Trouble with the car 47
   Für den Fall eines Unfalls – In case of an accident 48
   Im Hotel – At the hotel 50
   An der Rezeption – At the reception desk 50
   Hotelservice – Hotel services 52
   Wie man sich beschwert – How to complain 53
   Das Hotel verlassen – Checking out 54

4. **Allerlei Geschäfte – All sorts of odd jobs to do** 57
   In der Bank – At the bank 58
   Geld wechseln – Changing money 58
   Zahlungsverkehr – Money transfer 59
   Anlagen und Kredite – Investment and loans 61
   Probleme mit der Bank – Trouble with the bank 62

Auf der Post – At the post office 65
Briefe und Geld – Letters and money 65
Hinweise in Telefonzellen – Instructions in public phone boxes 67
Öffentliche Telefone – Public telephones 67
Einkaufen – Buying things 71
Die ersten Wortwechsel – First words 71
Die kleinen Dinge – Bits and pieces 71
Kleider kaufen – Buying clothes 72
An der Kasse – At the check out 73
Leben nach der Arbeit – Life after work 76
Die Stadt kennenlernen – Getting to know the town 76
Kulturelle Veranstaltungen – Cultural events 77
Andere Ereignisse – Other events 78
Menschen begegnen – Meeting people 80
Gesprächsanbahnung mit Fremden
– Starting a conversation with strangers 80
Sich vorstellen – Introducing oneself 80
Über den Beruf sprechen – Talking about one's job 81
Auf einem Kongreß – At a congress 82

5. **Messen und Firmen besuchen – Visiting fairs and companies** 85
Auf der Handelsmesse – At the trade fair 86
Informieren Sie sich – Get the right information 86
Ausstellungsfläche mieten – Renting exhibition space 87
Die Messeunterlagen – Trade fair documentation 89
Den Messestand aufstellen – Setting up the stand 89
Gespräche am Messestand – Conversations at the booth 90
In Verbindung bleiben – Keep in touch 92
Besuch bei Geschäftspartnern – Visiting business partners 95
Beim Empfang – At the reception 95
Pech gehabt – Bad luck 95
Glück gehabt – Good luck 96
Besucher in Empfang nehmen – Receiving visitors 97
Eisbrecher – Ice breakers 97
Die Firma vorstellen – Introducing the company 99
Zur Sache kommen – Getting down to brass tacks 100
Kollegen vorstellen – Introducing colleagues 101
Ein Firmenrundgang – A tour of the company 102
Geschäftsfreunde treffen – Meeting business partners 102
Gastfreundschaft – Hospitality 105
Seien Sie mein Gast – Be my guest 105
Fühlen Sie sich wie zu Hause – Make yourself at home 107
Gesprächsanbahnung – Conversation openers 109

Trinksprüche ausbringen – Suggesting toasts 110
Höflichkeiten austauschen – Making polite noises 111
Erinnerungen aufwärmen – Unlocking memories 112
Sich verabschieden – Taking one's leave 114
Sich bedanken – Saying thank you 115
Essen gehen – Dining out 117
Geschäftsfreunde einladen – Inviting business partners 117
Einen Tisch reservieren – Booking a table 118
Empfehlen und vorschlagen – Recommending and suggesting 118
Gespräch mit dem Ober – Talking to the waiter 119
Sich beschweren – Making a complaint 121
Die Rechnung, bitte – The bill, please 122

PART 2: Effektiv telefonieren – Telephoning effectively 127

1. Anrufe entgegennehmen – Answering the phone 128
2. Sagen Sie, wer Sie sind – Tell them who you are 128
Etiquette on the phone: First and last words 129
3. Den Anrufer identitifizieren – Identifying the caller 130
4. Wen wünschen Sie zu sprechen? – Who do you want to speak to? 132
5. Fragen, um was es geht – Asking what it's about 133
6. Der Grund des Anrufs – The reason for the call 134
7. Den Anrufer verbinden – Putting the caller through 135
Etiquette on the phone: Ten commandments 137
8. Wartezeiten überbrücken – Getting through the waiting periods 138
9. Ungeduldig werden – Getting impatient 139
10. Ein Gespräch annehmen – Taking a call 140
11. Keine Verbindung – No connection 141
12. Eine Nachricht hinterlassen – Leaving a message 142
Etiquette on the phone: 'Can you spell your name?' 143
13. Nachrichten entgegennehmen – Taking messages 144
14. Mißverständnisse ausschließen – Eliminating misunderstandings 145
15. Um einen Rückruf bitten – Asking to be called back 147
16. Den Rückruf vereinbaren – Arranging the return call 147
17. Jemanden zurückrufen – Calling someone back 148
18. Sich für einen Rückruf bedanken – Thank someone for calling back 149
19. Falsch verbunden – Wrong number 150
20. Höfliches am Telefon – Polite noises on the phone 151
21. Die Leitung ist schlecht – The line is bad 152
22. Verständigungsschwierigkeiten – Communication problems 153
23. Unter Zeitdruck stehen – To be under time pressure 154
24. Das Telefongespräch beenden – Ending the call 155
Strategies for secretaries: Screening off the boss 157
25. Den Chef abschirmen – Screening off the boss 159

26. Anrufbeantworter – Answering machines 161
27. Piepsen und Faxen – Beeping and faxing 162
28. Nummern buchstabieren – Spelling numbers 163
29. The British Telephone Alphabet 163

PART 3: Perfekt präsentieren – Perfect presentations 165

1. Den Redner vorstellen – Introducing the presenter 166
2. Stellen Sie sich vor – Introduce yourself 166
3. Freundliches Klima schaffen – Creating a friendly atmosphere 167
   Advice to presenters: Overcoming nervousness 168
4. Das Thema ankündigen – Announcing the subject 169
5. Tischvorlagen ansprechen – Referring to hand-outs 170
6. Einen Überblick geben – Giving an overview 170
7. Strukturieren Sie Ihre Präsentation – Structure your presentation 171
8. Den nächsten Schritt ankündigen – Announcing the next step 172
9. Zum Mitdenken aktivieren – Motivating them to think along with you 174
   Advice to presenters: Overcoming disasters 175
10. Gründe und Lösungen anbieten – Offering reasons and solutions 176
11. Alternativen aufzeigen – Showing alternatives 177
12. Beispiele anführen – Introducing examples 177
13. Anschauungsmaterial einsetzen – Using visual material 178
14. Um Fragen und Kommentare bitten – Inviting questions and comments 179
15. Um Wiederholung bitten – Asking for repetition 180
16. Um Zusatzinformationen bitten – Asking for additional information 181
   Advice to presenters: The OHP and the seven deadly sins 181
17. Fragen stellen – Asking questions 183
18. Wie Sie Einwände behandeln – How to deal with objections 183
   Advice to presenters: The presenter as an entertainer 185
19. So gewinnen Sie Zeit – How to play for time 186
20. Einer Frage ausweichen – Avoiding a question 187
21. Das Ende ankündigen – Announcing the end 187
22. Zusammenfassen – Summarising 188
   Advice to presenters: Use spoken English instead of written English 189
23. Sich verabschieden – Saying good-bye 190

PART 4: Erfolgreich verkaufen – Selling successfully 192

1. Am Telefon – On the phone 193
   Telefonische Anfragen – Queries over the phone 193
   Sales tactics: Getting through to the Purchasing Manager 194
   Sich an der Sekretärin vorbeimogeln – Getting round the secretary 196
   Sales tactics: How to get round the secretary 197
2. Kundenfang – Canvassing 199

Stellen Sie sich erneut vor – Reintroduce yourself 199
Verweisen Sie auf Ihre Broschüren – Refer to your brochures 200
Vereinbaren Sie einen Termin – Make an appointment 200
3. Ankunft beim Kunden – Arriving at the customer 201
Austausch von Höflichkeiten – Exchanging polite noises 201
Knüpfen Sie an Vorgespräche an – Refer to preparatory talks 202
Sales tactics: Creating the sales climate 203
Sales tactics: What selling is all about 205
4. Auf den Kundentyp eingehen – Handling various customer types 206
Tasten Sie den Kunden ab – Sound the customer out 206
Der hektische Kunde – The hectic customer 206
Der harte, faktenbewußte Kunde – The hard, factual customer 207
Der aggressive Kunde – The aggressive customer 207
Der ausweichende Kunde – The evasive customer 208
Der voreingenommene Kunde – The prejudiced customer 208
Sales tactics: Preparing product presentations 212
5. Präsentieren Sie Ihr Produkt – Present your product 213
Beschreiben Sie die Eigenschaften – Describe the features 213
Setzen Sie Ihre Unterlagen ein – Use your documents 214
Führen Sie Ihr Produkt vor – Give a live demonstration 215
6. Kundenvorteile ansprechen – Addressing benefits 216
Kundenvorteile hervorheben – Highlighting customer benefits 216
Kundenbedürfnisse zusammenfassen – Summarising customer needs 218
7. Den Auftrag an Land ziehen – Landing the contract 220
Preisauskünfte einholen – Inquiries about prices 220
Den Auftrag geben – Placing the order 220
Lieferbedingungen absprechen – Agreeing on delivery terms 221
Sales tactics: Overcoming objections 222
8. Reklamationen – Complaints 223
Gründe für Reklamationen – Reasons for complaints 223
Wie Sie reklamieren – How to make a complaint 224
Sales tactics: Defusing the angry customer 227
9. Was Sie dem verärgerten Kunden sagen
– What to say to the angry customer 228
Zuhören und fragen – Listen and ask 228
Zeigen Sie Verständnis – Show sympathy 228
Entschuldigen Sie sich, selbst wenn Sie recht haben
– Apologise even if you are right 229
Bieten Sie Lösungen an – Offer solutions 230
Die letzten Worte – Last phrases 230
Beleidigenden Kunden begegnen – Handling rude customers 231

PART 5: Professionell verhandeln – Negotiating professionally 233

1. Ein Preisangebot machen – Offering a price 234
   Advice to negotiators: Handling price and prospect 235
2. Preise aushandeln – Negotiating prices 236
3. Zeit gewinnen – Stalling for time 238
4. Den Preis rechtfertigen – Justifying the price 239
5. Einen Kompromiß vorschlagen – Suggesting a compromise 240
6. Kompromisse an Bedingungen knüpfen – Linking compromises to conditions 241
7. Zustimmung erbitten – Asking for consent 243
8. Dem Kompromiß zustimmen – Agreeing to the compromise 243
9. Kompromisse ablehnen – Rejecting compromises 244
10. Das Geschäft abschließen – Closing the deal 245

PART 6: Besprechungen meistern – Master your meetings 248

1. Die Eröffnung – The opening 249
   Meetings in Spain 250
2. Die Tagesordnung – The agenda 251
3. Ein angenehmes Klima schaffen – Creating a pleasant atmosphere 252
   Meetings in Britain 253
4. Das Protokoll – The minutes 255
5. Den Zweck erläutern – Explaining the purpose 255
6. Einige typische Anlässe – Some typical occasions 256
   Meetings in America 258
7. Tagesordnungspunkte – Items on the agenda 259
8. Gäste vorstellen – Introducing guests 260
   Meetings in Japan 261
9. Meinungen sammeln – Collecting opinions 262
10. Fragen weitergeben – Passing on questions 264
11. Disziplin halten – Maintaining discipline 264
12. Die Diskussion lenken – Conducting the discussion 265
13. Probleme vertagen – Putting off problems 266
14. Ergebnisse zusammenfassen – Summarising results 268
15. Sonstiges – Any other business 268
16. Eine Entscheidung blockieren – Blocking a decision 269
17. Abstimmen lassen – Putting it to the vote 270
18. Einigkeit betonen – Emphasising agreement 271
19. Die Sitzung beenden – Closing the meeting 271

PART 7: Gekonnt diskutieren – Discussing the clever way 274

1. Zu Worte kommen – Catching the chairman's eye 275
2. Das Wort ergreifen – Taking the floor 276

3. Seine Meinung sagen – Giving your opinion 277
Sagen, was man denkt – Saying what you think 277
Vorsichtige Meinungsäußerung – Giving your opinion carefully 277
Gewißheit ausdrücken – Expressing certitude 278
4. Argumentieren – Argumentation 280
Argumente einführen – Introducing arguments 280
Argumente stützen – Supporting arguments 281
Argumente abwägen – Balancing arguments 282
Verallgemeinern – Generalising 282
Das Thema wechseln – Changing the subject 283
Den Beitrag abschließen – Concluding the contribution 283
5. Vorschläge machen – Making suggestions 285
Vorschläge einleiten – Introducing proposals 285
Vorschlagen wie die Briten – Suggesting the British way 285
Vorschläge mit Nachdruck versehen – Emphasising proposals 286
6. Klarstellungen – Clarifying 288
Überprüfen, ob man richtig verstanden hat
– Checking understanding 288
Mißverständnisse aufzeigen – Pointing to misunderstandings 289
Unklarheiten beseitigen – Clarifying a point 289
7. Zustimmung – Agreement 292
Einverständnis ausdrücken – Expressing agreement 292
Volle Übereinstimmung – Complete agreement 292
Bedingte Zustimmung – Qualified support 293
8. Ablehnung – Disagreement 294
Ablehnung signalisieren – Signalling rejection 294
Zweifel anmelden – Raising doubt 295
Höfliche Ablehnung – Polite rejection 296
Neutrale Ablehnung – Neutral rejection 297
Entschiedener Widerspruch – Blunt rejection 298
Ablehnung begegnen – Responding to rejection 300
Enttäuschung ausdrücken – Expressing disappointment 300
9. Den Sprecher unterbrechen – Interrupting the speaker 302
Unterbrechen, um zu widersprechen – Interrupting to contradict 302
Unterbrechen, um einen Beitrag zu machen
– Interrupting to make a contribution 302
Auf Unterbrechung reagieren – Responding to interruption 303
Unterbrechungen ablehnen – Rejecting interruptions 304
Unterbrechungen vermeiden – Avoiding interruptions 305

Master your Business Phrases ist der zur Zeit wohl vollständigste englische Sprachführer für die Welt der Geschäfte. Seine Sprachmodule helfen Ihnen in allen Standardsituationen, mit denen Sie als Frau oder Mann der Industrie und Wirtschaft immer wieder zu tun haben. *Master your Business Phrases* begleitet Sie auf der Geschäftsreise und bereitet Sie auf Besprechungen, Verhandlungen oder Verkaufsgespräche vor. Es eignet sich sowohl für den Selbstlerner als auch für den Einsatz in Kursen und Seminaren (siehe Anhang). Und es ist das ideale Begleitbuch zu den anderen Bänden der Serie *Business English*.

Sprachtraining für Selbstlerner
Master your Business Phrases ist mehr als ein Nachschlagewerk. Wir haben Wert auf zahlreiche Übungen zu jedem Kapitel gelegt. Sie werden sehen, daß die *tasks* kurz, einprägsam und abwechslungsreich sind. Den Abschluß jeder Übungsreihe bildet *crossword power*, unser Kreuzworträtsel. Wenn Sie sich einen Lernpartner suchen, können Sie mit *Master your Business Phrases* wie in einem Sprachkurs arbeiten (siehe Anhang). Wenn *Master your Business Phrases* auf Ihrem Schreibtisch liegt oder in Ihrer Aktentasche steckt, können Sie sich anhand des Wegweisers schnell auf eine bevorstehende Situation einstellen.

Einsatz in Seminaren und Kursen
Kursleiter finden hier eine Fülle von Material und ein umfangreiches Repertoire an Übungen. Im Anhang geben wir Anregungen, wie Sie Kursteilnehmer selbsttätig, kreativ und praxisnah auf den Geschäftsalltag vorbereiten.

Anordnung nach Geschäftssituationen
Die *phrases* oder Redemittel der sieben Teile des Buches sind nach Situationen übersichtlich in kleine Einzelschritte angeordnet, in der chronologischen und sachlogischen Reihenfolge, in der sie voraussichtlich benötigt werden. Deshalb lesen sich die Beispielsätze, in denen sie verwendet werden, vielfach wie kleine Dialoge.

Strategie und Taktik
Nehmen Sie zum Beispiel Teil 4: 'Erfolgreich verkaufen'. Wenn Sie die Spalten überfliegen, erkennen Sie, daß Anordnung und Wortlaut auf Verkaufsstrategie und Verkaufstaktik beruhen. Auch bei den Kapiteln

über Telefonieren, Diskutieren, Verhandeln oder *small talk* mit dem Geschäftsfreund erwerben Sie das rechte Wort zur rechten Zeit sowie das taktische und psychologische Fingerspitzengefühl für die jeweilige Geschäftssituation.

Psychologie
Sie werden sich manchmal über unsere Wortwahl wundern. Sie hat etwas mit Psychologie zu tun. Um bei unserem Beispiel 'Erfolgreich verkaufen' zu bleiben: Warum sagt der versierte *sales rep* nicht: *How much money would you like to spend?*, sondern *How much would you like to invest?* oder statt *Wouldn't you like to buy a more powerful computer?* eher *Wouldn't you like to own a more powerful computer? Spend money* und *buy* erinnert den Kunden eben daran, daß man an seinen Geldbeutel will. Wer aber würde nicht gerne *besitzen* oder *investieren*?

Humor
Witz und Humor kommen in der Serie *Business English* nie zu kurz. Über hundert *jokes*, die auf das jeweilige Thema abgestimmt sind, laden Sie ein, in diesem Buch zu blättern und dabei jedesmal ein paar *phrases* mitzunehmen.

Die Serie Business English
Wollen Sie die Situationen in *Master your Business Phrases* vertiefen, nehmen Sie den entsprechenden Titel unserer Serie *Business English*. Dort informieren wir Sie gründlich und locker über Strategie, Taktik, Psychologie und Sprache der jeweiligen Bereiche des Wirtschaftslebens: über das Verkaufen in *Sell like Hell*, über das Telefonieren in *How to Phone Effectively*, über die Pflege von Kundenkontakten in *Small Talk for Big Business*, über Verhandeln und Präsentieren in *Get Through at Meetings*, über interkulturelle Unterschiede in *Going International*, über Rhetorik in *Spice up Your Speeches* (erscheint im Januar 2000). Schauen Sie doch mal bei uns rein!

GESCHÄFTSLEUTE UNTERWEGS

BUSINESS PEOPLE ON THE MOVE

Well that's it! You wanted to spend a quiet weekend with the family. No chance! The boss says you've got to go to New Ulm, Minnessota, for a meeting with the General Manager of the American subsidiary. No time to prepare. What do you do? Book flights, check connections, make a schedule. Thank God for the secretary! Better ask her to pack the suitcase. Your wife won't help you now that you've let her down.

1. *Die Geschäftsreise vorbereiten*
Preparing the business trip

Im Reisebüro
At the travel agency

Den Flug buchen – Booking the flight

Ich habe vor, nächste Woche nach Bangkok zu fliegen.	I'm planning to fly to Bangkok next month.
Und wie lange möchten Sie bleiben?	And how long would you like to stay?
Was kostet der Flug zur Zeit?	What's the price of the flight at the moment?
Ich möchte gerne einen Flug nach London buchen.	I'd like to book a flight to London.
Und wann möchten Sie fliegen?	And when is it you'd like to leave?
Erste Klasse oder Touristenklasse?	Do you want to fly first class or economy?
Und wie sieht es mit dem Rückflug aus?	And what about the return flight?
Wann ist Ihr Reisetag?	What date would you like to travel?

Don't worry, be happy!

Concorde travels at twice the speed of sound, which is fun, except that you can't hear the movie until two hours after you land.

Howie Mandel

Auf Nummer Sicher gehen – Make sure you've got it right

Wann sagten Sie, startet die Maschine der Malaysian Airlines?	When did you say that MAS 105 takes off?
MAS 105 startet um 9.40, Sie müssen also ungefähr um 7.30 einchecken.	MAS 105 leaves at 9.40, so check-in is at about half past eight.
Ist das Ortszeit?	Is that local time?
Ist es dort früher oder später als bei uns?	Are they ahead of us or behind us?
Ihr Anschlußflug ist um 14 Uhr.	The connecting flight is at 2.00 p.m.
Sie haben zwei Stunden Aufenthalt in Chicago.	You'll have a 2-hour layover in Chicago.
Bleibt mir genug Zeit, um zwischen den Flügen in den Flughafen zu gehen?	Will I have enough time to get into the airport between flights?
Ich hätte gerne eine Reiseversicherung.	I'd like some travel insurance.
Volle Deckung – das heißt Lebens-, Unfall-, Gepäckversicherung – macht £17.50.	For full cover – that's death, injury, baggage – it's £17.50.
Sollen wir ein Hotel für Sie reservieren?	Shall we make a hotel reservation for you?

Siehe auch *Unterwegs: Mit dem Flugzeug reisen*, Seite 29

(P) Master your phrases

Task 1: Complete the dialogue

You	Travel agent
I'd like .... to London.	What .... like to go?
What's .... of the flight?	.... or first class?
When .... the plane ....?	...... 9.40 a.m, sir.
I'd like some .... insurance.	Do you want full ...., sir?

Reisepläne ändern – Changing the itinerary

Tut mir leid, aber ich habe Ihren Flug nicht bekommen können. Aber Sie stehen auf der Warteliste.	I'm awfully sorry, but I couldn't get you on the flight you wanted. Your name's on the waiting list, though.
Nehmen Sie auch einen Standby-Flug, wenn ich Ihnen keine Reservierung geben kann?	Are you willing to travel stand-by if I can't get you a confirmed seat?
Entschuldigen Sie, aber wie es aussieht, muß ich meine Buchung ändern.	Sorry, it looks as if I'll have to change my booking.
Ich habe einen Flug nach London am Montag, aber ich kann nicht vor Freitag reisen.	I'm booked to London on Monday, but I can't leave before Friday.
Wie ist die Buchungsnummer?	What's your booking reference number?
Ich habe eine Reservierung für den ersten Juli. Leider muß ich sie stornieren.	I made a reservation for July 1st. I'm afraid I'll have to cancel it.
Leider muß ich meine Reservierung rückgängig machen.	I'm afraid I have to cancel my booking.
Ich habe einen Flug nach X für Montag gebucht und würde gerne am Sonntag fliegen.	I'm booked on a Monday flight to X and would like to change it to Sunday.
Eine Umbuchung ist nur gegen Zuschlag möglich.	I'm afraid it's only possible to change the booking by paying a supplement.
Ich komme eine Woche früher / später an.	I'll be arriving a week earlier / later.

Time for a smile

Come to Lapland for a honeymoon.
The nights last twenty-four hours.

Ein Zimmer reservieren – Booking a room

Ich möchte gern ein Zimmer reservieren.	I'd like to book a room, please.
Für wie lange, bitte?	How long would you like to stay?
Für eine Nacht, und zwar für den 12. Juli.	For one night, July 12.
Auf welchen Namen, bitte?	In what name, please?
Einzel- oder Doppelzimmer? Mit Bad oder Dusche?	Single or double? With bath or shower?
Haben Sie auch Nichtraucherzimmer?	Do you have no-smoking rooms?
Was kostet das für eine Nacht?	How much is that per night?
Ist das Frühstück inbegriffen?	Does that include breakfast?
Leider muß ich meine Reservierung verschieben / rückgängig machen.	I'm afraid I have to change / cancel my booking.
Würden Sie das bitte per Fax bestätigen?	Could you confirm that by fax, please?

P Master your phrases

Task 2: Preparing a flight

Find a suitable word to fill the gap.

1. I'm planning to .... to Bangkok next month.
2. Do you want to fly first class or ....?
3. What .... would you like to go?
4. I'd like some travel ....

Task 3: Making a reservation

1. I'd like to .... a room, please.
2. Single or ....?
3. With .... or shower?
4. How long would you like to ....?
5. Could you .... that by fax, please?

Einen Termin vereinbaren
Making an appointment

Time for a smile

Appointments used to be made days or even weeks in advance. Now appointments tend to be made the day after. You get a phone call from your boss or a business partner who says "If my wife asks, I was out to dinner with you last night, okay?"

Tag und Stunde – Day and hour

Ich möchte einen Termin mit Herrn / Frau ... vereinbaren.	I'd like to make an appointment with Mr / Ms ...
Könnte ich wohl einen Termin bei ... bekommen?	I was wondering if it would be possible to make an appointment with ...?
Darf ich fragen, worum es geht?	May I ask what it's about?
Wann würde es Ihnen passen?	When would it be convenient?
Wie wäre es mit Kalenderwoche 14?	How about week 14?
Wie wär's mit nächster Woche?	Shall we say next week?
Welcher Tag wäre für Sie am günstigsten?	What day would be the most convenient for you?
Welcher Tag paßt Ihnen am besten?	What day would suit you best?
Das paßt mir gut.	That suits me fine.
Sollen wir für Sie ein Zimmer reservieren?	Would you like us to arrange accommodation for you?
Wie lange werden Sie bleiben?	How long will you be staying?
Wir haben für Sie ein Zimmer im Ritz reserviert.	We've booked you into the Ritz.
Wann kommen Sie in ... an?	When will you be arriving in ...?
Ich fürchte, ich komme ziemlich spät an.	I'm afraid I'll be arriving quite late.
Haben Sie schon etwas vor?	Do you have anything planned?
Schön. Wenn Sie Zeit haben, würde ich Sie gerne zum Abendessen einladen.	Well, if you're free, I'd like to treat you to dinner.
Wie wär's mit heute abend?	Well, what about this evening?

Und um welche Uhrzeit?	And at what time of day?
Wie lange, glauben Sie, werden wir benötigen?	How long do you think we'll need?
Können wir eine Uhrzeit ausmachen?	Can we agree on a time?
Um wieviel Uhr? Sechs? Sieben?	What time? Six? Seven?
Sagen wir sieben Uhr.	Let's say seven o'clock.
Sieben Uhr, wenn Ihnen das recht ist.	Seven o'clock. If that's all right with you.
Einverstanden.	Fine with me.

Time for a smile

Manager: Do you know what the motto of our firm is?
Visitor: Of course, it's "Push".
Manager: What gave you that idea?
Visitor: I saw it on the door when I came in.

Treffpunkt vereinbaren – Arranging the meeting point

Was halten Sie davon, uns in meinem Hotel zu treffen?	How about if we meet at my hotel?
Schlagen Sie den Treffpunkt vor.	You suggest the place.
Wie wär's mit einem netten Restaurant?	What about meeting at a nice restaurant?
Ich schlage vor, wir treffen uns am Bahnhof.	I suggest we meet at the station.
Warum treffen wir uns nicht bei mir zu Hause?	Why don't we meet at my house / place?
Treffen wir uns (doch) in Ihrem Golfclub.	Let's meet at your golf club.
Wissen Sie, wie man dorthinkommt?	Do you know how to get there?
Ich schicke Ihnen einen Stadtplan.	I'll send you a map.
Soll ich ein Taxi nehmen?	Should I take a cab / taxi?
Wie komme ich am besten vom Flughafen zu Ihnen?	What's the best way to get to you from the airport?
Sie nehmen am besten die U-Bahn.	The easiest thing would be to take the underground.

Soll ich Sie vom Bahnhof abholen?	Shall I pick you up at the station?
Wir holen Sie ab.	We'll pick you up.
Herr / Frau ... wird Sie um 8.30 Uhr vom Hotel abholen.	Mr / Ms ... will call for you at the hotel at 8.30.
Wunderbar. Ich hole Sie (also) um fünf Uhr vom Hotel ab.	Great. I'll come and pick you up at your hotel at five o'clock.
Wir treffen uns also am 12. März in meinem Hotel um 17 Uhr.	So, we're meeting at my hotel on the 12th of March at 5 p.m.
Ich freue mich auf unser Treffen.	I look forward to meeting you.
Also, dann bis Freitag.	See you on Friday, then.

Food for thought

Punctuality is the thief of time.

Oscar Wilde

Termine verschieben – Rearranging appointments

Food for thought

Time flies like an arrow, fruit flies like a banana.

Groucho Marx

Ich rufe wegen der genauen Uhrzeit der Besprechung am Montag an.	I'm calling to check the exact time of Monday's meeting.
Kannst du zu der Konferenz am 20. kommen? – Leider nein.	Can you make the conference on the 20th? – No, I'm afraid I can't.
Ich fürchte, Dienstag geht bei mir nicht.	I'm afraid I can't make it on Tuesday.
Ich habe bis 3 Uhr zu tun.	I'm not free before 3 o'clock.
Leider bin ich schon ausgebucht.	Sorry, I'm already booked.
Leider habe ich schon einen anderen Termin.	I'm afraid I've got something else on.
Augenblick mal. Nein, tut mir leid, ich habe da schon einen Termin.	Wait a minute. No, sorry. I've got something else then.
Ist es möglich, daß wir uns später treffen?	Is there any chance of us meeting later?

Vielleicht könnten wir uns heute abend zu einem späteren Zeitpunkt treffen.	Well, perhaps we can arrange to meet later tonight.
Ich rufe an, um meinen Besuch am ... zu bestätigen.	I'm calling to confirm my visit on ....
Ich wollte mich vergewissern, daß ich Ort und Zeit richtig verstanden habe.	Just to make sure I've got the time and place right.
Ich muß das Treffen leider absagen.	I'm afraid I'll have to call off the meeting.
Ich muß den Termin leider absagen.	I'm afraid I have to cancel the appointment.
Könnten wir etwas anderes ausmachen?	Could we try to rearrange it?
Können wir den Termin auf nächste Woche verschieben?	Can we postpone the appointment until next week?
Könnten wir es auf heute abend verschieben?	Could we put it off till tonight?
Leider kann ich nun doch nicht am Donnerstag.	Unfortunately I won't be able to make on Thursday after all.
Könnten wir es eventuell auf Montag vorziehen?	Could we bring it forward to Monday, perhaps?
Leider bin ich an dem Tag außer Haus.	I'm afraid I'm out of the office on that day.
Ich habe zu der Zeit schon einen anderen Termin.	I'm afraid I already have another appointment then.
Könnten wir die Besprechung nächste Woche auf eine andere Uhrzeit legen?	Can we change the time of next week's meeting?

Siehe auch *Part 4: Erfolgreich verkaufen, 2. Kundenfang, Vereinbaren Sie einen Termin*, Seite 200.

Being on time

Punctuality is the art of guessing correctly how late the other party is going to be.

P Master your phrases

Task 4: Making an appointment

1. I was wondering if we could possibly (*uns treffen*) next week.
2. What day would (*passen*) you best?
3. (*Sagen*) we Tuesday?
4. Would you like us to arrange (*Unterkunft*) for you?

Task 5: Fit in the modals will, should, can, would, shall

1. .... you make the conference on the 20th?
2. .... I take a cab?
3. .... I pick you up at the station?
4. When .... it be convenient?
5. Ms Child .... call for you at the hotel at 8.30.

Task 6: Arranging place and time

Choose the correct verb form.

1. *I'm calling / call* to check the time of Monday's meeting.
2. How long are *you thinking / do you think* we'll need?
3. So, *we're meeting / we meet* at my hotel on the 12th of March.
4. I look forward *to seeing / see* you on the 12th.

Task 7: What you can do with meetings

Fit in the missing vowels.

I want to { c _ nf _ rm / c _ ll _ ff / c_nc _l / br _ ng f _ rw_ rd / p _ stp_ n _ / p _ t _ ff / r _ _ rr _ ng _ } our meeting

C Crossword power

Across

1. ✎ about week 14? 5. I'd like some travel ✎. 6 When does the plane take ✎? 7. You'll have a one hour ✎ in Boston. 12. I couldn't ✎ you on the flight you wanted. 15. Termin, Verabredung 17. I suggest we meet ✎ the station. 19. What day would ✎ you best? 22. Do you want to fly first class or ✎ ? 23. You ✎ the place and the time. 24. Could we ✎ the meeting off?

Down

2. When ✎ you be arriving? 3. Can you ✎ the conference on the 20th? 4. How much is that ✎ night? 7. Flug 9. Flughafen 10. I'm booked ✎ a Monday flight to X. 11. Could you ✎ that by fax? 13. When does the plane ✎ off? 14. Can we agree ✎ a time? 16. Besprechung 17. zustimmen, einer Meinung sein 18. What ✎ a breakfast meeting? 20. I'll pick you ✎ at the station. 21. Or shall I call ✎ you at your hotel?

2. *Unterwegs*
On the way

So there it is. Boss snaps his fingers and you have to jump. A trip off to Italy, England or Russia. Where are the tickets, when are the connections, what can you take with you, how do you get to the airport? Not to speak of those damned announcements at stations and airports.You can be sure nobody understands them because of the lousy acoustics.

Am Bahnhof
At the station

Let's start with a smile

The train to Kiev that Mr Foster was waiting for simply did not arrive. Finally he went to the stationmaster. "I'm beginning to worry! My train is almost one hour late!" The station master tried to calm him down. "That's no problem at all. Your ticket is valid for another four weeks."

Wie komme ich zum Bahnhof, bitte?	How do I get to the station, please?
Ich würde gerne in Glasgow um ungefähr 18 Uhr ankommen.	I'd like to arrive in Glasgow at about 6p.m.
Könnten Sie mir ein paar Abfahrtszeiten geben?	Could you tell me a few times?
Ich möchte am 21. fahren.	I'd like to travel on the 21st.
Es gibt nur einen Zug, und der kommt um 19.30 an.	There's only one train that arrives at 7.30 p.m.
Wann geht der nächste Zug nach X?	When's the next train to X?
Wie oft fahren die Züge nach X?	How often do the trains run to X?
Eine Fahrkarte nach London, bitte.	A ticket to London, please?
Einfach oder hin und zurück?	Single or return?
London hin und zurück, 2. Klasse, bitte.	London return, standard class, please.
Zweimal einfach nach Cardiff, bitte.	Two singles to Cardiff, please.
Wie lange dauert es?	How long does it take?
Zwei Stunden. Es ist ein Hochgeschwindigkeitszug.	Two hours. It's a high-speed train.
Kann ich über X nach Y fahren?	Can I go to X via Y?
Kann ich dort meine Reise unterbrechen?	Can I break the journey there?
Wann fährt der Zug ab?	When does the train leave?
Schauen wir einmal im Fahrplan nach.	Let's have a look at the timetable.
Muß ich umsteigen?	Do I have to change?

Nein, es ist ein durchgehender Zug.	No, it's a through train.
Wo muß ich umsteigen?	Where do I have to change?
Von welchem Bahnsteig fährt mein Zug ab?	From which platform does my train leave?
Hat der Zug einen Speisewagen?	Does this train have a restaurant car?
Dieser Zug ist immer sehr voll.	This train is always crowded.
Sie sollten lieber einen Sitzplatz reservieren.	You'd better reserve a seat.
Auf welchem Bahnsteig kommt der Zug aus München an?	Where does the train from Munich get in?
Ist dies der Bahnsteig für den Zug nach Glasgow?	Am I on the right platform for the Glasgow train?
Entschuldigen Sie, ist dieser Platz noch frei?	Excuse me madam, is this seat taken?
Sie können Ihren Koffer im Schließfach lassen.	You can leave your suitcase in a luggage locker.
Geben wir den schweren Koffer bei der Gepäckaufbewahrung ab.	Let's leave the heavy suitcase at the left-luggage office.
Hat der Zug aus X Verspätung?	Is the train from X running late?
Kommt der Zug pünktlich an?	Will the train be on time?
Der Zug aus X hat eine Verspätung von 15 Minuten.	The train from X is delayed by 15 minutes.
Erreiche ich meinen Anschlußzug in X noch?	Will I still be able to make my connection in X?
Der Zug hält in X lange genug, um den Anschlußzug zu erreichen.	The train stops at X long enough to catch the connection.

Time for a smile: Sign at a railway station

Toilets out of order.
Please use platforms 5 and 6.

Master your phrases

Task 1: At the ticket office

Fragen Sie

1. nach Zügen nach Glasgow.
2. wann der nächste Zug nach X geht.
3. ob Sie über Oxford fahren können.
4. ob Sie dort Ihre Reise unterbrechen können.
5. wo Sie umsteigen müssen.
6. nach der Abfahrtszeit.
7. von welchem Bahnsteig der Zug abfährt.
8. ob der Zug nach Glasgow Verspätung hat.
9. ob Sie Ihren Anschlußzug in Luton noch erreichen.
10. Nun verlangen Sie eine Rückfahrkarte zweiter Klasse.

Mit dem Flugzeug reisen
Going by air

Let's start with a smile

A fellow tried to get on a British Airways flight with a little Yorkshire terrier in his arms. The stewardess told him that dogs were not allowed on board, so he went to the airport shop and bought himself a pair of dark glasses and a white walking- stick. This time he was greeted by another stewardess who said, "It's quite unusual to see a Yorkshire terrier as a guide-dog, sir. They're usually Golden Labradors." – "You mean this isn't a Golden Labrador?" said the man in surprise.

Einchecken – Checking in

Der Koffer ist zu schwer.	This suitcase is too heavy.
Nehmen wir einen Gepäckwagen.	Let's get a trolley.
Ist es ein Linien- oder ein Charterflug?	Is it a scheduled flight or a charter flight?

Wo ist bitte der Lufthansa-Schalter?	Where is the Lufthansa desk, please?
In Halle A.	It's in hall A, sir.
Ist dies die Schlange für den Flug nach Dallas?	Is this the right queue for the plane to Dallas?
Ist die Maschine aus New York schon gelandet?	Has the plane from New York already landed?
Gibt es noch freie Plätze für einen späteren / früheren Flug?	Are there any seats free on a later / an earlier flight?
Das ist ein Ticket zum Sonderpreis.	This is a cut-price ticket.
Geben Sie mir bitte einen frühen Flug nach Paris.	Please book me an early flight to Paris.
Ich kann Ihre Buchung leider nicht ändern.	I'm afraid it's not possible to change your booking.
Ich muß meinen Flug nach Dublin leider stornieren.	I'm afraid, I have to cancel my flight to Dublin.
Welches ist Ihr Reiseziel?	What's your destination?
Raucher oder Nichtraucher?	Smoking or non-smoking, sir?
Ich hätte gerne einen Fensterplatz.	I'd like a seat at the window.
Ich sitze nicht gerne im Mittelgang.	I hate sitting at the aisle.
Bitte keinen Platz über dem Flügel, wenn möglich.	If possible, not a seat above the wing.
Wieviel Gepäck kann ich mitnehmen?	How much luggage can I take?
Stellen Sie Ihr Gepäck bitte auf die Waage.	Please put your luggage on the scales.
Kann ich das als Handgepäck mitnehmen?	Can I take this as hand luggage?
Ich fürchte, Sie haben zuviel Gepäck.	I'm afraid you've got excess luggage.
Sie haben leider 20 Kilo Übergewicht.	I'm afraid you've got 20 kilos excess baggage.
Ich brauche noch zwei Gepäckanhänger.	I need two more luggage labels, please.
Hier ist Ihre Bordkarte.	Here's your boarding card, sir.
Wo ist die Abflughalle?	Where's the departure lounge?
Begeben Sie sich bitte gleich zum Flugsteig 54.	Please proceed to gate 54 immediately.
Ihr Flugzeug hat bis zu einer Stunde Verspätung wegen Nebels.	Your plane has been delayed up to one hour by fog.
Ihr Flugzeug startet in 15 Minuten.	Your plane takes off in 15 minutes.

Time for a smile

Now they are working on a plane that'll seat 450 passengers. And that's just in the toilet.

Durchsagen verstehen – Understanding announcements

Passagiere mit Lufthansa, Flug 4556, werden gebeten, sich nach Flugsteig 54 zu begeben.	Passengers on Lufthansa flight 4556 are requested to proceed to Gate 54.
Die Passagiere für diesen Flug werden gebeten, sich zum Flugsteig 54 zu begeben.	Will all passengers for this flight please proceed to Gate 54?
British Airways, Flug Nummer 4456, nach London ist bereit zum Abflug.	British Airways announce the departure of flight 4456 to London.
Halten Sie bitte Ihre Bordkarte bereit.	Please have your boarding card ready.
Dies ist der letzte Aufruf für Lufthansa-Flug Nummer ... nach X.	This is the last call for Lufthansa flight .... to X.
Passagier Herr Bosy, gebucht nach London mit British Airways, Flug 646, wird dringend gebeten, sich zum Flugsteig 54 zu begeben.	Passenger Mr Bosy for London on British airways flight 656, please proceed to Gate 54 immediately.
Entschuldigen Sie bitte, mein Flug geht in wenigen Minuten.	Excuse me, my flight leaves in a few minutes.
Würden Sie mich wohl vorlassen?	Would you mind if I go first?
Aber sicher, bitte sehr.	No, go ahead.
Tut mir leid, aber ich habe es selbst eilig.	Sorry, but I'm in a hurry myself.

Don't worry, be happy

In the cockpit of a Boeing taking a hundred passengers to their Turkish holiday resort, the chief pilot is celebrating his birthday. After the fourth bottle of whisky he stammers, "I must stop drinking now – I've got my car at the airport."

Bei der Sicherheitskontrolle – At security control

Könnte ich bitte Ihren Flugschein sehen?	Could I see your ticket, please?
Was ist der Zweck Ihrer Reise?	What's the purpose of your journey?
Ist das Ihr Koffer?	Is that your case?
Haben Sie ihn persönlich gepackt?	Did you pack it yourself?
Haben Sie Ihren Koffer längere Zeit unbeaufsichtigt gelassen?	Did you leave your suitcase unattended any time?
Würden Sie bitte Ihre Taschen entleeren?	Would you empty your pockets, please?
Schalten Sie bitte Ihren Laptop ein.	Please switch on your laptop.
Die Gebühr für die Sicherheitskontrolle beträgt drei Dollar.	The security charge is three dollars.

Time for a smile

At the Security Control the officer asked me if I had any firearms with me. I said, "Well, what do you need?"

An Bord des Flugzeugs – On board the plane

Hier spricht Ihr Kapitän.	This is your captain speaking.
Willkommen an Bord unseres Airbus 320.	Welcome on board our Airbus 320.
Wir sind startbereit.	We are ready for take-off.
Bitte schnallen Sie sich an.	Please fasten your seat belts.
Unsere Reisegeschwindigkeit beträgt ungefähr 900 km/h.	Our cruising speed is about 600 mph.
Unsere durchschnittliche Flughöhe beträgt 10 000 Meter.	We're flying at an average altitude of 10,000 metres.
Stellen Sie bitte das Rauchen ein.	Please put out any cigarettes.
Wir geraten in Turbulenzen.	We are going to encounter some turbulence.

Die Schwimmwesten sind unter Ihrem Sitz.	The lifevests are under your seats.
Im Falle eines Druckverlusts fallen die Atemmasken von der Decke.	If there is a loss of pressure, the oxygen masks will drop from the ceiling.
Pressen Sie die Sauerstoffmasken gegen das Gesicht.	Press the oxygen masks to your face.
Mir ist nicht gut. Bringen Sie mir bitte etwas gegen Luftkrankheit.	I feel sick. Please bring me something for airsickness.
Füllen Sie bitte Ihre Landekarten aus.	Please fill in your landing cards.
Bleiben Sie bitte sitzen, bis das Flugzeug seine endgültige Position erreicht hat.	Please remain seated until the plane has come to a standstill.
Wann ist die voraussichtliche Ankunftszeit?	When is the estimated time of arrival?
Wenn Sie Ihre Uhren stellen wollen, es ist jetzt 14 Uhr Ortszeit.	If you want to set your watches, it's now 2p.m. local time.
Gibt es einen Zubringerbus in die Stadt?	Is there a shuttle-service to the city?
Hatten Sie einen angenehmen Flug?	Did you have a good flight?
Nein, es war sehr unruhig.	No, it was very bumpy.

Murphy's law about flying

- The distance to the gate is inversely proportional to the time available to catch your flight.
- As soon as the stewardess serves the coffee, the airliner encounters turbulence.
- When the plane you are on is late, the plane you want to transfer to is on time.
- Whichever conveyer belt you stand by, your baggage will come in another one.

Ⓟ Master your phrases

Task 2: Complete these questions

1. Excuse me, could you .... my ....? I'd prefer an earlier flight.	I'm afraid it's not possible change your booking.
2. How much ....?	Thirty kilos, all in all.
3. Can I take this as ....?	I'm afraid it's too big for the rack, sir.
4. When .... my plane ....?	In 15 minutes, sir.

Task 3: Ask the right questions

1. Bitten Sie die Stewardeß um ein Mittel gegen Luftkrankheit.	....
2. Fragen Sie nach der voraussichtlichen Ankunftszeit.	....
3. Fragen Sie nach der Ortszeit.	....
4. Fragen Sie nach der Gepäckausgabe.	....
5. Fragen Sie, ob es einen Pendelbus in die Stadt gibt.	....

The joy of flying

I flew over on Concorde. That plane is so fast it gives you an extra couple of hours to look for your luggage.
Bob Hope

Sit back and smile

I took a plane trip to Barbados last week. One chap sitting in the plane was trembling and biting his nails. He had turned bright green. It worried me a bit – it was the pilot.

Eine Seereise machen
Going on a voyage

Let's start with a smile

My wife and I have recently returned from a luxury cruise. On our first day at sea we received a note from the captain asking us to sit with him at dinner. We didn't join him as my wife thought it was outrageous that we should pay a small fortune to go on the cruise and then be expected to eat with the staff.

Wann geht eine Fähre nach Dover?	When is there a ferry for Dover, please?
Wie lange dauert die Überfahrt?	How long does the crossing take?
Können Sie mir sagen, wo die Queen Elizabeth vor Anker liegt?	Can you tell me where the Queen Elizabeth is berthed?
In einer Stunde legen wir ab und segeln nach Boston.	In one hour we'll weigh anchor and set sail for Boston.
Wo machen wir Zwischenlandung auf der Reise?	Where does the ship stop on the voyage?
Machen wir eine Zwischenlandung in Honolulu?	Will there be a stop-over at Honolulu?
Können wir auf Santorini an Land gehen?	Is it possible to go ashore at Santorin?
Legen Sie die Schwimmwesten an, bevor Sie sich in die Rettungsboote begeben.	Put on the life-jackets before you get into the life-boat.
Wir gehen wegen des Sturms eine Meile vor der Küste vor Anker.	We'll drop anchor one mile off the coast because of the storm.
Wann legen wir in Marseille an?	When do we dock in Marseilles?
Sind die Ausflüge im Preis inbegriffen?	Are the excursions included in the price of the cruise?
Könnte ich eine andere Kabine haben?	Could I have a different cabin, please?
Geben Sie mir bitte ein Mittel gegen Seekrankheit.	Could you give me something for sea-sickness, please?

Time for a smile

"I've a complaint to make," said a woman to the steward on a holiday cruise. "A sailor peeped into my cabin last night when I was undressing. I think that's absolutely scandalous." –"What do you expect in second class," replied the steward, "the captain himself?"

Ⓟ Master your phrases

Task 4: Get your terms right

Fill in the table.

By train	By air	By boat
train	plane	boat
railway	....	....
journey	....	....
station	....	sea port / harbour
platform	....	....
engine driver		....

A bad surprise on the cruise

"Steward – about that washing machine in my cabin.
Everytime I put clothes in, they disappear."

Typical German

A German on a cruise on the Amazon is watching the native fishing boats on the huge river. Suddenly one of the boats capsizes and the three natives are howling desperately for help. Immediately some crocodiles approach them. "Typical!" the German exclaims. "Nothing to eat, but lifeboats from Lacoste!"

C Crossword power

Across

1. Where does a train leave from? 6. Can I go to Dover ✎ Hovercraft? 7. This is the last ✎ for flight LH 646 to Boston. 9. Two ✎ to Cardiff, please. 12. I hate to sit ✎ the aisle. 13. reisen 16. You'd better reserve a ✎. 17. Is it a ✎ flight or a charter flight? 19. Please proceed to ✎ A54 immediately. 20. My plane takes ✎ in 5 minutes. 21. When is the next ✎ to Dover, please?

Down

2. Let's leave the suitcases in the luggage ✎. 3. Will my train be ✎ time? 4. Don't ✎ your train. 5. How often do the trains ✎ to Hastings? 6. Can I ✎ my trip in Chicago? 8. From which platform does my train ✎? 10. Where does my train from Munich ✎ in? 11. The train from is ✎ by 20 minutes. 12. I prefer a seat at the ✎. 13. How long does it ✎ to get to Glasgow? 14. Is this the right ✎ for the plane to Dallas? 15. What's the best ✎ to get to Perth? 17. Please put your luggage on the ✎. 18. We'll ✎ anchor one mile off the coast.

3. *Ankunft im Ausland*
Arrival in a foreign country

Swedish customs officials at Arlanda airport were puzzled by the behaviour of a gentleman who, long after all the passengers had passed through the immigration control, ran up and down with a bewildered look on his face. Finally, one of the Swedes went up to him and asked why he had not come through the passport control. "I don't know where my line is," replied the gentleman. "There it says 'Swedes' and there it says 'Foreigners'. But I am neither a Swede nor a foreigner. I'm an Englishman."

Richard D. Lewis. When Cultures Collide

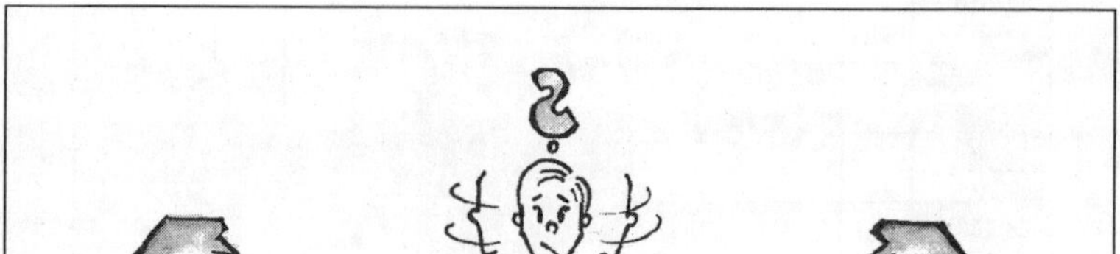

Ein fremdes Land betreten
Entering a foreign country

Bei der Paßkontrolle – At the passport control

Würden Sie bitte Ihre Landekarte ausfüllen?	Would you please fill in your landing-card?
Ihren Ausweis bitte.	Could I see your passport please?
Kann ich bitte Ihre Reiseunterlagen sehen?	Can I see your travel documents, please?
Was ist der Zweck Ihrer Reise?	What's the purpose of your visit?
Ich gehöre zu einer Reisegesellschaft. Unser Führer ist bei der Paßkontrolle.	I belong to a party. Our guide is at the passport control.
Ich bin geschäftlich hier.	I'm here on business.
Ich besuche einen Geschäftsfreund in Tokio.	I'm going to visit a business friend in Tokyo.
Wie lange haben Sie vor zu bleiben?	How long will you be staying?
Ich bleibe eine Woche.	I'll be staying for a week.
Ich mache eine Rundreise.	I'm making a round trip.
Ich habe leider kein Visum.	I'm afraid I haven't got a visa.
Kann ich mit meinem Konsulat telefonieren?	Can I phone my consulate?
Würden Sie bitte das Einwanderungsformular ausfüllen?	Would you please fill in the immigration form?
Sind Sie gegen Pocken geimpft?	Have you been vaccinated against small pox?
Welche Staatsangehörigkeit haben Sie? – Ich bin Deutscher.	What's your nationality? – I'm German.

What not to say to the customs official

"Any alcohol?" demands the Saudi customs official.
"No, thanks," answered Klaus, "I've got enough in my suitcase."

Am Zoll – At the customs

Haben Sie etwas zu verzollen?	Have you got anything to declare?
Ich habe nur Waren für meinen persönlichen Gebrauch.	I only have articles for my personal use.
Würden Sie bitte diesen Koffer öffnen?	Would you open this suitcase, please?
Was befindet sich in Ihrer Tasche?	What is in your bag?
Nur ein paar Geschenke und Souvenirs.	Only a few presents and souvenirs.
Entschuldigen Sie bitte. Muß ich diese Zigarren verzollen?	Excuse me sir, do I have to pay duty on these cigars?
Haben Sie zollfreie Waren gekauft?	Did you buy anything tax free?
Wieviel ist zollfrei?	What's the duty-free allowance?
Für dieses Paket müssen Sie eine Zollerklärung ausfüllen.	For this parcel you have to fill out a customs' declaration.
Tut mir leid, aber Parfum ist ein zollpflichtiger Artikel.	Sorry, but perfume is a dutiable item.
Die 20 Uhren, die ich gekauft habe, sind immer noch in der Zollabfertigung.	The 20 watches I bought are still in customs clearance.

Why things go wrong

Air traffic controller: "What is your height and position?"
New pilot: "I'm about five feet ten inches, and I'm sitting in the pilot's seat."

Erste-Hilfe-Kasten – Survival kit

Wie komme ich zur Gepäckausgabe?	Where's the baggage claim, please?
Ich fürchte, ich habe meinen Flug-/ Fahrschein verloren.	I'm afraid I've lost my ticket.
Ich habe meinen Flug / Zug verpaßt.	I've missed my flight / train.
Wann geht der nächste Flug nach Boston?	When's the next flight to Boston?

Ich fürchte, Ihr Paß ist abgelaufen.	I'm afraid your passport has expired.
Ich habe leider vergessen, meinen Paß zu verlängern.	I'm afraid I forgot to have my passport renewed.
Kann ich mit meinem Konsulat telefonieren?	Can I phone my consulate?
Ich habe leider kein Visum.	I'm afraid I haven't got a visa.
Könnten Sie mir eine Aufenthaltsgenehmigung ausstellen?	Could you issue me with a residence permit?
Ich kann mein Gepäck nicht finden.	I can't find my luggage.
Mein Koffer war nicht dabei.	My case hasn't turned up.
Gehen Sie zum Fundbüro.	Go to Lost and Found / the Lost Property Office.
Jemand hat meinen Koffer vertauscht.	Someone has switched suitcases with me.
Mein Koffer ist beschädigt worden.	My suitcase has been damaged.
An wen kann ich mich wenden?	Where can I report it?

In case of trouble, get an efficient lawyer!

My lawyer's beyond brilliant. In a recent case some of you may have read about, he told his client, "Don't worry. The judge is my cousin. Their chief witness goes with my secretary. And I'm planning to bribe four of the jurors. Meanwhile, try to escape!"

Ⓟ Master your phrases

Task 1: Give the right answers

What's your nationality?	I'm ....
What's the purpose of your visit?	I'm here on ....
I'm afraid your passport has expired.	Too bad! Can I .... my consulate?
How long are you planning to stay?	I'll .... a week.
Have you got anything to declare?	No, I've only articles .... use.
Where will you be staying?	I'm .... with a .... partner in Kiev.

Task 2: At security control. What did they ask you?

.... your flight ticket please?	Here you are.
Is that your ....?	Yes, it is.
What .... case?	Only presents and souvenirs.
.... it yourself?	Yes, I did.
Did you .... at any time?	No, I stayed with it all the time.
Please .... your laptop.	Where can I plug it in?

Task 3: Let's go *woggling* again

1. I'm afraid I've *woggled* my ticket.
2. Could you *woggle* me a residence permit?
3. My case hasn't *woggled* up.
4. Someone has *woggled* suitcases with me.
5. Where can I *woggle* the loss?

Time for a smile

It takes over 3,000 bolts and screws to assemble a car
– but it takes only one nut to scatter it all over the road.

Mit dem Auto unterwegs
Going by car

Let's start with a smile

On the motorway at night, a driver is informed by the radio traffic service: "Attention please, watch out for a driver going in the wrong direction." The driver grumbles: "One driver? There are hundreds, hundreds of them."

Einen Wagen mieten – Renting a car

Entschuldigen Sie, wo ist hier ein Autoverleih?	Excuse me, where is a car rental, please?
Ich möchte gerne einen Wagen mieten.	I'd like to rent a car, please.
Wie lange brauchen Sie den Wagen?	How long do you want it for?
Ich möchte einen Wagen für heute mieten.	I'd like to hire a car for the day.
Wünschen Sie einen bestimmten Wagentyp?	Do you want a certain class, sir?
Wie groß soll der Wagen sein?	What size car do you want?
Mir genügt ein Mittelklassewagen.	A family car will do.
Welche Preisklasse hätten Sie gerne?	Which group would you like?
Wieviel kostet ein BMW pro Tag?	How much is the daily rental for a BMW?
Ich bin automatische Schaltung nicht gewöhnt.	I'm not used to an automatic transmission / gearbox.
Ich hätte lieber einen Wagen mit Gangschaltung.	I'd prefer a car with a gear change.
Und wieviel macht das pro Woche?	How much is that per week?
Sind die Kilometer inbegriffen?	Is the mileage included?
Ja, Sie haben unbegrenzte Kilometerzahl.	Yes, you've unlimited mileage.
Ist Vollkaskoversicherung im Preis inbegriffen?	Is fully comprehensive insurance included in the price?

Unsere Autos sind haftpflichtversichert.	Our cars are insured for third party.
Was deckt die Versicherung ab?	What does the insurance cover?
Vollkasko müssen wir gesondert berechnen.	For comprehensive insurance we have to charge you extra.
Wie hoch ist die Selbstbeteiligung?	How much is the excess?
Wie hoch ist die Kaution?	How much is the deposit?
Darf ich bitte Ihren Führerschein sehen?	May I have a look at your driving licence, please?
Könnten Sie mir bitte Ihren ständigen Wohnsitz geben?	Could I have your permanent address?
Bitte unterschreiben Sie hier.	Please sign here.
Diese Kopie ist für Sie.	That's your copy.
Und hier sind Ihre Schlüssel.	And here are your keys.
Kann ich eine Straßenkarte haben?	Could I have a road map, please?
Das Auto steht auf dem Parkplatz.	The car is in the car park.
Der Wagen wird vor dem Flugplatz stehen.	The car will be waiting outside the airport.
Was mache ich, wenn ich eine Panne habe?	What do I do in case of a breakdown?
Wo kann ich das Auto in Glasgow zurückgeben?	Where can I return the car in Glasgow?

(P) Master your phrases

Task 4: Complete these sentences

1. I'm not used to automatic ....
   I'd prefer a car with a ....
2. What does the insurance ....?
3. Is fully .... insurance .... in the price?
4. How much is the daily .... for a Ford Cortina?
5. Where can I .... the car in Glasgow?

Unterwegs im Auto – On the road

Können Sie mir helfen? Ich fürchte, ich habe mich verfahren.	I wonder if you can help me. I'm afraid I've lost my way.
Ist dies die Straße nach York?	Is this the road to York?
Entschuldigen Sie, wie komme ich von hier auf die Autobahn?	Excuse me, how do I get to the motorway from here?
Könnten Sie es mir bitte auf der Karte zeigen?	Could you please show me on the map?
Fahren Sie geradeaus, und biegen Sie die dritte Straße nach links ab.	Go straight on and take the third turning to the left.
Seien Sie vorsichtig. Die Straßen sind eisglatt.	Be careful, the roads are icy.
Der Paß ist offen, aber Sie brauchen Winterreifen oder Ketten.	The pass is open, but you need winter tyres or snow chains.
Wie komme ich von hier zum Verkehrsverein?	How do I get to the tourist information office from here?
Fahren Sie geradeaus. Das Krankenhaus ist gegenüber dem Bahnhof.	You go straight on. The hospital is opposite the station.

An der Tankstelle – At the petrol station

Time for a smile

Tourist, at a petrol station: "Could you change the oil, please?"
Mechanic: "If I were you, I would keep the oil and change the car."

Ich habe kein Benzin mehr. Ist hier irgendwo eine Tankstelle?	I've run out of petrol. Is there a petrol station anywhere around here?
Volltanken, bitte.	Fill her up, please.
Prüfen Sie bitte auch den Ölstand und den Reifendruck.	Would you also check the oil level, and the tyre pressure.
Sie sollten auch die Wischerblätter auswechseln.	You'd better change the wiper blades as well.

Die Kupplung rutscht. Könnten Sie sie nachstellen?	The clutch is slipping. Could you adjust it, please?
Könnten Sie die Batterie bitte aufladen? Sie ist leer.	Could you recharge the battery, please? It's flat.
Das Profil ist abgefahren. Montieren Sie bitte den Ersatzreifen.	The tyre is worn down. Could you put the spare on, please?
Der Kühler leckt. Können Sie ihn abdichten?	The radiator is leaking. Can you seal it?
Der Keilriemen ist locker. Könnten Sie ihn bitte spannen?	The fanbelt is slipping. Could you tighten it?
Könnten Sie bitte die Zündung einstellen? Der Motor läuft unrund.	Could you adjust the ignition? The motor sounds rough.
Wann hatten Sie das Auto zuletzt beim Kundendienst?	When did this car last have a service?
Im Auspuff ist ein Loch. Kann man es schweißen?	There's a hole in the exhaust pipe. Is it possible to weld it, please?
Wann ist mein Wagen fertig?	When will my car be ready?
Bis Dienstag nächster Woche.	By Tuesday next week, sir.

P Master your phrases

Task 5: Match problems and phrases

Typical problems ...		and what to say at the garage	
1	you've run out of petrol	A	put on / fit the spare
2	there isn't enough oil	B	make it watertight /seal it
3	the clutch is slipping	C	recharge it / charge it up
4	you have a puncture	D	try to bump-start it
5	the battery is flat	E	adjust it
6	the radiator is leaking	F	tighten it
7	the car won't start	G	weld the hole in the exhaust pipe
8	the fanbelt is slipping	H	try to seal the sump
9	the motor is too loud	I	top it up
10	the oil is leaking	J	adjust the ignition /check the plugs
11	the engine sounds rough	K	fill her / it up

Be polite and add 'please' each time you ask for help.

Ärger mit dem Auto – Trouble with the car

Technology

Four-wheel-drive means getting stuck in inaccessible places.

Könnten Sie mich bitte zur nächsten Notrufsäule mitnehmen?	Could you give me a lift to the next emergency telephone?
Wir hatten einen Unfall. Ob Sie uns wohl abschleppen könnten?	We had an accident. I wonder if you could tow our car?
Könnten Sie uns zur nächsten Reparaturwerkstätte schleppen?	Could you tow us to the nearest service garage / repair shop?
Wie ruft man einen Pannendienst?	How do I call a breakdown service?
Ich habe eine Reifenpanne. Können Sie mir bitte beim Reifenwechsel helfen?	I've got a puncture. Could you help me to change the wheel / put on the spare, please?
Könnten Sie mich anschieben? Der Motor springt nicht an.	Could you give the car a push? The engine won't start.
Mein Auto ist im Schlamm steckengeblieben. Könnten Sie mich herausziehen?	My car is stuck in the mud. Could you pull me out?

Time for a smile

A Trabi makes your average Skoda look like a Ferrari.

How do you double the price of a Trabi?
Fill up the petrol tank.

I once bought a car designed for five people:
one had to drive while the other four pushed.

Master your phrases

Task 6: Are you a gentleman? Well, then help the young lady.

She is walking on the road.	Give her a ....
Her car got stuck in the mud.	.... it out of it.
And it has got a puncture.	Help to .... on the ....
The engine of her car won't start.	Give her a .... to .... start it.
Hopeless! The car won't start.	Call the .... service.
The breakdown service is too busy.	Then you have to .... her to the next ....

One for the road

Bad luck. I had the right of way,
but the other had the truck.

Für den Fall eines Unfalls – In case of an accident

Bitte rufen Sie die Polizei und einen Krankenwagen.	Please call the police and an ambulance.
Herr Wachtmeister, könnten Sie bitte den Unfall aufnehmen?	Officer, could you please make a protocol?
Entschuldigen Sie, dürfte ich Ihren Führerschein sehen?	Excuse me sir, may I have a look at your driving licence?
Ihre Kfz-Zulassung, bitte.	Your log book, please.
Wo ist Ihr Auto versichert?	Where is your car insured?
Es ist bei HUK versichert.	It's insured with HUK.
Wie ist der Unfall passiert?	How did the accident happen?
Der andere Wagen hat in einer Kurve überholt.	The other car was overtaking on a bend.
Ich war geblendet.	I was blinded by the light.
Er hat die Scheinwerfer nicht abgeblendet.	He didn't dim the headlights.
Das Auto vor uns hat ohne Grund gebremst.	The car in front of us braked without any reason /cause.

Ich mußte bremsen, und er ist auf uns aufgefahren.	I had to brake and he drove into the back of us.
Es war Ihre Schuld. Ich hatte Vorfahrt.	It was your fault. I had the right of way.
Ich bestehe auf einen Alkoholtest.	I insist on a breathalyser test.
Ich wollte nur einem Fußgänger ausweichen.	I only tried to avoid a pedestrian.
Sie haben doch den Unfall gesehen.	You saw the accident, didn't you?
Würden Sie für mich aussagen?	Would you act as my witness?
Sie machen besser ein Photo und schreiben einen Unfallbericht.	You'd better take a photo and make a damage report.

The joy of driving in Britain

There was a terrible fog in Glasgow. Two drivers collided. They groped their way out of their cars and approached each other.
"I had right of way!" says the first. "Possibly, but it doesn't matter," replies the other. "We're in my garage."

Im Hotel
At the Hotel

An der Rezeption – At the reception desk

Let's start with a smile

"Excuse me, do you have a room for tonight?"
"Certainly, sir. It'll be fifteen pounds a night. Or I can let you have room for only five pounds, if you make your own bed."
"I'll take the five-pound room."
"Right. I'll just go and fetch the wood, the hammer and the nails for the bed."

Haben Sie Zimmer frei?	Do you have any vacancies?
Wir sind leider ausgebucht.	I'm afraid we're fully booked.
Aber Sie haben meine Buchung per Fax bestätigt.	But you confirmed my booking by fax.
Können Sie mir ein ruhiges Hotel im Zentrum empfehlen?	Can you recommend a quiet hotel in the centre?
Wie lange bleiben Sie? – Ich weiß noch nicht.	How long will you be staying? I don't know yet.
Ich habe ein Zimmer für mich reservieren lassen.	There is a room reserved for me here.
Ich habe ein Zimmer für Meier reservieren lassen.	I've had a room reserved in the name of Meier.
Ich habe ein Zimmer für zwei Nächte reserviert.	I booked a room for two nights.
Wünschen Sie ein Doppel- oder Einzelzimmer?	Do you want a double room or a single room?
Ich hätte gerne ein Zimmer mit Dusche oder Badezimmer.	I'd like a room with shower or with bathroom.
Hat das Zimmer Toilette?	Does the room have a private toilet?
Hat das Zimmer Klimaanlage?	Is the room air-conditioned?
Wie teuer sind Ihre Zimmer?	What are your hotel rates?
Ist das Frühstück inbegriffen?	Does that include breakfast?

Könnte ich mir das Zimmer vorher ansehen?	Could I have a look at the room first?
Dieses ist zu laut. Zeigen Sie mir bitte ein anderes Zimmer.	This one is too noisy. Show me another room, please.
Ich nehme dieses Zimmer. Wieviel kostet es?	I'll take this room. How much is it?
Möchten Sie Vollpension oder nur Frühstück?	Do you want full board or only breakfast?
Vollpension ist nicht im Preis mit eingeschlossen.	Full board isn't included.
Wie hoch ist der Aufpreis für ein zweites Bett?	What's the surcharge for an extra bed?
Haben Sie etwas Billigeres?	Don't you have anything less expensive?
Kann ich die Anmeldung in meinem Zimmer ausfüllen?	Can I fill in the registration form in my room?
Was muß ich hier reinschreiben?	What do I have to fill in here?
Ich brauche Ihre Unterschrift.	I need your signature, sir.
Unterschreiben Sie bitte hier.	Would you please sign here?
Entschuldigen Sie, Sie haben vergessen zu unterschreiben.	Excuse me sir, you have forgotten to sign the form.
Gibt es eine Ermäßigung für Geschäftsleute?	Is there a reduction for businessmen?
Angenehmen Aufenthalt.	Enjoy your stay.

Time for a smile

A man walked up to the desk of a resort hotel and asked for a room.
"Have you got a reservation?" asked the indifferent clerk.
"No. But I've been coming here every year for twelve years, and I've never needed a reservation."
"Well, there is nothing available. We are fully booked, and without a reservation you can't get a room."
"Suppose the President of the United States came in. You would have a room for him, wouldn't you?"
"Of course, for the President we would find a room."
"Alright," said the man. "Well, the President isn't coming here tonight. So give me his room."

Hotelservice – Hotel services

Time for a smile

The pretty bell girl at the Hilton in Boston showed Renny Bosy to his room. Renny asked her what the rates were.
"Eighty dollars," said the girl.
"That's reasonable," said Renny, "I'll pay the eighty dollars with pleasure ..."
"With pleasure," interrupted the girl, "it'll be five hundred."

Liegt eine Nachricht für mich vor?	Are there any messages for me?
Sind Briefe für mich da?	Are there any letters for me?
Hat jemand nach mir gefragt?	Did anyone inquire for me?
Ja, hier ist eine Nachricht für Sie.	Yes, here's a message for you.
Wo kann ich parken?	Where can I park my car?
Der Parkplatz ist hinter dem Hotel.	The car park is behind the hotel.
Könnten Sie meine Wertsachen in den Safe tun?	Could you please put my valuables in your safe?
Können Sie mein Gepäck auf das Zimmer bringen lassen?	Could you have my luggage sent up / taken up to my room?
Kann ich meine Kleider reinigen lassen?	Is there a laundry service?
Kann ich bei Ihnen Geld wechseln oder einen Euroscheck einlösen?	Can I change money here or cash a eurocheque?
Sie nehmen doch Kreditkarten, oder?	You accept credit cards, don't you?
Wann wird Frühstück serviert?	When is breakfast served, please?
Ich bräuchte ein Ferngespräch nach München.	I need a long-distance call to Munich.
Ich erwarte ein Ferngespräch.	I'm expecting a long-distance call.
Legen Sie es auf mein Zimmer.	Put it through to my room.
Wie bekomme ich ein Amt?	How do I get an outside line?
Könnte ich einen Stadtplan haben?	Could I have a map of the town?
Wo ist das Konferenzzimmer?	Where's the conference room?
Würden Sie mir bitte ein paar deutsche Zeitungen besorgen?	Would you be so kind as to get me some German newspapers?

Können wir auf unserem Zimmer frühstücken?	Could we have breakfast in our room?
Wir wollen nicht gestört werden.	We don't want to be disturbed.
Können Sie mir das Abendessen auf meinem Zimmer servieren?	Can you send the dinner to my room?

Wie man sich beschwert – How to complain

Let's take a break and smile

Lady Wilberforce rang for the hotel manager who came up immediately. "I've a complaint to make," she said, "In the room opposite, there's a man doing sit-ups – completely naked. It's disgraceful!" The manager looked out of the window. "Excuse me, but I'm afraid I can only see his head," he said.
"Well," said the lady angrily, "you just stand on this chair."

Sie haben mir einen falschen Schlüssel gegeben. Dieser hier paßt nicht.	I'm afraid you've given me the wrong key. This one doesn't fit.
Ich würde gerne den Geschäftsführer sprechen. Ich habe eine Reklamation.	I'd like to see the manager. I've a complaint to make.
Ich möchte mich über den Service in Ihrem Hotel beschweren.	I want to make a complaint about the service at your hotel.
Ich möchte mich beschweren.	I've a complaint to make.
Der Wasserhahn tropft.	The tap drips.
Ich hätte gerne ein anderes Zimmer.	Could I have a different room, please?
Die Toilettenspülung funktioniert nicht.	The lavatory won't flush.
Entschuldigen Sie, aber ich glaube, mit der Rechnung stimmt etwas nicht.	Excuse me, but I'm afraid there's something wrong with the bill.

Das Hotel verlassen – Checking out

A joke for the road

A businessman visiting Brighton stopped at a hotel for an early evening drink. In the bar he got to know a very attractive girl. After a few drinks, he took her over to the reception desk and booked a double room for the night, signing in as Mr and Mrs Doorbar.
The next morning after breakfast he was presented with a bill for £950. "What's all this?" he exclaimed. "I've only been here one night, haven't I?"
"You're quite right, Mr Doorbar," said the clerk, "but your wife has been here for a week."

Ich reise morgen ab. Könnten Sie bitte meine Rechnung fertig machen?	I'm leaving tomorrow. Could you get my bill ready?
Ich möchte abreisen. Machen Sie mir bitte meine Rechnung bis 16.00 Uhr fertig.	I'd like to check out. Please have my bill ready by 4p.m.
Wie möchten Sie zahlen?	How would you like to pay?
Ich hätte gerne eine getrennte Rechnung für meine Telefongespräche.	Could I have a separate bill for my telephone calls, please?
Setzen Sie es auf meine Rechnung.	Put it on my bill.
Führen Sie bitte alle Posten einzeln auf.	Can you let me have an itemised bill, please?
Schicken Sie die Rechnung bitte an Dolittle Ltd., Bristol.	Please send the bill to Dolittle Ltd in Bristol.
Bis wann muß ich das Zimmer räumen?	When do I have to check out?
Kann ich meinen Koffer für ein paar Stunden unterstellen?	Could I leave my suitcase here for a couple of hours?
Wecken Sie mich bitte um 7 Uhr.	Could you please wake me at 7a.m.
Ich muß meinen Zug erreichen.	I've a train to catch.
Könnten Sie mir ein Lunchpaket mitgeben?	Could I have packed lunch, please?
Würden Sie mir bitte ein Taxi für sieben Uhr morgens bestellen?	Would you please order a taxi for me at seven o'clock?

Ⓟ Master your phrases

Task 7: Let's test your memory

1. I've a (*Reservierung auf den Namen Meier*).
2. Is there a (*Ermäßigung für*) businessmen?
3. Is there a (*Nachricht für*) me?
4. Do you want (*Vollpension*) or only (*Frühstück*)?
5. I'd like to (*sprechen*) the manager. I've a (*Reklamation*) to make.
6. I'm leaving tomorrow. Could you (*meine Rechnung fertig machen*)?
7. Could I have a (*getrennte Rechnung*) for the calls?
8. Excuse me, (*mit meiner Rechnung stimmt etwas nicht*).

Task 8: A mixed bag of questions

1. What do you put into the hotel safe?	your ....
2. Another word for booking:	....
3. What's the document called you have to fill in:	....
4. Three meals at the hotel:	....
5. They clean and iron you clothes:	....
6. Bookings are either	co .... or ca ....
7. If you are not satisfied, you make a	....
8. You want a detailed bill. Ask for an	.... bill

Task 9: Get your prepositions right

1. I've had a room reserved .... the name of Meier.
2. Could I have a look .... the room first?
3. Could you have my luggage sent .... my room?
4. I want to make a complaint .... the service at your hotel.

C Crossword power

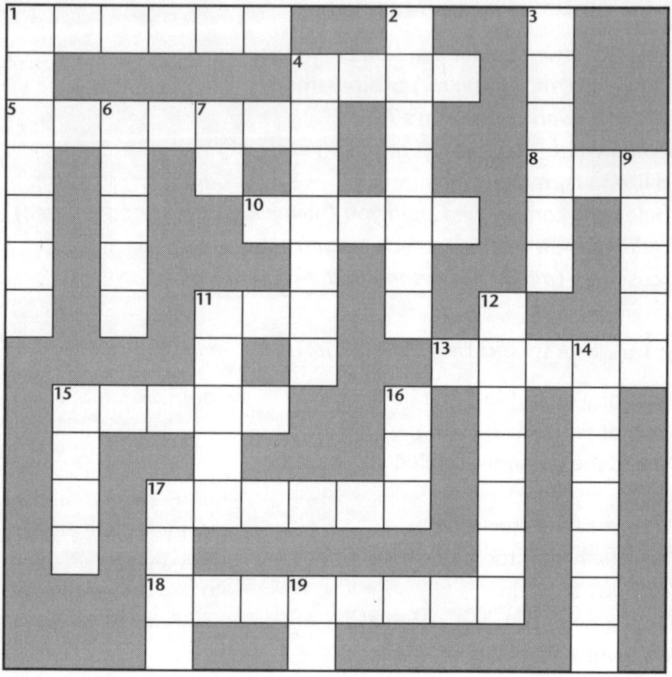

Across

1. Selbstbeteiligung (bei Kaskoversicherung) 4. Do I have to pay ✎ on these cigars? 5. What's the ✎ of your visit? 8. Could I have a ✎ of the town? 10. Where's the baggage ✎, please? 11. I'd like to hire a car ✎ the day. 13. Could you get my bill ✎ ? 15. Could you ✎ me with a residence permit? 17. I'd prefer a car with a gear ✎ . 18. Someone has ✎ suitcases with me.

Down

1. I'm afraid your passport has ✎. 2. How long will you be ✎? 3. Could you issue me a residence ✎? 4. Have you got anything to ✎ ? 6. I'm making a ✎ trip. 7. I'm here ✎ business. 9. Our cars are third ✎ insured. 11. The lavatory won't ✎. 12. I'm afraid I forgot to have my passport ✎. 14. Kaution 15. Perfume is a dutiable ✎. 16. I only have articles for my personal ✎. 17. Can I ✎ a eurocheque? 19. I complained ✎ Mr Smith.

4. *Allerlei Geschäfte*
All sorts of odd jobs to do

Now you're there – safe and sound, but exhausted from the trip. You check your schedule in the hotel room. There's the trade fair you have to attend, three customers to visit, a meeting with the manager of the subsidiary, the presentation of the new product lines, postcards to write, phone calls to make and lots more. And there are the problems with the bank to sort out.
Of course your wife forgot the extra shirts. You'll have to buy some first thing in the morning – and the ties to match. Will there be time for some sightseeing?

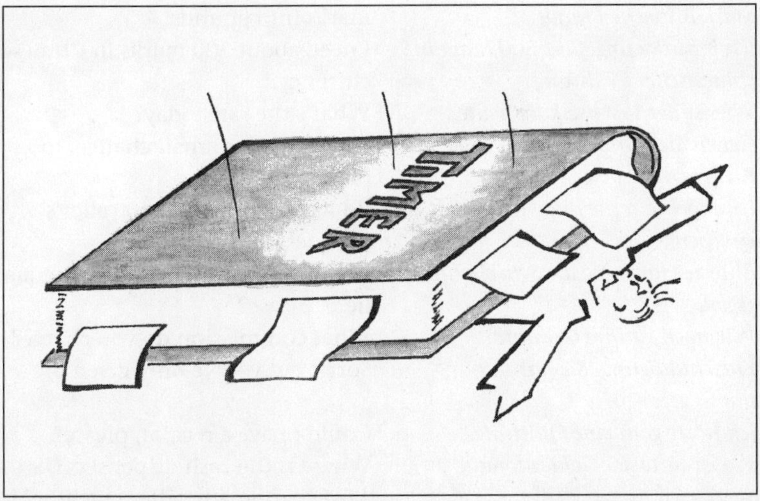

In der Bank
At the bank

Let's start with a smile

Bridget O'Leary was trying to cash a cheque in a Dublin bank. "Can you identify yourself, madam?" asked the clerk. "Certainly," said Bridget, reached into her handbag, took out a little mirror, looked in it and declared confidently, "Yes, it's me all right. I'd recognise me anywhere."

Geld wechseln – Changing money

Ich habe kein Bargeld mehr.	I have run out of cash.
Wo kann ich sonntags mein Geld wechseln?	Where can I change my money on Sundays?
Wo ist bitte die nächste Bank?	Where is the nearest bank, please?
Wann sind die Banken hierzulande geöffnet?	When do the banks open and close in this country?
Ich hätte gerne für 500 Deutsche Mark Britische Pfund.	I'd like to change 500 German marks into pounds.
Ich brauche ungefähr 500 Mark in chinesischer Währung.	I need about 500 marks in Chinese currency.
Wie ist der Wechselkurs heute?	What's the rate today?
Geben Sie mir bitte auch etwas Kleingeld.	Give me some small change, too, please.
Ich möchte gerne diese Reiseschecks einlösen.	I'd like to cash these traveller's cheques.
Bitte zeichnen Sie die Schecks hier gegen.	Could you countersign the cheques here, please?
Wie hoch ist Ihre Gebühr?	What commission do you charge?
Entschuldigung, Sie haben mir nur ... gegeben.	Sorry, but you've only given me ...
Ich hätte gern eine Quittung.	Could I have a receipt, please?
Wo ist bitte der Geldautomat?	Where is the cash dispenser (US: ATM = automatic teller machine)?

Kann ich Bargeld mit meiner Kreditkarte abheben?	Can I draw cash with my credit card?

Zahlungsverkehr – Money transfer

Don't worry, be happy!

Tom: My wife had her credit card stolen.
Bob: That's terrible.
Tom: It could be worse. The thief has been spending less than she did.

Ich möchte ein Girokonto eröffnen.	I'd like to open a current account.
Geben Sie uns bitte hier eine Unterschriftsprobe.	Please fill in your specimen signature here.
Ich erwarte eine Überweisung aus Deutschland.	I'm expecting a transfer from Germany.
Kann ich Geld auf ein Konto in Libyen überweisen?	Can I transfer money to an account in Libya?
Wer ist der Empfänger?	Who's the recipient?
Ich möchte ein Sparbuch eröffnen.	I'd like to open a savings account.
Hier ist Ihr Sparbuch.	Here's your passbook.
Haben Sie schon ein Konto bei uns?	Do you already have an account with us?
Wieviel möchten Sie einzahlen?	How much would you like to pay in?
Ist Geld für mich eingezahlt worden?	Has money been paid in for me?
Ich möchte Geld auf mein Konto in Deutschland überweisen.	I'd like to have money transferred to my account in Germany.
Füllen Sie bitte den Überweisungsvordruck aus.	Please fill in the transfer form.
Bei welcher Bank sind Sie?	Who do you bank with?
Ich habe ein Konto bei der City Bank.	I have an account with the City Bank.
Wissen Sie die Bankleitzahl?	Do you know the bank sorting code?
Ich möchte 200 Dollar von meinem Konto abheben.	I'd like to withdraw 200 dollars from my account.
Wo bekomme ich meine Kontoauszüge?	Where do I get my bank statements?

Ich möchte einen Dauerauftrag geben / ändern.	I'd like to place / change a standing order.
Ich möchte mein Konto schließen.	I want to close my account.

Time for a smile

A bank is a place where they lend you an umbrella in fair weather and ask for it back when it begins to rain.

Mark Twain

Ⓟ Master your phrases

Task 1: Are you fit to have an account?

1. What should you not do with a cheque?
   A. countersign B. cash C. lose D. fake
2. What can you not do with an account?
   A. overdraw B. debit C. balance D. commission
3. What does the bank charge you for money transfer?
   A. commission B. interest C. rate D. customs

Task 2: Can you match up these phrases?

	Customer		Bank clerk
1	I'd like to have money transferred to Germany.	A	Here's your passbook.
2	Who do you bank with?	B	Please go to counter 7.
3	Where do I collect my bank statements?	C	I have an account with the City Bank.
4	I'd like to open a savings account.	D	Please fill in the transfer form.

Time for a smile

A banker is a person who is willing to make a loan, if you present sufficient evidence to show that you don't need it.

Herbert V. Prochnow

Anlagen und Kredite – Investment and loans

Everything is relative

A German businessman entered a Swiss bank. He looked carefully around, went to the reception desk and whispered,
"I want to invest 300,000 marks."
"You needn't whisper," said the bank clerk, "poverty is nothing to be ashamed of."

Ich möchte einen Kredit beantragen.	I'd like to apply for a loan.
Einen langfristigen oder kurzfristigen Kredit?	A long term or short term loan?
Haben Sie Sicherheiten?	Have you got any security?
Wie hoch ist der Zinssatz?	What's the interest rate?
Ich möchte eine größere Summe investieren?	I'd like to invest a lump sum.
Was raten Sie mir, zu kaufen?	What do you advise me to buy?
Denken Sie an Aktien oder festverzinsliche Wertpapiere?	Are you thinking of stocks or bonds?
Wo bekomme ich die beste Rendite?	Where do I get the highest return on my money?
Sie sollten Ihre Investition lieber streuen.	You'd better spread your investment.
Möchten Sie ein Limit angeben?	Do you want to fix a limit?
Welches Konto darf ich belasten?	Which account may I debit?
Ich möchte ein Schließfach mieten.	I'd like to rent a safe deposit box?
Folgen Sie mir bitte zum Banktresor.	Please follow me to the bank vault.

No use arguing with bankers

Customer: I'd have to be an idiot to buy stock in your company.
Director: Well, how many shares do you want?

Probleme mit der Bank – Trouble with the bank

Banking is serious business

The American humorist James Thurber once overdrew his bank account and was summoned by the bank manager, who was stunned to hear that he didn't keep a note of the cheques he wrote. "Then how do you know how much money is in your account?" he asked. "I thought that was your business," replied Thurber.

Wer leitet diese Zweigstelle?	Who's in charge of this branch?
Ich habe eine Reklamation.	I've got a complaint to make.
Der Automat hat meine Karte einbehalten.	The machine's taken my card.
Haben Sie die richtige Geheimnummer eingegeben?	Did you type in the correct PIN (personal identity number)?
Ich fürchte, Sie haben Ihr Konto überzogen.	I'm afraid you've overdrawn your account.
Ich habe meine Kreditkarte verloren. Was soll ich tun?	I've lost my credit card. What shall I do?
Sperren Sie bitte mein Konto.	Please bar my account.
Ich dachte, mein Konto sei ausgeglichen.	I thought my account was balanced.
Auf meinem Kontoauszug ist keine Überziehung ersichtlich.	My statement does not show an overdraft.
Die Überziehungszinssatz beträgt 16 %.	The overdraw charge is 16 %.
Wie hoch ist mein Überziehungskredit?	What's my overdraft facility?
Sie haben einen Überziehungskredit bis zu einem Monatsgehalt.	We grant you an overdraft facility of one month's salary.

How to balance one's account

My bank sent me a bank statement last week saying that I was seven hundred pounds overdrawn. I reacted promptly. I immediately wrote them a cheque for the money.

(P) Master your phrases

Task 3: How did the manager respond?

Rearrange the dialogue.

Customer	Bank manager
1. I'd like to invest a lump sum.	A. Have you got any security?
2. What do you advise me to buy?	B. In that case you should take bonds. Which account may I debit?
3. I prefer a long term investment.	C. Are you thinking of a long term or a short term investment?
4. I was thinking of applying for a loan.	D. You'd better spread your investment. It's less risky.

Do you really need a bank?

The French dramatist, Tristan Bernard, hit hard times towards the end of his life and was obliged to withdraw all his savings from his account at the Banque de France. As he was leaving the bank with every penny he owned in his pocket, he turned to the guard who was standing outside. "Thank you, my friend," he said. "You may go home now."

C Crossword power

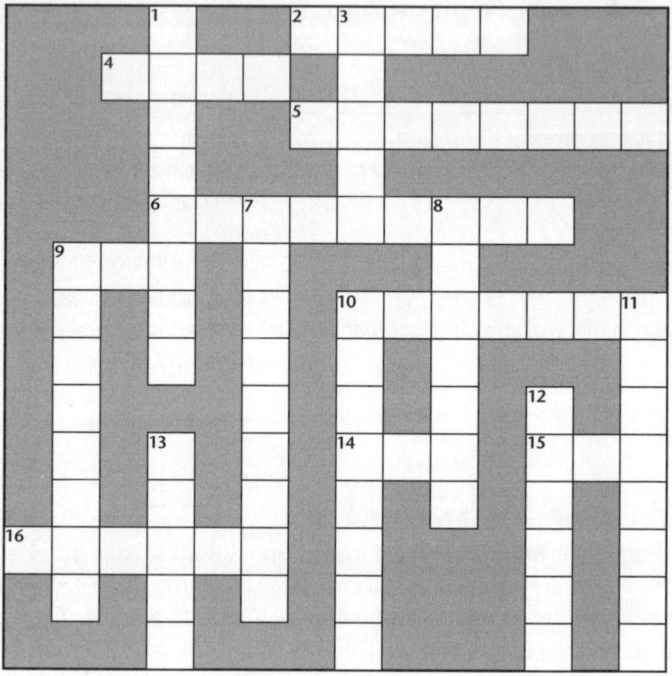

Across

2. I'd like to ✎ for a loan. 4. Please ✎ in the transfer form. 5. Sparbuch 6. Where is the nearest cash ✎ ? 9. I lost my credit card. Please ✎ my account. 10. I'd like to open a ✎ account. 14. I have ✎ out of cash. 15. Did you type in the correct ✎ ? 16. Where do I get the highest ✎ on my money?

Down

1. I'd like to ✎ 200 dollars from my account. 3. I'd like to ✎ a standing order. 7. Where do I get my bank ✎ ? 8. Do you know the bank ✎ code? 9. I thought my account was ✎ . 10. Währung 11. Can I ✎ money to an account in Libya? 12. You'd better ✎ your investment. 13. Please follow me to the bank ✎ .

Auf der Post
At the post office

Let's start with a smile

The head of the sales department asked the new apprentice, "Have you posted those two things I gave you? You know, the letter to Sydney and that little parcel of components to Manchester."
"I have," said the apprentice full of pride, "and what's more, I put right that mistake you made with the postage."
"What do you mean?" said the boss surprised.
"Well, you put £8.20 worth of stamps on the local parcel and only an 80p stamp on that letter to Australia. Don't worry, I sorted it out. I just changed the addresses."

Briefe und Geld – Letters and money

Können Sie mir helfen? Ich suche einen Briefkasten.	Can you help me, please? I'm looking for a letter-box.
Wie teuer ist ein normaler Inlandbrief?	How much is a normal domestic letter?
Ich möchte diesen Brief postlagernd nach Leeds schicken.	I'd like to send this letter poste restante to Leeds.
Was kostet ein Brief per Luftpost nach Deutschland?	How much is an airmail letter to Germany?
Was kostet ein Eilbrief nach Deutschland?	What's the postage on an express letter to Germany?
Wann ist dieser Eilbrief in Kanada?	When will this express letter arrive in Canada?
Ich möchte dies per Einschreiben schicken.	I'd like to send this as a registered letter.
Ist dieser Brief nach Dänemark richtig frankiert?	Is there enough postage on this letter to Denmark?
Dieses Paket braucht ungefähr vier Wochen nach Italien.	This parcel will take approximately four weeks to Italy.
Was kostet es als Luftpost?	How much is it by airmail?

Wo kann ich dieses Päckchen aufgeben.	Where can I send off this parcel?
Muß ich eine Zollerklärung ausfüllen?	Do I have to fill out a customs declaration?
Vier Briefmarken für Ansichtskarten nach Deutschland, bitte.	Four stamps for picture postcards to Germany, please.
Haben Sie Sondermarken?	Have you got any special-issue stamps?
Geben Sie mir den ganzen Satz.	Give me the whole set.
Schicken Sie mir bitte meine Post an diese Adresse nach.	I'd like to have my mail forwarded to this address.
Eine Postanweisung bitte. Ich möchte 1000 Dollar an diese Adresse schicken.	A postal order, please. I'd like to send $1000 to this address.
Eine Postanweisung über 1000 Dollar an eine Firma in den USA.	A 1000 dollar postal order to a firm in the USA, please.
Haben Sie ein Postgirokonto?	Do you have an account with the post office bank?

P Master your phrases

Task 4: What is it?

Things the postman brings ....
You put presents into it ....
An urgent letter ....
A letter for which you get a receipt ....
Money transferred by post ....
The price you pay for a letter ....
Not a local phone call ....
You put postcards into it ....

Task 5: Guess the meaning and match the phrases

Stamps you can find on letters

1 Einschreibebrief	A By air mail
2 Eilzustellung	B Insured letter
3 Wertbrief	C Special Delivery
4 Luftpost	D Recorded Delivery

Hinweise in Telefonzellen – Instructions in public phone boxes

Nehmen Sie den Hörer ab.	Lift the receiver.
Werfen Sie das Geld ein.	Insert your money in the slot.
Es sind mindestens 10 Pence erforderlich.	A minimum of 10p is required.
Warten Sie auf das Amtszeichen.	Listen for the dialling tone.
Wählen Sie die gewünschte Nummer.	Dial the number required.
Werfen Sie kein Geld ein. Dieses Gespräch ist gebührenfrei.	Do not insert money. This call is free.
Das Gespräch ist gebührenfrei.	This call is free of charge.
Notrufe: Wählen Sie 999.	Emergency calls: dial 999.
Die Nummer hat sich geändert.	The number has been changed.
Wählen Sie zuerst die internationale Vorwahlnummer	First dial the international code ...
... dann die regionale Vorwahlnummer ohne die Null ...	... then the area code minus the initial '0' ...
... dann die Nummer des Teilnehmers.	... then dial the subscriber's number.

Öffentliche Telefone – Public telephones

Geben Sie mir bitte eine Telefonkarte.	I'd like a telephone card.
Kann ich von hier ein Ferngespräch führen?	Can I make a long-distance call from here?
Gehen Sie in Kabine 6.	Go to booth number 6.
Kann ich nach München in Deutschland durchwählen?	Can I dial straight through to Munich in Germany?
Kann ich nach München durchwählen?	Can I dial / get Munich direct?
Ab wann beginnt der Nachttarif?	What time does the cheap rate begin?
Die Vermittlung hilft Ihnen.	The operator will assist you in making the call.
Könnten Sie mir bitte die Vermittlung geben?	Could you please give me the telephone exchange?

Ist dort die Bahnhofsauskunft?	Is that the Central Station Information?
Geben Sie mir bitte die Störungsstelle.	Please give me the operator. There's a fault on the line.
Ein Ferngespräch nach Heidelberg in Deutschland, bitte.	A long-distance call to Heidelberg in Germany, please.
Muß ich lange darauf warten?	Will I have to wait long?
Vermittlung, würden Sie bitte mein Gespräch nach München streichen?	Operator, will you please cancel my call to Munich?
Ich habe es wiederholt versucht, aber ich bekomme keine Antwort.	I've tried again and again, but there is no answer.
Die Verbindung ist furchtbar.	It's a terrible connection.
Ich glaube, sie ist gestört.	I think it's out of order.
Wir sind unterbrochen worden.	We have been cut off.
Die Leitung ist tot.	The line is dead.
Ich hätte gerne ein Ferngespräch nach Bristol.	I'd like to make a long-distance call to Bristol.
Ich hätte gerne ein Gespräch mit Voranmeldung.	I'd like to place a person-to-person call.
Ich möchte ein R-Gespräch nach New York führen.	I'd like to make a reversed / transferred charge call to New York.
Wie ist der Name des Teilnehmers?	What is the name of the party / person you are calling?
Wie lautet die Telefonnummer?	What's the number, please?
Können Sie mir eine Verbindung nach Zürich herstellen?	Can you get me a line to Zurich, please?
Wissen Sie zufällig die Vorwahlnummer?	Do you happen to know the dialling code (am: area code)?
Haben Sie ein Telefonbuch?	Do you have a directory / phone book?
Ich brauche das Branchenverzeichnis.	I need the yellow pages.
Könnten Sie mir die Nummer des Strandhotels geben?	Could you give me the telephone number of the Beach Hotel?
Teilen Sie mir bitte mit, wieviel das Gespräch kostet.	Please let me know what the call comes to.
Ich möchte das Gespräch bezahlen.	I'd like to pay for the call.

Die Vermittlung ruft zurück und sagt Ihnen, wieviel das Gespräch macht?	The operator will ring you back and tell you how much the call comes to.
Wann muß ich die Münze einwerfen?	When do I have to insert the money?
Wenn Sie den hohen Signalton hören, müssen Sie Geld nachwerfen.	When you hear the high-pitched tone, you have to insert more money.
Vermittlung, ich bin unterbrochen worden. Können Sie mich bitte wieder verbinden?	Operator, I've been cut off. Could you connect me again, please?

Siehe auch *Effektiv telefonieren*, Seite 127ff.

P Master your phrases

Task 6: These sentences are in a mess.

Can you correct them? Put the right word next to the phrase.

1. Insert the receiver. ....
2. Listen for your money in the slot. ....
3. Dial the dialling tone. ....
4. Lift the number required. ....
5. First dial the subscriber's code. ....
6. Then the international code minus initial '0'. ....
7. Then dial the area number. ....

Task 7: Guided translation

1. Can I make a (*Ferngespräch*) from here?
2. I'd like to make a (*R-Gespräch*) call to New York.
3. I'd like to place a (*Gespräch mit Voranmeldung*).
4. Could you let me have the (*Branchenverzeichnis*)?

C Crossword power

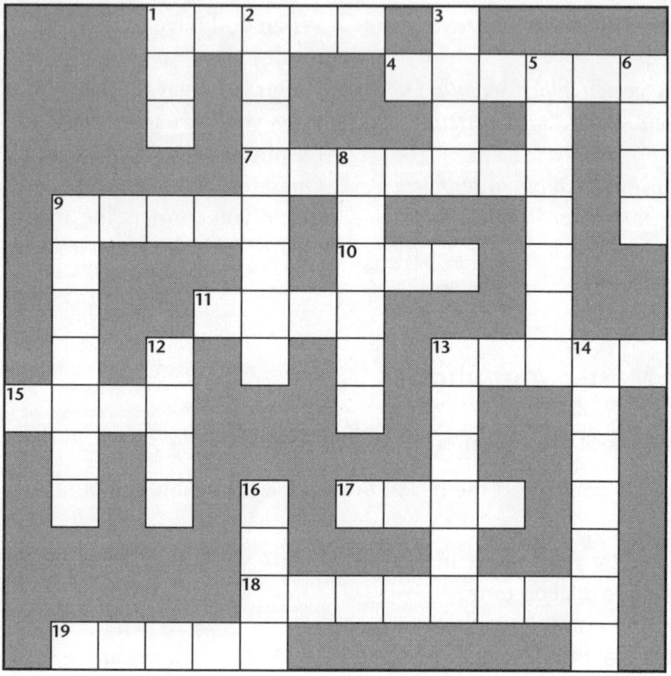

Across

1. A $1000 postal ✎ to a firm in the USA, please. 4. Päckchen 7. What's the postage on an ✎ letter to Germany? 9. I need the yellow ✎ . 10. I'm looking for a letter-✎ . 11. ✎ the number required. 13. I'd like to send this letter ✎ restante to Leeds. 15. What time does the cheap ✎ for international calls begin? 17. Do you have an account ✎ the post office bank? 18. Listen for the ✎ tone. 19. Have you got any special-✎ stamps?

Down

1. Where can I send ✎ this parcel? 2. How much is a normal ✎ letter? 3. This parcel will ✎ four weeks to Italy. 5. Do I have to fill out a ✎ declaration? 6. Can you get me a ✎ to Zurich, please? 8. Instructions in ✎ phone boxes 9. What's the ✎ on an express letter to Germany? 12. We have been cut off. The line is ✎ . 13. A ✎ order to a firm in the USA, please. 14. Can I dial straight ✎ to Munich in Germany? 16. First dial the international ✎ .

Einkaufen
Buying things

Time for a smile

After a tiring day's shopping, the perfect purchase is either in the first or the last shop you've been into.

Die ersten Wortwechsel – First words

Guten Morgen. Kann ich Ihnen helfen?	Good morning. What can I do for you?
Werden Sie schon bedient?	Are you being served?
Nein, danke. Ich schaue mich bloß um.	Thanks. I'm just looking around.
Wer ist der nächste?	Who's next, please?
Ich glaube, ich bin jetzt an der Reihe.	Excuse me, I think it's my turn.
Entschuldigung. Nach Ihnen.	Oh, I'm sorry. After you.
Könnten Sie mir vielleicht helfen?	I wonder if you could help me.
Ich suche ...	I'm looking for ...

Die kleinen Dinge – Bits and pieces

Wo bekomme ich Filme für meine Videokamera?	Where can I buy films for my video camera?
Haben Sie Diafilme für diese Kamera?	Have you got slide films for this camera?
Können Sie diesen Film entwickeln? Einen Abzug pro Negativ.	Could you develop this film? One print from every negative.
Würden Sie mir zeigen, wie man den Film einlegt?	Would you show me how to put the film in?
Ich brauche eine Straßenkarte von London.	I need a map of London.
Ist hier ein Optiker in der Nähe?	Is there an optician near here?
Könnten Sie diese Brille reparieren?	Could you repair these glasses / spectacles?

Wie lange dauert es?	How long will it take?
Wann ist meine Uhr fertig?	When will my watch be ready?
Wie teuer wird die Reparatur werden?	What will it cost to repair?
Ich brauche eine Zahnbürste, Zahnpasta und Sonnenöl.	I'd like a toothbrush, toothpaste and sun-tan lotion, please.

Kleider kaufen – Buying clothes

Murphy's Law about buying clothes

1. If you like it, they don't have it in your size.
2. If you like it and it's in your size, it doesn't fit anyway.
3. If you like it and it fits, you can't afford it.
4. If it fits, it's ugly.
5. If you like it, it fits and you can afford it, it falls apart the first time you wear it.

Der Pullover gefällt mir. Kann ich ihn anprobieren?	I like this pullover. Could I try it on?
Haben Sie etwas Billigeres?	Haven't you got anything cheaper?
Ich würde gerne dieses Sporthemd anprobieren?	I'd like to try this sports shirt on?
Was für eine Größe tragen Sie?	What size do you take?
Ich habe Größe 52.	I take a size 52.
Dieses Hemd ist leider zu weit an den Schultern.	I'm afraid this shirt is too wide across the shoulders.
Versuchen Sie es mit Größe 48.	Try a size 48.
Ich möchte diese Hose umtauschen.	I'd like to change these trousers.
Sie ist nicht meine Größe.	They are not my size.
Ich fürchte, dieser Anzug sitzt nicht gut.	I'm afraid the suit doesn't fit me very well.
Könnten Sie das Jackett ändern?	Could I have the jacket altered?
Die Ärmel sind zu lang.	The sleeves are too long.
Ich suche eine Bluse.	I'm looking for a blouse.
Diese Bluse paßt gut zu Ihrem Rock.	This blouse goes nicely with your skirt.

Den Rock kann man ändern, ohne Aufpreis.	The skirt can be altered at no extra charge.
Gibt es diese Strickjacke in anderen Farben?	Is this cardigan available in other colours?
Wie wäre es mit Gelb?	What about something in yellow?
Ich hätte gerne ein paar Schuhe, Größe 42.	I'd like a pair of shoes, size 42.
Diese Schuhe sind zu eng. Ich brauche die nächste Größe.	I'm afraid these shoes are too small. I need the next size.
Sehen Sie diesen Regenmantel hier? Das ist wirklich ein gutes Angebot.	Look at this raincoat. It's a real bargain.
Kosten Änderungen extra?	Do I have to pay for alterations?
Ich möchte diesen Regenmantel reinigen lassen.	I'd like to have this raincoat cleaned.

Good bargains

A bargain is something you buy that is cheaper than something you really want or need.

An der Kasse – At the check out

Wieviel macht das alles zusammen?	How much is that altogether?
Wollen Sie im voraus bezahlen?	Do you want to pay in advance?
Nehmen Sie Deutsche Mark?	Do you accept German marks?
Ich möchte mit Kreditkarte zahlen.	I'd like to pay by credit card.
Wir benötigen eine Anzahlung von 10 %. Sie bezahlen den Rest nach Lieferung.	We require a deposit of 10 %. You can pay the rest after delivery.
Könnte ich eine Plastiktüte haben?	Could you give me a carrier bag, please?
Können Sie es bitte als Geschenk einpacken?	Could you gift-wrap it, please?
Könnten Sie mir diese Sachen ins Hotel schicken?	Could you send these things to the hotel, please?
Könnten Sie es mir an diese Adresse schicken lassen?	Could I have it sent to this address?

Master your phrases

Task 8: Find a phrase that has the same meaning

Can I help you?	What ....?
I think I was next.	I think ....
We need a deposit of 10 %.	We .... a deposit of 10 %.
When will it be ready?	How ....?

Task 9: One word for four idioms

1. How long will it	....................................?
2. What size do you	....................................?
3. I'll	this cardigan.
4. Do you	German marks?

Task 10: What to say in these situations?

The problem	What to say
Your raincoat is dirty.	I'd like to ....
The skirt doesn't fit, but you want it after all.	Could you .... this skirt?
The article is a bit too expensive.	....?
You want to send it as a present.	Can you .... it, please?
It's too heavy and your hotel is far away.	Could you ....?

C Crossword power

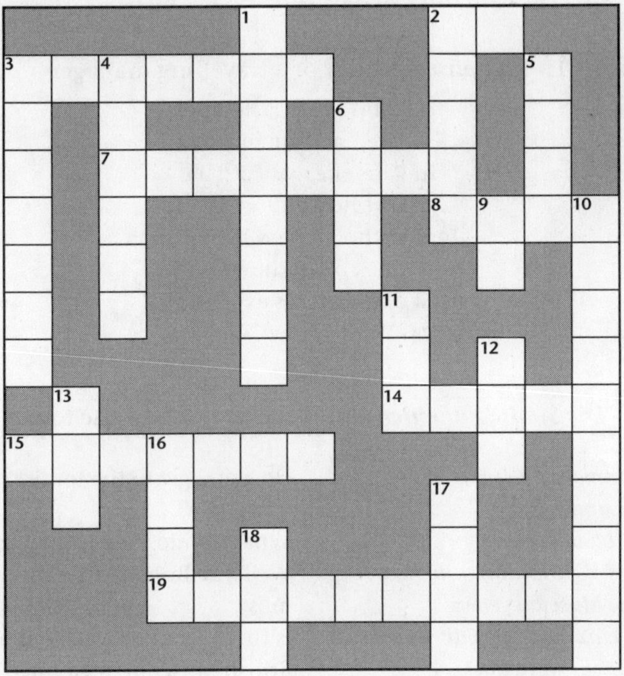

Across

2. Can I pay ✎ credit card? 3. Could you repair these ✎ 7. You buy spectacles at the ✎ 8. This blouse ✎ nicely with your skirt. 14. One ✎ from each negative, please. 15. This raincoat is really a good ✎. 19. I'd like a toothbrush and ✎, please.

Down

1. You can pay the rest after ✎. 2. Are you ✎ served? 3. They help you see better. 4. I'm just looking ✎. 5. What size do you ✎? 6. I take a ✎ 52. 9. Could I try it ✎? 10. Could you repair these ✎? 11. I need a ✎ of London. 12. This suit doesn't ✎ me very well. 13. ✎ I help you? 16. Another word for '*present*' 17. Could you gift-✎ this, please? 18. What are you looking ✎?

Leben nach der Arbeit
Life after work

The expense account of a travelling manager

In Berlin she was Belinda,
She was Patsy up in Perth,
In Paris she was Patricia,
The sweetest girl on earth.
In Stockholm she was Stella,
The pick of all the bunch,
But down on his expenses,
It was Petrol, Hotel, Lunch ...

Die Stadt kennenlernen – Getting to know the town

Wie komme ich von hier zum Verkehrsamt?	How do I get to the tourist office from here?
Was ist besonders sehenswert hier?	What should I see while I'm here?
Sie müssen (unbedingt) in das Britische Museum gehen.	Well, the British Museum is a must.
Gibt es eine deutsche Führung durch das Britische Museum?	Is there a guided tour of the British Museum in German?
Könnten wir einen Deutsch sprechenden Führer bekommen?	Could we have a German-speaking guide for this tour?
Können Sie uns eine Stadtführung empfehlen?	Can you recommend us a guided tour of the town?
Kommen wir auch in die Altstadt?	Will we also be visiting the old part of the city?
Wie wäre es mit einer geführten Busrundfahrt durch die Altstadt?	What about a guided bus tour of the old city?
Was sind die wichtigsten Sehenswürdigkeiten in London?	What are the most important sights in London?
Können Sie mir einen interessanten Bummel auf der Karte zeigen?	Can you show me an interesting walk on the map?

Holt uns der Ausflugsbus vom Hotel ab?	Will the bus for the excursion pick us up at the hotel?
Wann brechen wir zu dem Ausflug auf?	When do we set off for the excursion?
Um wieviel Uhr kommen wir zum Hotel zurück?	What time do we get back to the hotel?
Haben wir Zeit, um etwas einzukaufen?	Do we have any time to do any shopping?
Haben Sie einen Katalog auf deutsch?	Do you have a catalogue in German?
Darf man photographieren?	Are we allowed to take photos?

Sightseeing the American way

An American tourist was visiting a zoo in London. In front of the kangaroo house he stopped dead and exclaimed, "One thing I really grant you Brits. Your grasshoppers are really a lot bigger than ours back in Texas."

Kulturelle Veranstaltungen – Cultural events

Könnte ich bitte einen Blick in Ihren Veranstaltungskalender werfen?	Excuse me, could I have a look at your calendar of events?
Was läuft im Kino?	What's on at the cinema?
Können Sie mir einen Film empfehlen?	Can you recommend a film?
Wann beginnt der Hauptfilm?	When does the main film start?
Wann beginnt die (Abend-) Vorstellung?	When does the (evening) performance start?
Wo bekomme ich die Karten?	Where do I get the tickets?
Beim Kartenvorverkauf.	At the booking office.
Ich möchte Plätze für heute abend reservieren.	I'd like to reserve seats for tonight.
Wann beginnt der Vorverkauf für Hamlet?	When does the booking for Hamlet start? / When can you start booking for Hamlet?

Zwei Karten für morgen abend.	Two tickets for tomorrow evening, please.
Haben Sie noch Karten für heute abend?	Have you got any tickets left for tonight?
Tut mir leid. Sonntags finden in England keine Vorstellungen statt.	Sorry. There aren't any performances on Sunday in England.
Tut mir leid, wir sind ausgebucht.	Sorry, we're sold out.
Können Sie mir sagen, wie ich zur Oper komme?	Can you tell me where the opera house is?
Wo ist die Garderobe?	Where's the cloakroom?

Sightseeing the German way

A group of German tourists makes its way to the top of Mount Etna and looks into the smoke-filled crater. One of them turns to his neighbour and says, "It looks just like hell." The Italian guide hears this, shakes his head and mutters, "Oh, these Germans. They've been everywhere!"

Andere Ereignisse – Other events

Können Sie mir einen guten Nachtclub empfehlen?	Can you tell me where to find a good night-club?
Um wieviel Uhr beginnt die Show?	What time does the show start?
Ist Abendgarderobe erforderlich?	Do you need to dress up?
Gibt es hier einen Golfplatz?	Do you have a golf-course here?
Wollen wir tanzen gehen?	Shall we go dancing?
Ich würde lieber einen Bummel machen.	I'd rather go for a walk.
Darf ich Sie zu einer Party einladen?	Would you like to come to a party?
Darf ich Sie nach Hause begleiten?	May I walk / drive you home?

C Crossword power

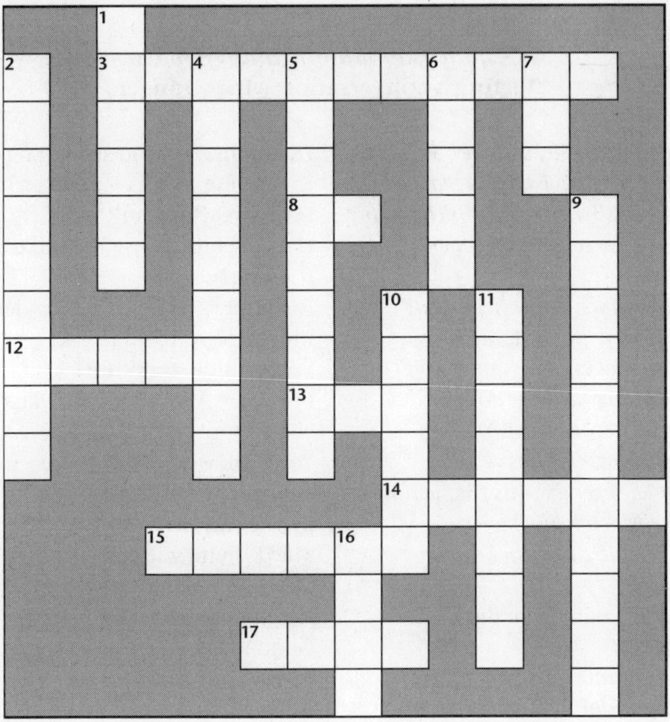

Across

3 German for *'tourist office'*
8 When do you pick us ✎ ?
12 he explains the sights to you.
13 When do we set ✎ ?
14 you watch a film there.
15 Is there a golf ✎ here?
17 English for *'Bummel'*

Down

1 the calendar of ✎
2 you buy it at the museum
4 English for *'empfehlen'*
5 sightseeing trip
6 a place of interest
7 plan of a city
9 you watch it at the theatre
10 you ask for tickets there
11 it tells you the date
16 Sorry, we're ✎ out.

Menschen begegnen
Meeting people

Gesprächsanbahnung mit Fremden
Starting a conversation with strangers

Entschuldigen Sie, sprechen Sie Englisch?	Excuse me, do you speak English?
Entschuldigung, ist dieser Platz besetzt?	Excuse me, is this seat taken?
Ein scheußliches Wetter, nicht wahr?	Nasty weather, isn't it?
Regnet es so schon lange hier?	Has it been raining here like this for long?
Es ist ziemlich kalt / heiß / voll hier, finden Sie nicht auch?	It's rather cold / hot / crowded in here, don't you think?
Das ist aber ein langsamer Zug!	What a slow train it is!
Entschuldigung, war das Ihr Glas / Stuhl / Fuß?	I'm sorry. Was that your glass / chair / foot?
Sie sehen besorgt aus. Kann ich irgend etwas für Sie tun?	You look worried. Is there anything I can do for you?
Übrigens, ich heiße Meier.	By the way, my name is Meier.
Darf ich Sie zu einem Drink einladen?	May I invite you for a drink?
Wie wär's mit einem Bier? – Gute Idee!	How about a beer? – Good idea!
Sind Sie zum ersten Mal in Deutschland?	Is this your first visit to Germany?
Sind Sie geschäftlich hier oder zum Vergnügen?	Are you here on business or pleasure?

Sich vorstellen – Introducing oneself

"How do you do?" is a greeting, not a question.
So don't tell people about your indigestion.

Darf ich mich vorstellen?	Can / May I introduce myself?
Darf ich bekannt machen?	May I introduce you?

Ich heiße Hans Krug.	I'm Hans Krug.
Ich sollte mich vielleicht vorstellen.	Perhaps I should introduce myself.
Mein Name ist Tom Dobson.	Tom Dobson's the name.
Verzeihung, ich habe Ihren Namen nicht verstanden.	Sorry. I didn't catch /get your name.
Ich glaube, wir sind uns schon einmal begegnet.	I think we've met before.
Ich bin aus Bonn. Wo kommen Sie her?	I'm from Bonn. Where are you from?
Ich bin auf Urlaub / Geschäftsreise hier.	I am here on holiday / a business trip.
Freut mich, Ihre Bekanntschaft zu machen.	Pleased to make your acquaintance.
Freut mich, Sie kennenzulernen.	Pleased / Glad to meet you.
Es war nett, Sie kennenzulernen.	It's been nice meeting you.
Ich hoffe, wir sehen uns mal wieder.	See you again, I hope.

Time for a smile

Two businessmen were having lunch one day when two women entered the restaurant. "Oh, dear," whispered one. "My wife and my lover have just walked in." The other hid behind his newspaper and whispered, "So have mine."

Über den Beruf sprechen – Talking about one's job

Ich arbeite in der Buchhaltung.	I'm from accounts.
Ich bin von IBM in Berlin.	I'm from IBM in Berlin.
Was machen Sie beruflich?	What line of business are you in?
Ich bin Handelsvertreter.	I'm a sales rep.
Ich arbeite für eine Firma, die Maschinen baut.	I work for an engineering company.
Wir produzieren Teile für die Autoindustrie.	We make parts for the car industry.
Meine Firma vertreibt Computerprogramme.	My firm markets computer software.

Siehe auch *Introducing the company*, Seite 99.

Auf einem Kongreß – At a congress

Entschuldigen Sie, wo ist das Konferenzzimmer?	Excuse me, where is the conference room?
Sie sehen ein bißchen verloren aus. Kann ich Ihnen helfen?	You look a bit lost. Can I help you?
Sind Sie zum erstenmal hier? – Ich auch.	Are you here for the first time? – So am I.
Es ist nett hier. Kommen Sie oft hierher?	Nice place. Do you come here often?
Wissen Sie zufällig, wer der Gastredner ist?	Do you happen to know who the guest speaker is?
Was erwarten Sie von dem Kongreß?	What do you expect from the congress?
Darf ich mich zu Ihnen setzen, falls Sie niemanden erwarten?	If you aren't expecting anybody, do you mind if I join you?
Darf ich fragen, warum Sie hier sind?	May I ask why you are here?
Ich bin aus Deutschland. Wo kommen Sie her?	I'm from Germany. Where are you from?
Sind Sie auch im Hilton?	Are you also staying at the Hilton?
Ist es angenehm? – Ja, sehr.	Is it comfortable? – Yes, very.
Wie ist das Essen?	What's the food like?
Wie lange bleiben Sie? – Nur für zwei Tage.	How long are you staying? – Just for two days.
Darf ich Ihnen meine Karte geben?	Let me give you my card.
Wir könnten zusammen zu Abend essen, wenn Sie wollen.	We could have dinner together, if you like.

Time for a smile

I surprised my wife with a mink coat.
She'd never seen me in one.

P Master your phrases

Task 11: A *woggle* exercise to test your memory

Each *woggle* stands for a word.

1. May I *woggle* myself? Peter Smith is the *woggle*.
2. Sorry. I didn't *woggle* your name.
3. Are you here on *woggle* or pleasure?
4. I think we've *woggled* before.
5. It's been nice *woggling* you.
6. *Woggled* to meet you, too.
7. Do you woggle to know who the guest *woggler* is?
8. Are you also *woggling* at the Hilton?

Task 12: How to say 'Entschuldigen Sie'

Match them			
1	*Excuse me,*	A	for being late again. I had a breakdown.
2	*Sorry,*	B	for saying so, but I don't like your smoking.
3	*I beg your pardon,*	C	was that your foot?
4	*I apologise*	D	I'm afraid I didn't catch your name.
5	*Forgive me*	E	do you speak English?

Time for a smile

One girl told her friend:
"He not only lied to me about his yacht,
but I had to do most of the rowing."

C Crossword power

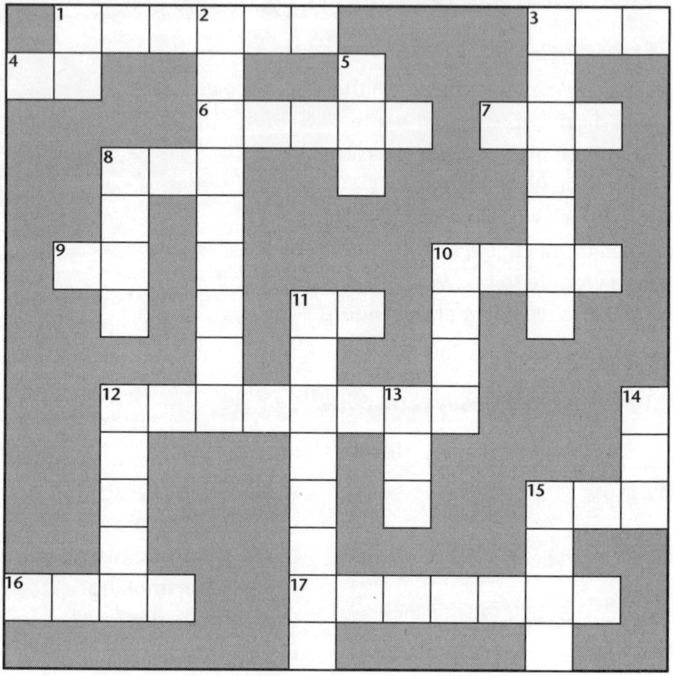

Across

1. May I ✎ you for a drink? 3. I think we've ✎ before. 4. Are you here ✎ business or pleasure? 6. Excuse me, is this seat ✎ ? 7. ✎ me give you my card. 8. May I invite you ✎ a drink? 9. Are you here for the first time? – ✎ am I. 10. Has it been raining here like this for ✎ ? 11. Did you come ✎ train? 12. Are you here on business or ✎ ? 15. ✎ I ask why you are here? 16. You look a bit ✎ . Can I help you? 17. Are you also ✎ at the Hilton?

Down

1. What line of business are you ✎ ? 2. May I ✎ myself? 3. It's been nice ✎ you. 5. I didn't ✎ your name. 8. I'm ✎ Germany. Where are you ✎ ? 10. What ✎ of business are you in? 11. Are you here on ✎ ? 12. We make ✎ for the car industry. 13. I'm a sales ✎ . 14. By the ✎ , my name is Meier. 15. Do you ✎ if I join you?

5. *Messen und Firmen besuchen* Visiting fairs and companies

Receptionists, don't judge by appearance!

Receptionists, waiters and policemen tend to judge people by their appearance, which can be a mistake – as this story illustrates.
A shabby gentleman turned up at the National Gallery one day with a painting under his arm. He asked to see the director, but was rudely turned away, and only after he had waited patiently and repeated his request was he allowed in. The old man tried to persuade the director to take a quick look, but he firmly refused and was on the verge of having him removed from the office when the covering fell off – revealing a masterpiece that the director had tried but failed to buy at an auction. "My name is Sir William Wallace," said the shabby gentleman, a well known millionaire, quietly. "I came to offer this picture to the National Gallery."

Auf der Handelsmesse
At the trade fair

Let's start with a smile

At a computer fair, James Kelly was shown a computer that could answer every question. He asked it where his father was. It answered: "Your father is playing poker in a saloon in Las Vegas."
"Wrong," said James. "My father is dead and his body lies in a Baptist cemetery in Ohio." The salesman was surprised, and hurriedly typed in: "Where exactly is Mr Kelly senior?" The computer flashed its answer up on the screen:
"Mr Kelly senior's body lies in a Baptist cemetery in Ohio, but this bastard's father is still sitting in that saloon in Las Vegas."

Informieren Sie sich – Get the right information

Wann soll die Ausstellung stattfinden?	When is the exhibition to be held?
Wann findet die Ausstellung statt?	When will the exhibition take place?
Wo genau liegt das Ausstellungsgelände?	Where exactly is the exhibition site?
Wie lange dauert die Ausstellung?	What is the duration of the fair?
Die Messe wird am Montag eröffnet.	The fair will open on Monday.
Die Messe ist von 9.30 bis 18.45 geöffnet.	The opening hours of the fair are from 9.30 a.m. to 6.45 p.m.
Wann wird die Öffentlichkeit zur Messe zugelassen?	When is the fair open to the public?
Wieviel Besucher erwarten Sie?	How many visitors are you expecting?
Wir hatten 100000 Besucher letztes Jahr.	Last year, we had 100,000 visitors.
Wie viele Stände wird es geben?	How many stands will there be?
Haben Sie schon Reservierungen von Firmen aus unserer Branche bekommen?	Have you already received any bookings from firms active in our field?

Welche Veranstaltungen gibt es während der Messe?	What events will be held while the trade fair is on?
Kann man im Ausstellerverzeichnis werben?	Is it possible to have advertising in the catalogue?
Vermitteln Sie Dolmetscher und Hostessen?	Do you organise interpreters and hostesses?
Sorgen Sie auch für die Erfrischungen?	Do you also supply refreshments?
Könnten Sie uns bei der Zollabfertigung behilflich sein?	Could you help us with the customs clearance?
Könnten Sie uns die Informationen zufaxen?	Could you send us the information by fax?

Ausstellungsfläche mieten – Renting exhibition space

Wir möchten an der Ausstellung teilnehmen.	We'd like to take part in the exhibition.
Möchten Sie sich zur Messe anmelden?	Would you like to register to take part at the fair?
Wir möchten uns um eine Ausstellungsfläche bewerben.	We wish to apply for exhibition space.
Wie buche ich einen Stand?	How do I book a booth?
Wann ist der letzte Termin, um einen Stand zu buchen?	When is the last date we can book a stand?
Wann ist Anmeldeschluß?	When's the application deadline?
Was kostet es, einen Stand zu mieten?	How much does it cost to book a stand?
Wie hoch ist die Standmiete?	What's the stand rental?
Können Sie uns ein Angebot für den Quadratmeterpreis machen?	Can you quote us the price per square meter?
Wieviel Quadratmeter benötigen Sie?	How many square meters do you need?
Ist die Versicherung im Preis des Standes inbegriffen?	Does the cost of the stand include insurance?
Wollen Sie mehr als einen Stand aufstellen?	Do you want to erect more than one booth?

Wir möchten uns mit einem größeren Stand an der Messe beteiligen.	We want to participate at the fair with a bigger stand.
Ich würde gerne Stand Nummer 18 buchen.	I would like to book stand number 18.
Wann steht er uns zur Verfügung?	When will it be available?
Ich möchte einen Stand in der Nähe des Haupteingangs.	I'd like a stand near the main entrance.
Ist es möglich, per Fax zu reservieren?	Is it possible to fax you a reservation?
Wir müssen unsere Anmeldung leider zurückziehen.	I'm afraid we have to withdraw our application.

P Master your phrases

Task 1: Let's go *woggling* again

1. We'd like to take *woggle* in the exhibition.
2. When is the exhibition to be *woggled*?
3. Where exactly is the exhibition *woggle*?
4. The fair will *woggle* on Monday.
5. Do you also *woggle* refreshments?

Task 2: Beef up your word power

Find an expression that has almost the same meaning.

stand	b . . . .
booking	r. . . . .
take part in a fair	p . . . . in a fair
free tickets	c . . . . tickets
withdraw an application.	c . . . . . an application

Time for a smile

The newest kind of computer was presented at the Cebit in Hannover. Somebody asked it, "What will Germany be like in 2020?"
The answer came back in Japanese.

Die Messeunterlagen – Trade fair documentation

Bitte nehmen Sie uns in den Ausstellerkatalog auf.	Please list us in the catalogue of exhibitors.
Bis wann brauchen Sie das Werbematerial für die Pressemitteilungen?	When do you need the promotional material / sales literature for the press release?
Wann ist letzter Termin für Einträge in den Messekatalog?	When's the deadline for entries in the exhibition catalogue?
Ich möchte mich vergewissern, daß Sie unsere Produktmappe erhalten haben.	I'd just like to make sure you've received our portfolio.
Schicken Sie uns bitte den Veranstaltungskalender.	Please send us the calendar of events.
Wir würden gerne eine Podiumsdiskussion organisieren.	We'd like to organise a panel discussion.
Wie viele Freikarten können Sie uns überlassen?	How many complimentary tickets will you let us have?
Wie viele Ausstellerausweise kann unsere Firma bekommen?	How many badges can our company have?
Die Messeleitung wird die Messeausweise am Montag ausstellen.	The fair authorities will issue the fair passes on Monday.
Schicken Sie uns bitte eine Besucherliste nach der Messe.	Please send us a list of visitors after the fair.

Den Messestand aufstellen – Setting up the stand

Kann ich kommen, um den Standort für unseren Stand auszusuchen?	Can I come and choose the location for our booth?
Uns wurde zuwenig Ausstellungsfläche zugewiesen.	We were assigned too little exhibition space.
Wir sind nicht mit der Zuteilung der Ausstellungsfläche zufrieden.	We are not satisfied with the allocation of exhibition space.
Wir hätten lieber einen Messestand im Hauptgebäude.	We'd prefer a stand in the main exhibition building.

Gibt es Parkmöglichkeiten für Aussteller?	Are there parking facilities for exhibitors?
Wann können wir unseren Stand aufstellen?	When can we put up our stand?
Werden Sie den Stand selber aufstellen?	Are you going to assemble the stand yourself?
Können wir uns einen Stand aufbauen lassen?	Can we arrange to have a stand built for us?
Beauftragen Sie lieber eine Firma für Messebedarf.	You'd better commission an exhibition contractor.
Wir bringen unsere eigenen Möbel mit.	We'll be bringing our own furniture.
An wen wenden wir uns wegen der Stromanschlüsse?	Who do we talk to for arranging power points?
Wünschen Sie Anschlüsse für Computer?	Do you require connections for computers?
Ich gehe davon aus, daß der Stand Telefon- und Faxanschluß hat.	I assume that the stand is fitted with telephone and fax lines.
Wann müssen wir unseren Stand abbauen?	When do we have to dismantle our stand / pull our stand down?
Sie müssen Ihr Material am Dienstag bis 14.30 abtransportiert haben.	You must remove your material by 14.30 on Tuesday.

Advert at a fashion fair:

Our clothes not only make girls slim,
they also make men look round.

Gespräche am Messestand – Conversations at the booth

Kann ich Ihnen behilflich sein?	Can I help you?
Hätten Sie einen Augenblick Zeit für mich?	Excuse me, could you spare me a minute?
Sind dies Werbegeschenke?	Are these freebies / give-aways?
Sie können diese Disketten mitnehmen.	You can take these floppies with you.
Es sind Messegeschenke.	They're presents from the fair.

Tut mir leid, dies ist ein Ausstellungsstück.	Sorry, but this is a sample and not for sale.
Wie groß ist Ihre Firma ungefähr?	Could you give me some idea about the size of your company?
Wie viele Mitarbeiter beschäftigt Ihre Firma?	How many people are employed by your company?
In wie viele Länder exportieren Sie?	How many countries do you export to?
Wie sieht Ihre Produktreihe aus?	What exactly is your product range?
Welches Modell verwenden Sie denn zur Zeit?	Which model are you using at the moment?
Wie sind Sie damit zufrieden?	How are you getting on with it?
Wie ich sehe, suchen Sie etwas Schnelleres.	As I see it, you're looking for something faster.
Ich glaube, wir haben genau das Richtige für Sie.	I think we've exactly the right solution for you.
Könnte man das Modell auch für ... verwenden?	Could this model also be used for ...?
Ist das Gerät auch für ... geeignet?	Is this device also suitable for ...?
Glauben Sie, daß man diese Version auch für ... verwenden kann?	Do you think this version could be used for ...?
Ich führe es Ihnen vor.	Let me demonstrate it to you.
Dies ist unser neuestes Modell.	This is our latest model.
Wie schneidet es im Vergleich mit der Konkurrenz ab?	How does it compare with its competitors?
Ab wann ist es lieferbar?	When will it be available?
Könnten Sie uns ausführliches Material zu dieser Maschine zusenden?	Could you please send us full details of this machine?
Ich interessiere mich für die technischen Angaben.	I'm interested in its technical details.
Was für eine Kapazität hat es?	How about its capacity?
Gibt es das Werkzeug auch in anderen Größen?	Is this tool available in different sizes?
Wir haben mehrere Produkte, die Ihren Anforderungen entsprechen würden.	We've got several products that would meet your requirements.

Ich glaube, dieses Modell wäre für Sie am besten geeignet.	I'd say the best one for you is this model.
Können Sie die Möbel auch nach Maß anfertigen?	Can you also make customised furniture?
Glauben Sie, daß man diese Serie für unsere Zwecke abändern kann?	Do you think this series could be modified to suit our needs?
Haben Sie ein paar Prospekte für mich?	Do you have any brochures I could have?
Sie erhalten auf alle Produkte einen Messerabatt von 15 %.	You get all products at a trade fair discount of 15 %.
Wir haben Geschäftsstellen in allen europäischen Ländern.	We have offices in every European country.
Diese Einführungspreise gelten nur während der Messe.	These introductory prices are only available during the fair.
Könnten Sie mir Verkaufsliteratur überlassen?	Perhaps you might have some sales literature you could let me have?

Siehe auch *Introducing the company* und *Selling successfully*, Seite 99 und 192 ff.

Advert seen at the Frankfurt Car Saloon

Perhaps the reason why so many people are satisfied with our cars is because we aren't. (HONDA)

In Verbindung bleiben – Keep in touch

Wie können wir Sie erreichen?	How can we reach you?
Ich rufe Sie gleich nach der Messe an.	I'll call you up right after the fair.
Hier ist meine Karte.	Here's my card.
Haben Sie eine Vertretung in unserer Stadt?	Do you have a representative in our town?
Besuchen Sie uns doch einmal in unserem Werk.	Why don't you come and have a look at our plant?
Ich bin nächste Woche in ... Ich könnte dann bei Ihnen vorbeischauen.	I'll be in ... next week. Perhaps I could visit you then.
Schicken Sie uns ein Angebot über 500 Stück.	Please send us a quote for 500 items.

Time for a smile

Selling is the most exciting thing you can do with your clothes on.
John Fenton

Master your phrases

Task 3: Definition exercise

1. Money you need to rent a stand ....
2. The area the fair is to be held on ....
3. Last date for the application ....
4. Number of square meters for the stand ....
5. Lady who helps the visitors ....
6. Free gifts for visitors ....
7. He erects the booth for you ....

Task 4: Printed material

Can you match them?

1	catalogue of	A	material
2	sales	B	literature
3	promotional	C	visitors
4	list of	D	exhibitors

Task 5: Scrambled sentences

Can you get the word order right?

1. Sorry / sale / but / not / sample / this / a / for / is / and.
2. What / product / is / range / exactly / your?
3. How / this / its / with / competitors / compare / does / product?
4. Is / sizes / this / in / available / different /tool?

C Crossword power

Across

1 Please ✎ us the price for a booth. 5. Which model are you ✎ at the moment? 6 Do you ✎ refreshments? 9 Do you require ✎ for computers? 13 When is the fair open to the ✎ ? 15 When will the fair take ✎ ? 16 Is this your latest ✎ ? 17 Where exactly is the exhibition ✎ ? 19 When does the ✎ open? 20 When's the application ✎ ? 21 What exactly is your product ✎ ?

Down

2 A hammer is a ✎ . 3 Please send us a ✎ of visitors after the fair. 4 What is the ✎ of the fair? 7 We'd like to organise a ✎ discussion. 8 How many countries do you export ✎ ? 10 We wish to apply for exhibition ✎ . 11 Could you help us with the customs ✎ ? 12 When can we put ✎ our stand? 14 How do I book a ✎ ? 18 When will the exhibition be ✎ ?

Besuch bei Geschäftspartnern Visiting business partners[1]

Beim Empfang – At the reception

Guten Tag. Was kann ich für Sie tun?	Good morning. How can I help you?
Herzlich willkommen bei PELC. Was kann ich für Sie tun?	Welcome to PELC. What can I do for you?
Hallo, ich bin Tina Trump. Was kann ich für Sie tun?	Hello, my name's Tina Trump. How can I help you?
Mein Name ist ... Ich habe einen Termin mit Herrn/Frau ...	My name's ... I've an appointment with Mr / Ms ...
Würden Sie Frau Smith bitte sagen, daß ich hier bin?	Would you tell Ms Smith that I'm here?
Ach ja. Herr / Frau ... erwartet Sie.	Ah, yes Mr / Ms ... is expecting you.
Nehmen Sie bitte Platz.	Please take a seat.
Ich schaue nach, ob er da ist.	I'll just check if he's in.
Ich sehe nach, ob er am Platz ist.	I'll see if he's at his desk.
Einen Moment bitte. Ich sehe im Computer nach.	Just a moment sir. I'll look on the computer / check on the screen.

Pech gehabt – Bad luck

Erwartet Sie Mr Bews?	Is Mr Bews expecting you?
Tut mir leid. Ich kann Ihren Namen hier nicht finden.	Sorry, I don't seem to have your name here.
Tut mir leid, Mr Bews ist nicht im Büro.	I'm afraid Mr Bews is not in the office.
Tut mir leid, Mr Bews ist heute nicht im Haus / in einer Besprechung.	Sorry, Mr Bews is out today / is at a meeting.

1 Mehr darüber in *Small Talk for Big Business. Business Conversation für bessere Kontakte* (mit Kassette / Audio-CD), rororo 60577.

Ich höre gerade, er ist im Urlaub.	I've been told he's on vacation.
So ein Pech! Mr Brain ist nicht mehr in der Firma.	Oh dear, Mr Brain is no longer with the company.
Er arbeitet nicht mehr für uns.	He doesn't work for us any more.
Tut mir leid. Herr Smith ist aufgehalten worden.	Sorry, sir, Mr Smith has been held up.

Glück gehabt – Good luck

Tragen Sie sich bitte ein / aus.	Please sign yourself in / out.
Sie brauchen einen Ausweis. Bitte unterschreiben Sie das Formular.	You'll need an identity card. Please sign this form.
Würden Sie bitte das Formular ausfüllen?	Could you fill in / out this form, please?
Hier ist Ihre Sicherheitsplakette / Besucherplakette.	Here's your security badge / visitor's badge.
Stecken Sie die Karte in den Schlitz.	Put your card in the slot.
Ziehen Sie die Karte durch den Schlitz.	Swipe / pull the card through the slot.
Finden Sie den Weg zu ihm?	Do you know your way up to him?
Wie komme ich zu ihrem Zimmer?	How do I get to her room?
Wie komme ich zu Mr Sharks Abteilung?	How do I get to Mr Shark's department?
Sein Büro ist im sechsten Stock, Zimmer 606.	His office is on the sixth floor, room 606.
Der Fahrstuhl ist dort drüben.	The elevator's over there.
Wenn Sie aus dem Fahrstuhl kommen, gehen Sie gleich nach links.	Turn left when you come out of the elevator.
Gehen Sie den Korridor entlang. Es ist dann auf der linken Seite.	Go down the corridor and it's on the left.
Ich sage ihm / ihr Bescheid, daß Sie hier sind.	I'll just tell him / her you're here.
Er / Sie holt Sie gleich ab.	He / She'll be down / with you in a moment.

Time for a smile

Etiquette is knowing how to yawn with your mouth closed.

Besucher in Empfang nehmen – Receiving visitors

Guten Tag. Ich bin Tom Prox. Sie müssen Herr Meier sein.	Good morning. My name is Tom Prox. You must be Mr Meier.
Sie sind Herr X? Mein Name ist Brain.	Mr X, isn't it? How do you do? My name is Brain.
Entschuldigen Sie, aber ich bin aufgehalten worden.	Sorry sir. I was held up / detained.
Vielen Dank, daß Sie gekommen sind.	Thank you for coming.
Es freut mich, daß Sie uns besuchen.	So glad you've come to visit us.
Wir tagen in einem anderen Gebäude.	Our meeting is in a different building.
Wenn Sie mir bitte folgen würden.	If you'd like to come this way.
Hier entlang, bitte.	Would you please come this way?
Darf ich Ihnen das Gepäck abnehmen?	Can I give you a hand with your luggage?
Darf ich Ihren Mantel nehmen?	Please let me take your coat.
Da wären wir. Möchten Sie ablegen?	Here we are. May I take your coat?

Time for a smile

This man is an incurable liar,
except when he compliments me.

Eisbrecher – Ice breakers

Nehmen Sie doch Platz.	Do sit down. / Please take a seat.
Machen Sie es sich bequem.	Do make yourself comfortable.
Sind Sie zum ersten Mal bei uns?	Is this is the first time you've been here?
Hatten Sie eine angenehme Reise?	Did you have a good trip?
Der Zug war etwas überfüllt.	The train was rather overcrowded.
Ich hoffe, Sie hatten einen guten Flug / Überfahrt.	I hope you had a pleasant flight / crossing.
Der Flug war ziemlich unruhig.	The flight was rather bumpy.

Sind Sie gut durch den Zoll gekommen?	Did you get through the customs alright?
Haben Sie problemlos hergefunden?	Did you have any trouble finding us?
Haben Sie unsere Firma gleich gefunden?	Did you find our company straight away?
Dank Ihrer genauen Beschreibung hatte ich keine Probleme.	I didn't have any trouble thanks to your clear instructions.
Wo übernachten Sie?	Where are you staying?
Wie war der Transfer zum Hotel?	How was the transfer to the hotel?
Aber bitte, setzen wir uns doch.	Let's sit down, shall we?
Wir haben uns ja schon eine Ewigkeit nicht mehr gesehen.	We haven't seen each other for ages.
Wie geht es Ihrer Familie?	How is the family?
Danke, sehr gut. Und wie steht's bei Ihnen?	Very well, thanks. And yours?
Übrigens, vielen Dank für Ihre Weihnachtsgrüße.	By the way, many thanks for your Christmas greetings.
Lassen wir die Förmlichkeiten beiseite.	Let's forget the formalities.
Ich schlage vor, wir lassen die Förmlichkeiten beiseite.	I suggest we drop the formalities.
Darf ich Ihnen etwas zum Trinken anbieten?	May I offer you something to drink?
Kaffee, Tee oder etwas anderes?	Coffee, tea or something else?
Stört es Sie, wenn ich rauche?	Do you mind if I smoke?
Ich nehme das gleiche wie Sie.	I'll have the same as you.
Trinken wir zuerst ein Tröpfchen zum Aufwärmen?	Shall we have a drop of something to keep the cold out first?

Time for a smile

Bob: "How do you like your change from salesman to teacher?"
Ron: "Fine. The pay is regular and the hours are satisfactory.
But what I like best is that the pupil is always wrong."

Die Firma vorstellen – Introducing the company

Unsere Firma wurde 1895 gegründet.	Our company was founded in 1895.
Wir sind eine Firmengruppen, die Seife vertreibt.	We're a group that markets soap.
Wir sind Hersteller / Produzent von Autoersatzteilen.	We're a manufacturer / maker / producer of spare parts for cars.
Wo ist die Zentrale Ihrer Firma?	Where's your company's head office?
Unsere Zentrale ist in Frankreich.	Our head office / headquarters is located in France.
Unsere Muttergesellschaft hat ihren Sitz in der Schweiz.	Our parent company is Swiss-based.
Unsere Firma hat sich schnell vergrößert.	Our company has grown rapidly.
Wir haben immer die Anforderungen des sich wandelnden Markts erkannt.	We've always recognised the requirements of the changing market.
Wir modernisieren ständig unsere Produktreihe.	We're continuously innovating our product range.
Wir sind innerhalb von 40 Jahren zum Marktführer aufgestiegen.	We've become the market leader within 40 years.
Wir sind einer von Europas führenden Weinlieferanten.	We're one of Europe's leading suppliers of wines.
Wir beschäftigen über 300 Angestellte.	We employ over 300 people.
Wir haben Tochtergesellschaften in zehn Städten.	We've subsidiaries located in ten cities.
Wir richten eine Filiale in Ihrer Stadt ein.	We'll set up a branch in your town.
Unsere Firma ist im Computergeschäft tätig.	Our company is involved / is active in the field of computers.
Unsere Produktpalette enthält auch Flugzeugmotoren.	Our range of products includes aircraft engines.
Wir machen viele Geschäfte im Fernen Osten.	We do a lot of business in the Far East.
Die Firma hatte 1998 einen Umsatz von 10 Milliarden Mark.	The company had a turnover of DM 10 billion in 1998.
Wir haben einen Reingewinn von 5 Milliarden erzielt.	We made a net profit of 5 billion.

Wir haben 10 Millionen in Forschung und Entwicklung investiert.	We invested 10 million in R&D.

Zur Sache kommen – Getting down to brass tacks

Ist es Ihnen recht, wenn wir gleich über das Geschäftliche sprechen?	Is it alright with you if we get straight down to business?
Sollen wir mit der Arbeit anfangen, falls Sie bereit sind?	Well, if you're ready, shall we get down to business?
Können wir anfangen, wenn es Ihnen recht ist?	Can we make a start then, if you don't mind?
Erst die Arbeit, dann das Vergnügen, ist meine Devise.	Business before pleasure is my motto.
Ich freue mich über diese Gelegenheit, ein paar Dinge zu klären.	I'm glad we have this opportunity to settle a few details.
Ich bin froh, daß wir Gelegenheit haben, ein paar offene Fragen zu klären.	I'm pleased we have this chance to discuss a few unresolved questions.
Ich hoffe, wir kommen heute zu einer Einigung.	I hope we can reach an agreement today.

Ⓟ Master your phrases

Task 6: At the reception (rec): Translate

Sie: Könnten Sie Frau Child sagen, daß ich hier bin?
Rec: Erwartet Sie Frau Child?
Sie: Ich habe einen Termin für 10 Uhr bei ihr.
Rec: Nehmen Sie bitte Platz. Sie holt Sie gleich ab.

Task 7: Formalities

1. Could you (*ausfüllen*) this form, please?
2. Here's your (*Besucherabzeichen*).
3. (*Ziehen Sie*) your visitor's card through the (*Schlitz*).

Task 8: Find the right words

You	Your visitor
I hope	Yes, but I'm still suffering from jet lag.
Did you ....?	I didn't have any trouble thanks to your clear instructions.
How ....?	Very well, thanks. And yours?
May I ....?	Thanks. A coffee would be fine.
Is it alright with you if we get ....?	Why not? Business before pleasure is my motto.

Kollegen vorstellen – Introducing colleagues

Mr Pitt, darf ich Ihnen Ms Bell vorstellen?	Mr Pitt, may I introduce you to Ms Bell?
Ms Bell arbeitet in der Personalabteilung.	Ms Bell works in the personnel department.
Paul, ich möchte dich mit Peter Smith bekannt machen. Peter, das ist Paul Lavery.	Paul, I'd like you to meet Peter Smith. Peter, this is Paul Lavery.
Sagen Sie einfach Paul zu mir.	Oh, just call me Paul.
Gerne. Ich heiße Tom.	Right. I'm Tom.
Freut mich, Sie kennenzulernen.	Pleased to meet you.
Ganz meinerseits.	The pleasure is mine ./ Glad to meet you, too.
Peter ist unser Computerspezialist.	Peter is our computer expert.
Tim ist unser Experte in Rechtsfragen.	Tim is the our expert on legal matters.
Tim wird Ihnen gerne alle Ihre Fragen über Produkthaftung beantworten.	Tim will be happy to answer any questions you may have about product liability.
Ms Child bearbeitet Reklamationen.	Ms Child deals with complaints.
Herr Bosy übernimmt die Verkaufsabteilung.	Mr Bosy will take over the sales department.

Ein Firmenrundgang – A tour of the company

Ich glaube, ich sollte Ihnen etwas über unsere Firma erzählen.	I think I ought to tell you something about the company.
Unsere Produktionsstätte befindet sich auf dem Gelände.	Our production facility is on site.
Hier sehen Sie ...	Here you can see ...
Hier fertigen / produzieren wir ...	This is where we produce ...
Das Gebäude da drüben ist ...	That building over there is ...
Vor uns sehen Sie ...	In front of us you can see ...
Neben / gegenüber dem Lager befindet sich ...	Next to / opposite the warehouse there is ...
Leider dürfen wir da nicht rein.	I'm afraid we can't go in there.
Man darf hier nicht fotografieren.	You can't take photos in there.
Handys sind in diesem Gebäude nicht erlaubt.	Mobile phones (cell phones) are forbidden in this building.
Dies ist eine Nichtraucherzone.	This is a no-smoking area.
Wir müssen hier unsere (Schutz-) Helme aufsetzen.	We have to wear our helmets here.

Geschäftsfreunde treffen – Meeting business partners

Hallo, Peter! Lange nicht gesehen!	Hello Peter! Long time no see!
Hallo Tom. Ich habe dich eine Ewigkeit nicht gesehen.	Hello Tom. I haven't see you for ages.
Wie geht es Ihnen?	How are you?
Wie geht's so?	How are things? / How are you doing? / How's life? How are you these days?
Wie geht's uns heute morgen?	How are we this morning?
Danke, gut. Und wie geht's dir?	Fine, thank you. And you?
Es könnte mir schlimmer gehen.	It could be worse.
Ich kann nicht klagen.	I can't complain.
Es gibt nichts, worüber ich klagen könnte.	I have nothing to complain about.

Mir geht's gut.	I'm getting on nicely.
Mir geht es großartig.	I'm feeling great.
Es könnte mir nicht besser gehen.	I couldn't feel better.

Siehe auch *Telephoning effectively: Polite noises*, Seite 151.

P Master your phrases

Task 9: What to say

1. You enter a British company. What would the receptionist say?
   A. How do you do? Can I help you?
   B. Good afternoon. Can I have your name?
   C. Welcome to Lamy. How can I help you?
2. You are introduced to the purchasing manager. He says 'How do you do?' What's your reaction?
   A. Fine thank, you. B. How are you? C. How do you do?
3. One of his salesmen arrives. He greets you: 'How are you, Bob?' How do you react?
   A. Thank you, fine. B. Fine, thank you. C. How are you?

Task 10: Presenting the company

Complete the verbs.

1. Our company was *f.* . . . . . in 1895.
2. We're a *m.* . . . . of spare parts for cars.
3. Our head office is *l.* . . . . . in France.
4. We *e.* . . . . over 300 people.

Long time no see

Two elderly ladies met at a banquet after an absence of ten years. Said the first, "Good gracious, Elizabeth, I haven't seen you for ages. You certainly look a lot older."
"You look much older too, Dorothy, dear. I wouldn't have recognised you except for the dress and hat."

C Crossword power

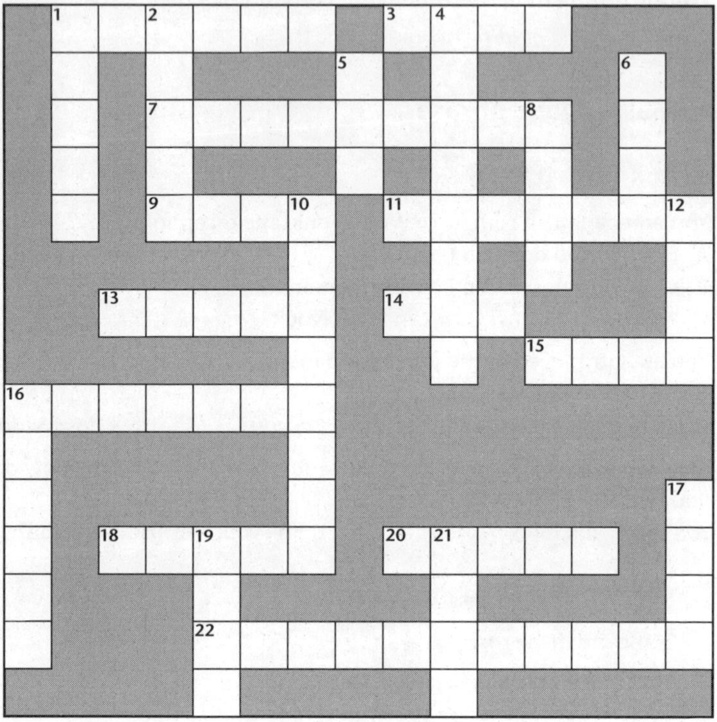

Across

1 Let's ✎ formalities.
3 Paul, I'd like you to ✎ Tom.
7 I'm sure we'll reach an ✎ .
9 How can I ✎ you?
11 What about ✎ business?
13 Here's your visitor's ✎ .
14 Thank you ✎ coming.
15 Do you ✎ if I smoke?
16 I got through the ✎ alright.
18 I'm glad you came to ✎ us.
20 Let's get started, ✎ we?
22 I've an ✎ with Mr Dobson.

Down

1 My office is on the 6th ✎ .
2 Let's ✎ an agreement.
4 Take the ✎ to the 6th floor.
5 Long time no ✎ !
6 Let's get ✎ to business.
8 Please ✎ a seat.
10 Did you have a ✎ flight?
12 ✎ to meet you.
16 Thank you for ✎ .
17 May I take your ✎ ?
19 Do have a ✎ .
21 Let me take your ✎ .

Gastfreundschaft
Hospitality

Let's start with a smile: A difficult guest

James Peabody, director of a company in the Midlands, welcomed an important customer from Germany. "We're so pleased to have you with us. I do hope you'll enjoy your stay. On Monday night you'll be my guest at the club. You'll meet a lot of interesting people and there'll be a lot of drinking and ..."
"I'm sorry, sir," interrupted the German. "I don't drink." "Oh really? Let me see. Tuesday night – you'll like that. We always have a dance. There are lots of pretty girls. You'll really enjoy that."
"No, sir," said the German, "I don't go in for that sort of thing."
"Really? Hmm ... excuse me if I'm being indiscreet. Are you homosexual?" asked Peabody.
"Certainly not, sir."
"What a pity! In that case you won't enjoy Friday night either."

Seien Sie mein Gast – Be my guest

Was haben Sie heute abend vor?	What are you doing this evening?
Ich möchte einen geruhsamen Abend verbringen.	I'm thinking of having a quiet evening.
Haben Sie schon etwas für heute abend vor?	Have you got anything planned for tonight?
Möchten Sie heute abend zu uns zum Essen kommen?	Would you like to join us for dinner this evening?
Vielen Dank, das hört sich gut an.	Thank you, that sounds very nice.
Ich würde mich freuen, wenn Sie mir Gesellschaft leisten würden.	I would be pleased if you would keep me company.
Darf ich Sie heute abend zu mir einladen?	May I invite you to my place tonight?
Hätten Sie Lust, heute abend auf ein Glas Wein zu uns zu kommen?	Would you like to come over for a glass of wine?

Gerne, um wieviel Uhr?	I'd love to; what time?
Paßt es Ihnen zwischen acht und halb neun?	Would between eight and half past suit you?
Wir haben ein paar Kollegen für Freitag abend eingeladen.	We've invited a few colleagues over for Friday evening.
Möchten Sie nicht auch dazukommen?	Wouldn't you like to join us, too?
Ich würde gerne kommen, aber leider kann ich nicht.	I'd love to, but unfortunately I won't be able to.
Ich würde sehr gerne, aber ich habe schon eine Verpflichtung.	I'd love to, but I've got an another engagement.
Warum bringen Sie Ihren Kollegen nicht mit?	Why don't you bring your colleague along with you?
Meine Frau würde Sie gerne kennenlernen.	My wife would like to meet you.
Ich kann leider heute abend nicht.	I'm afraid I can't make it tonight.
Ich fürchte, ich muß ablehnen. Ich muß mal wieder früh ins Bett.	I'm afraid I'll have to say no. I need an early night.
Sie wird sehr enttäuscht sein, wenn Sie unsere Einladung ablehnen.	She'll be very disappointed, if you turn us down.
Vielen Dank. Ich komme gerne.	Thank you very much. I'll look forward to that.
Ich freue mich darauf, Ihre Familie kennenzulernen.	I'm looking forward to meeting your family.

Rejecting invitations the English way

Lady Astor sent George Bernard Shaw the following letter of invitation: "My husband and I would like to invite you to my fortieth birthday party. We are looking forward to seeing you again after all this time." The famous author wrote back: "I very much regret that I won't be able to come to your fortieth birthday party. But I can't tell you how much I enjoyed that same party five years ago."

Fühlen Sie sich wie zu Hause – Make yourself at home

Aber bitte, kommen Sie doch herein.	Please, come on in.
Schön, dich wieder bei uns zu haben.	It's good to see you here again.
Darf ich Ihren Mantel abnehmen?	May I take your coat?
Aber setzen Sie sich doch.	Do sit down.
Darf ich Ihnen einen Aperitif anbieten?	May I offer you an aperitif?
Die Bar ist dort drüben. Bitte bedienen Sie sich.	The bar is over there. Please help yourself.
Möchten Sie einen Sherry?	Would you like a sherry?
Gießen Sie sich noch etwas ein.	Help yourself to some more.
Sie haben eine gemütliche Wohnung.	You've got a cosy flat.
Sie haben ein wundervolles Haus.	You have a wonderful house.
Möchten Sie, daß ich Ihnen das Haus zeige?	Would you like me to show you around the house?
Was für ein schöner Garten!	What a nice garden you have!
Setzen wir uns noch etwas in den Garten.	Let's go and sit in the garden.
Ich würde auch gerne auf dem Land leben.	I'd like to live in the country, too.
Darf ich Sie mit meiner Frau bekannt machen?	May I introduce you to my wife?
Ich habe Ihnen eine Kleinigkeit mitgebracht.	I've brought you a little something.
Herzlichen Dank. Aber das war doch nicht nötig.	Thank you. You shouldn't have.
Mein Mann hat mir schon viel von Ihnen erzählt.	My husband has told me a lot about you.
Ich hoffe nur Gutes.	Only good things, I hope.
Fühlen Sie sich ganz wie zu Hause.	Make yourself at home.
Entschuldigen Sie, wo ist bitte die Toilette?	Excuse me, where is the toilet, please?

Master your phrases

Task 11: Fill in those nasty little words

1. Would you like to join us .... dinner this evening?
2. Why don't you bring your colleague .... you?
3. I'm looking .... meeting your family.
4. Please, come ....

Task 12: Get your tenses right

1. What (*you / do*) this evening?
2. My husband (*tell*) me a lot about you.
3. I (*love*) to join you, but I've got another engagement.
4. My wife (*be / very*) disappointed if you (*turn*) us down.

Task 13: Say it in other words

Have you got anything planned for tonight?	What .... evening?
Why don't you come for dinner this evening?	Would you .... us for dinner this evening?
Would eight o'clock be alright?	Would eight o'clock ....?
I'd love to, but unfortunately I won't be able to.	I'd love to, but I'm........................ .... it.

Time for a smile

There was a young lady of Kent
Who said that she knew what it meant
When men asked her to dine
Upon lobster and wine,
She knew, Oh, she knew! But she went.

Gesprächsanbahnung – Conversation openers

Advice from the expert

The best opener for any conversation is a bottle opener.

Haben Sie uns gleich gefunden?	Did you find us straight away?
Wie war Ihr Aufenthalt in England bis jetzt?	How has your stay in England been so far?
Wann sind Sie angekommen?	When did you arrive?
Waren Sie schon mal in England?	Have you been to England before?
Sind Sie gut untergebracht?	Do you like your accommodation?
Sind Sie mit Ihrem Hotel zufrieden?	Are you satisfied with your hotel?
Haben Sie sich schon eingelebt?	Have you settled in here yet?
Ja, alle hier sind sehr hilfsbereit.	Yes, everybody here is very helpful.
Wie gefällt Ihnen unsere Stadt?	How do you like our town?
Ich habe noch keine Zeit für einen Stadtbummel gefunden.	I haven't yet had time to walk around the city.
Die Altstadt ist wirklich wundervoll.	The ancient city is really marvellous.
Die Menschen sind alle ausgesprochen freundlich.	The people are all really friendly.
Wie gefällt es Ihnen in Deutschland?	How are you finding things in Germany?
Es ist noch zu früh, um darüber etwas zu sagen.	It's a bit early to form an opinion.
Stammen Sie aus dieser Gegend?	Are you from here originally?
Ich bin vor 20 Jahren hierhergezogen.	I moved here about 20 years ago.
Bonn? Wo liegt das?	Bonn? Whereabouts is that?
Das Essen ist fertig. Gehen wir ins Wohnzimmer.	Dinner is ready. Let's move to the living room.
Wir können uns beim Essen weiter unterhalten.	We can continue our conversation at dinner.

Trinksprüche ausbringen – Suggesting toasts

Advice from the expert

You don't say "Cheers" when you drink a cup of tea in the jungle; you say "Christ, the flies!"

Prince Charles

Prost!	Cheers!
Auf Ihr Wohl!	To your good health!
Ich schlage vor, wir trinken auf den Abschluß unseres Vertrags.	I'd like to propose a toast to the conclusion of our contract.
Erheben wir unsere Gläser und trinken auf die Zukunft unserer Firma.	Let's raise our glasses to the future of our company.
Ich erhebe mich, um auf das Wohl unserer Gäste zu trinken.	I rise to toast our guests.
Ich möchte einen Toast auf unseren neuen Kollegen ausbringen.	I'd like to make a toast to our new colleague.
Meine Damen und Herren, begießen wir es mit einem Glas Champagner.	Ladies and gentlemen, let's celebrate this with a glass of champagne.
Auf das Wohl unseres neuen Direktors!	Here's to our new director!
Ich wünsche dem neu ernannten Produktionschef viel Glück und Erfolg.	I'd like to wish the newly designated head of production good luck and every success.
Viel Glück euch beiden.	Best of luck, you two.
Und nun hoch die Tassen.	And now everybody. 'bottoms up!'

Advice to after-dinner speakers:

If after ten minutes you don't strike oil, stop boring.

A gossip talks about others, a bore talks about himself and a brilliant small-talker talks about you.

Höflichkeiten austauschen – Making polite noises

How things can go wrong

During a dinner party the hostess sitting at the opposite end of the table to a great friend scribbled a note to her and asked the butler to deliver it discreetly. Unfortunately, the lady couldn't read without her glasses. So she asked the man seated on her left to help her out. "Please be a dear," he read, "and try to liven up the man on your left. He's a terrible bore, but see if you can talk to him."

Auf ein so gutes Abendessen war ich nicht gefaßt.	I hadn't expected such a good dinner.
Das war wirklich ausgezeichnet.	That was really excellent.
Das ist einmalig!	That's second to none!
Das ist absolute Spitze!	It's out of this world!
Sie müssen mir das Rezept geben.	You must let me have the recipe.
Ich muß wirklich sagen, du verstehst zu leben.	I must say you certainly know what's what.
Ich habe viel von Ihrer Briefmarkensammlung gehört.	I have heard a lot about your stamp collection.
Mir gefällt Ihre Waffensammlung wirklich sehr.	I like your collection of arms.
Zu Beginn möchte ich Tom zu seiner Leistung gratulieren.	I'd like to begin by congratulating Tom on his performance.

A famous anti-small-talker

Calvin Coolidge, the taciturn thirtieth President of the United States, was nicknamed Silent Cal.
"I've made a bet, Mr President," said a young woman next to him, "that I can get more than two words out of you."
"You lose," replied her host.

Erinnerungen aufwärmen – Unlocking memories

Ich hoffe, du gewöhnst dich allmählich an deinen neuen Job.	I hope you're settling in at your new job.
Wie ist dein neuer Chef?	How's your new boss?
Reden wir nicht vom Geschäft.	Let's not talk business.
Wie lange kennen wir uns jetzt schon?	How long have we known each other?
Das müssen gut und gerne zehn Jahre sein.	That must be a good ten years.
Erinnerst du dich, wann wir uns zum ersten Mal begegnet sind?	Do you remember the day when we first met?
Das muß eine Ewigkeit her sein.	That must have been ages ago.
Wo war das doch gleich wieder?	Where was that again?
War das nicht auf Toms Party?	Wasn't it at Tom's party?
Nein, ich glaube, das war in der Vorlesung über ... von Professor X.	No, I think it was at Professor X's lecture on ...
Daran kann ich mich überhaupt nicht mehr erinnern.	I can't remember any of that at all.
Ich erinnere mich noch gut an unsere Studienzeit.	I remember our student days well.
Ach ja, jetzt fällt es mir langsam wieder ein.	Oh yes, it's gradually coming back to me.
Jetzt dämmert es mir wieder.	Now it's beginning to dawn on me.
Das waren noch Zeiten.	Those were the days.
Denkst du noch manchmal an unsere Zeit in Paris?	Do you still think about our days in Paris?
Unser gemeinsamer Urlaub ist mir unvergeßlich.	I'll never forget our holiday together.
Weißt du noch, wie wir zusammen unseren ersten Job gefeiert haben?	Do you remember how we celebrated our first job together?
Erinnerst du dich noch an die alte Dobson?	Can you remember old Dobson?
War das nicht die Wirtin vom Roten Löwen?	Wasn't that the landlady from the Red Lion?
Dein Gedächtnis möchte ich haben.	What a memory you've got!

Hast du noch Kontakt mit Tony?	Are you still in contact with Tony?
Tony, die Ratte? Wie könnte ich den vergessen?	Tony, the rat? How could I forget him?
Was ist eigentlich aus der langbeinigen Jane geworden?	Whatever happened to long-legged Jane?
Es tut gut, die alten Erinnerungen wieder aufzufrischen.	It's nice to remember old times.
Wir müssen uns unbedingt mal wieder treffen.	We really must see each other again.

P Master your phrases

Task 14: Get your tenses right

1. When (*you / arrive*)?
2. (*you / be*) to England before?
3. I (*enjoy*) every single day.
4. How long (*we / know*) each other?
5. (*you / remember*) the day when we first met?

Task 15: Test your toasts

1. I'd like to .... a toast to the conclusion of our contract.
2. Let's .... our glasses to the future of Europe.
3. Id like to .... a toast to our new colleague.
4. .... to our new director!

Leaving the French way

The inventor Thomas Alva Edison had little time for formal dinners. Once, finding himself surrounded by people with whom he had nothing in common, he wanted to escape as soon as possible. But as he was inching towards the door he was approached by his hostess who said, "I'm so pleased that you could come, Mr Edison. Tell me what are you working on now?"
"My exit," replied the inventor.

Sich verabschieden – Taking one's leave

Mein Gott, ist es schon so spät?	Goodness, is it that time already?
Ich glaube, es ist an der Zeit, daß ich mich auf den Heimweg mache.	Well, I think it's about time I started making my way home.
Ich glaube, ich sollte langsam aufbrechen.	I think I should be going now.
Nun, ich glaube, ich sollte mich langsam verabschieden.	Well, I'd better think about leaving.
Ich fürchte, ich muß nun gehen.	I'm afraid I've got to leave now.
Ich muß meinen Zug erreichen.	I've got a train to catch.
Ich kann wirklich nicht länger bleiben.	Well, I really can't be staying any longer.
Schade, aber ich muß mich jetzt wirklich auf die Socken machen.	It's a pity, but I'm afraid I really must be getting along now.
Ich muß mich nun leider verabschieden.	I'm afraid I must be going now.
Aber Sie sind doch gerade erst gekommen.	But you've only just arrived.
Ich fürchte, ich muß langsam aufbrechen.	I'm afraid I must be setting off now.
Wie schade, daß Sie schon gehen müssen. Nun, ich will Sie nicht aufhalten.	Such a shame you have to go already. Well, I mustn't keep you.
Ich möchte Ihre Gastfreundschaft nicht überstrapazieren.	I don't want to overstay my welcome.
Sie wollen doch nicht etwa schon gehen?	You're not thinking of going already?
Müssen Sie wirklich schon gehen?	Do you really have to go already?
Ich kann wirklich nicht länger bleiben.	I really can't stay any longer.
Ich habe morgen einen anstrengenden Tag vor mir.	Tomorrow is going to be a hard day for me.
Es ist schon spät, und wir müssen morgen wieder früh raus.	It's already late and we have to make an early start tomorrow morning.

Time for a smile

Guest: "I'm afraid I've got to leave now. I'd like to thank you for this wonderful evening. Don't trouble to show me out."
Host: "It's no trouble. It will be a pleasure."

Sich bedanken – Saying thank you

Vielen herzlichen Dank für den netten Abend.	Thanks so much for the delightful evening.
Gern geschehen.	My pleasure.
Freut mich, daß es Ihnen gefallen hat.	Glad you enjoyed it.
Keine Ursache. Wir hoffen, es hat Ihnen gefallen.	Don't mention it. We hope you enjoyed yourself.
Ich finde es schade, daß Sie nicht länger bleiben können.	I'm sorry you can't stay a bit longer.
Schade, daß Sie nicht bleiben können.	It's a pity you can't stay.
Ich hoffe, wir sehen uns bald einmal wieder.	Well, I hope we meet again in the very near future.
Lassen Sie bald wieder etwas von sich hören.	I'm looking forward to hearing from you soon.
Ich freue mich schon darauf, Sie auf der Messe in Berlin wiederzusehen.	I'm looking forward to seeing you at the trade fair in Berlin.
Wir hoffen, bald wieder von Ihnen zu hören.	We hope to hear from you soon.
Sie müssen uns bald wieder besuchen kommen.	You must come and see us again soon.
Kann ich Sie vielleicht nach Hause begleiten?	Can I see you home, perhaps?

Time for a smile

Groucho Marx was leaving a particularly boring party.
At the door he said to the hostess, "I've had a wonderful evening – but this wasn't it."

C Crossword power

Across

1. My wife would like to ✎ you. 4. Would you like to ✎ us for dinner this evening? 6. I ✎ to toast our guests. 8. I'd ✎ to come. At what time? 11. I rise to ✎ our guests. 12. Make yourself at ✎ . 14. Let's ✎ to the living room. 15. I'm afraid I've got to ✎ now. 17. Have you got anything ✎ for tonight? 20. I don't want to ✎ my welcome. 21. ✎ you enjoyed it. 22. I quite ✎ your collection of arms. 23. May I ✎ you an aperitif?

Down

2. I'd love to, but I've got an another ✎. 3. Let's not ✎ business. 5. May I ✎ you to my place tonight? 7. Would eight o'clock ✎ you? 9. I'm afraid I can't ✎ it tonight. 10. ✎ your good health! 12. ✎ yourself to some more wine. 13. Let's ✎ this with a glass of champagne. 16. I really ✎ the evening? 19. It's ✎ a delightful evening.

Essen gehen
Dining out

VIPs on food

I just love Chinese food. My favourite dish is 27.
Clement Atlee

I will not eat oysters. I want my food dead.
Not sick, not wounded, dead.
Woody Allen

McDonald's in Tokyo is a terrible revenge for Pearl Harbour.
S. I. Hayakawa

Geschäftsfreunde einladen – Inviting business partners

Was halten Sie von einem Arbeitsessen?	What about a working lunch?
Haben Sie schon zu Mittag / Abend gegessen?	Have you had lunch / dinner?
Darf ich Sie heute zu einem Abendessen einladen?	May I take you out tonight?
Darf ich Sie zu einem guten Abendessen einladen?	May I take you out for a nice dinner?
Hätten Sie Lust, mit mir einmal zum Essen zu gehen?	Would you care to join me for dinner one day?
Wir würden Sie gerne zum Mittagessen einladen.	We'd like to invite you for lunch.
Kennen Sie eine nette Kneipe?	Do you know a good pub?
Wir haben ein gutes Restaurant hier ganz in der Nähe.	There's a good restaurant near here.
Die haben eine gute heimische Küche.	They do good local meals there.
Es gibt dort sehr gute regionale Spezialitäten.	They do / serve very good local cuisine.
Das hört sich gut an.	That sounds good.

Einen Tisch reservieren – Booking a table

Ich möchte für Freitag abend einen Tisch für zwei Personen bestellen.	I'd like to reserve a table for two for Friday night, please.
Könnte ich einen Tisch im Nichtraucherbereich bekommen?	Could I please have a table in the no-smoking area?
Ich hätte gern den Tisch in der Ecke.	I'd like the table in the corner.
Haben Sie einen Tisch für eine Person?	Have you got a table for one, please?
Haben Sie einen Tisch reserviert?	Have you reserved / booked a table?
Ich habe einen Tisch für acht Uhr reserviert.	I reserved a table for eight o'clock.
Auf welchen Namen, bitte?	What name is it, please?
Ein Tisch für drei, bitte.	A table for three, please.
Tut mir leid, wir sind heute ausgebucht.	Sorry, we're full this evening.
Ist dieser Tisch frei?	Is this table free?

Time for a smile

A tourist saw an advertisement for a restaurant which claimed that any dish requested could be served. The man decided to test this restaurant. He entered and ordered an elephant on toast. The waiter took the order and went away into the kitchen. A few minutes later, he returned and said calmly, "We do apologise, sir, but we have run out of bread."

Empfehlen und vorschlagen – Recommending and suggesting

Herr Ober! Ich hätte gerne die Speisenkarte und die Weinkarte.	Excuse me, waiter, could I have the menu and the wine list, please?
Was essen / trinken Sie?	What would you like?
Essen Sie lieber Schweine- oder Kalbfleisch?	Do you prefer pork or veal?
Essen Sie gerne Muscheln?	Do you like mussels?

Nein, ich mache mir nicht viel aus Meeresfrüchten.	No, I don't care much for seafood.
Ich nehme hier immer die Spezialität des Hauses.	I always have the chef's special here.
Was für Fisch essen Sie am liebsten?	What kind of fish do you like best?
Was würden Sie empfehlen?	What would you recommend?
Sie haben sehr gute Weine aus der Gegend.	They serve very good wines from this region.
Es gibt hier einige empfehlenswerte Gerichte / Speisen.	There are several dishes worth eating here.
Sie machen sehr gute regionale Fleischgerichte.	They do very good local meat dishes.
Sie bekommen hier ausgezeichnete Schweinshaxe.	You can get excellent pork knuckle.
Meiner Meinung nach schmeckt Wild hier am besten.	The tastiest thing here in my opinion is the game.
Der Rehbraten ist hier sehr gut.	They serve very good venison.
Sie sollten einen trockenen Rotwein dazu trinken.	You should try a dry red wine with it.

Gespräch mit dem Ober – Talking to the waiter

Here's to the waiter

We had been waiting for ages for the waiter. "Gentlemen," said my host, raising an empty glass, "I rise to toast absent friends, among whom I include the waiter of this table."

Haben Sie schon gewählt?	Are you ready to order?
Entschuldigen Sie, kann ich bitte die Speisenkarte haben?	Excuse me, can I have the menu?
Was sind Ihre Spezialitäten?	What are your specialities?
Gibt es heute etwas Besonderes?	Is there anything special today?
Was ist die Spezialität des Kochs?	What's the chef's special?
Ich habe mich noch nicht entschieden.	Sorry, I haven't decided yet.

Was gibt es heute als Tagesgericht?	What's today's special?
Womit wollen Sie anfangen? Was möchten Sie als erstes?	What would you like to start with?
Ich glaube, ich nehme als erstes einen Shrimpcocktail.	I think I'll have shrimp cocktail to start with.
Und danach?	And to follow?
Was ist das hier genau?	Can you tell me what that is exactly?
Lammrostbraten mit einer Minzsoße.	It's roast lamb with mint sauce.
Lammfleisch wird in England mit einer Minzsoße gegessen. Haben Sie das schon probiert?	In England lamb is eaten with a mint sauce. Have you ever tried it?
Ich habe noch nie Wildschwein gegessen.	I've never eaten wild boar.
Und ich nehme die Ente.	And I'll have the duck.
Ich versuche mal das Lamm.	I'll try the lamb.
Ich nehme das Schweinekotelett.	I'll have the pork chop.
Ich hätte gern die Suppe und danach ein Steak.	I'll have the soup and a steak to follow, please.
Wie hätten Sie das Steak gern?	How would you like the steak?
Englisch (blutig) / medium / durchgebraten.	Rare / medium / well done.
Und als Gemüse / Beilage?	And the vegetables?
Nur einen kleinen Salat, bitte,	Just a side salad, please.
Was möchten Sie trinken?	What would you like to drink?
Ich schlage vor, wir bleiben beim Rotwein.	I suggest we stay with red wine.
Eine halbe Flasche Chablis, bitte.	I'll have a half bottle of the Chablis, please.
Fangen Sie doch an, lassen Sie es nicht kalt werden.	Do start, don't let it get cold.
Ich hätte gerne noch eine Portion.	I'd like a second helping.
Würden Sie mir bitte noch ein Brötchen bringen?	Would you bring me another roll, please?
Könnten Sie mir bitte (noch) etwas Brot bringen?	Could I have some (more) bread, please?

Könnte ich bitte noch einen Löffel haben?	Could I have another spoon, please?
Würden Sie mir bitte den Senf geben?	Would you mind passing the mustard, please?
Schmeckt Ihnen der Wein?	Is the wine to your liking?
Könnten wir jetzt unser Dessert bestellen?	Could we order our sweet / dessert now?
Ein großes Dunkles, bitte.	A pint of bitter, please.
Ein kleines Helles.	A half of lager.
Diese Runde geht auf mich. Was möchten Sie?	This round's on me. What are you having?
Danke, keinen Alkohol für mich, bitte. Ich muß noch fahren.	No alcohol for me, thanks. I'm driving.
Zum Wohl! / Prost!	To our health! / Cheers!
Es ist Zeit, wir schließen gleich!	Time, ladies and gentlemen, please.
Dürfen wir um Ihre letzten Bestellungen bitten?	Last orders, please!

Sich beschweren – Making a complaint

Time for a smile

"Waiter! Look at that! You've brought me a lobster with only one claw."
"I'm ever so sorry, sir, but it lost its claw in a fight."
"Never mind! Take it away and bring me the winner."

Entschuldigen Sie bitte, ich warte immer noch auf mein Steak.	Excuse me! I'm still waiting for my steak.
Entschuldigen Sie, aber dauert es noch lange?	Excuse me, will it be much longer before we're served?
Entschuldigen Sie, aber hier muß ein Irrtum vorliegen. Das habe ich nicht bestellt.	Excuse me, there must be some mistake. This is not my order / this is not what I ordered.
Das ist aber völlig verkocht / nicht durchgebraten.	I'm sorry but this is overcooked / it isn't properly cooked.

Ich habe es medium bestellt, es ist aber fast roh.	I asked for it medium but this is rare.
Es tut mir leid, aber ich kann das so nicht essen.	I'm sorry, I can't eat it done like this.
Ich werde die Rechnung nicht bezahlen, wenn Sie nicht ...	I'm not going to pay this bill if you won't ...
Ich möchte bitte den Geschäftsführer sprechen.	I'd like to speak to the manager, please.

Time for a smile

"Waiter! Waiter! What is this fly doing in my soup?"
"Hm ... Breaststroke, I think."

Die Rechnung, bitte – The bill, please

Zahlen, bitte!	Could I have the bill, please?
Ich möchte bitte zahlen.	Could I have the bill (US: check), please?
Bitte getrennte Rechnung.	Separate bills, please. / We're going Dutch.
Das übernehme ich.	Let me get this.
Nein, nein, Sie sind unser Gast.	No. No. This is on us!
Haben Sie vielen Dank!	Well. Thank you very much.
Das geht auf meine Rechnung.	It's my treat.
Wieviel Trinkgeld gibt man der Kellnerin?	How much do you give the waitress?
Kann ich mit der Karte bezahlen?	Can I pay by credit card?
Nehmen Sie Kreditkarten?	Do you take credit cards?
Nehmen Sie Schecks?	Do you accept cheques?
Ich glaube, mit der Rechnung stimmt etwas nicht.	I think there's something wrong with the bill.
Könnte ich bitte einen Beleg haben?	Could I have a receipt, please?
Einhundert, bitte.	Make it a hundred.
Behalten Sie das Wechselgeld.	Keep the change.

A short list of what you might eat

STARTERS – VORSPEISEN

ham and melon	Melone mit Schinken
prawn cocktail	Krabbencocktail
smoked salmon	Räucherlachs
lobster	Hummer

MAIN COURSE – HAUPTSPEISE

Mutton	Hammel
lamb	Lamm
lamb chops	Lammkoteletts
lamb roast	Lammbraten

PORK – SCHWEIN

cutlet	Kotelett
bacon	Speck

BEEF – RIND

beef burgundy	Burgunderbraten
brains	Hirn
veal	Kalb
minced meat	Hackfleisch

POULTRY – GEFLÜGEL

roast duck	gebratene Ente
roast chicken	gebratenes Hähnchen
partridge	Rebhuhn
turkey	Pute

GAME – WILD

wild boar	Wildschwein
venison	Reh
rabbit	Kaninchen

FISH – FISCH

trout	Forelle
perch	Barsch
pike	Hecht
salmon	Lachs
plaice	Scholle
sole	Seezunge

VEGETABLES – GEMÜSE

boiled vegetables	gekochtes Gemüse
stir-fried vegetables	Wok-Gemüse
peas	Erbsen
cabbage	Kohl
cauliflower	Blumenkohl

sprouts	Rosenkohl
fried potatoes	Bratkartoffeln
chipped potatoes	Pommes frites
mashed potatoes	Kartoffelbrei
SALAD – SALAT	
mixed salad	gemischter Salat
cucumber salad	Gurkensalat
lettuce	grüner Salat
DESSERTS – NACHSPEISEN	
pancake	Pfannkuchen
stewed fruit	Kompott
fruit salad	Obstsalat

How to complain about your steak

I did not say this meat was tough. I just said I didn't see the old horse that usually stands outside.

W. C. Fields

Ⓟ Master your phrases

Task 16: Cross out the wrong verb

1. They *do / serve / make* good meals there.
2. What would you *recommend / assume / suggest*?
3. I think I'll *try / take / test* the T-bone steak.
4. Could I have the *bill / check / invoice*, please?
5. Do you *take / allow / accept* credit cards?

Task 17: How are they normally served?

1 duck	A boiled
2 salmon	B mashed
3 vegetable	C smoked
4 meat	D mixed
5 fruit	E stewed
6 salad	F roast
7 potatoes	G minced

Task 18: They mean almost the same

1. Have you *reserved* a table?	Have you .... a table?
2. Is this table *taken*?	Is this table ....?
3. *Separate bills*, please,	We're ....
4. *Let me get this.*	.... me.
5. Do you *take* credit cards?	Do you .... credit cards?

Time for a smile

The managing director was looking over the expense accounts of the purchasing department.

"What are these items here?" he asked his purchasing manager. "They seem a bit excessive."

"Oh, those are our restaurant bills"

"Well, in future," said the managing director, "don't buy any more restaurants."

C Crossword power

Across

1. Have you ✎ a table? 3. Erbsen 5. Are you ready to ✎ ? 7. There are several dishes worth ✎ here. 10. What ✎ of fish do you like best? 11. Speisenkarte 12. Kalbfleisch 14. Schweinefleisch 16. What would you ✎ ? 20. German for '*working lunch*'.

Down

1. I've never eaten wild ✎ . 2. I'm sorry, I can't eat it ✎ like this. 3. A ✎ of lager, please. 4. They serve good ✎ cuisine here. 6. May I invite you to wine and ✎? 8. Could I please have a table in the no-smoking ✎ ? 9. Wild 10. ✎ the change, please. 13. Rehbraten 15. Kaninchen 17. Ente 18. Would you care to ✎ me for dinner? 19. May I ✎ you out tonight?

EFFEKTIV TELEFONIEREN

TELEPHONING EFFECTIVELY[1]

The first impression a client gets of your company is often over the phone. So don't be caught speechless when it rings. It could mean either the beginning or the end of a business relationship.

Time for a smile

Not knowing who you are talking to can be dangerous, as this phone story shows:
Tom and Tina had been married for twenty years without children. One day, the doctor told Tina that she was expecting a baby. Excitedly she rang up Tom at his office. "Tom, imagine, I am pregnant." "That's great ...," exclaimed Tom. Then, after a long silence, Tom stuttered, "I beg your pardon, who is speaking?"

1 Telefonieren mit Pfiff und Witz, *How to Phone Effectively. Business English am Telefon* (mit Audio-CD oder Kassette), rororo 60139.

1. *Anrufe entgegennehmen* – Answering the phone

Living Models. Guten Morgen. Sie wünschen?	Living Models. Good morning. Can / May I help you?
Ruver Ltd. Guten Tag. Kann ich Ihnen helfen?	Ruver Ltd. Hello. Can I be assistance?
Guten Tag. Was kann ich für Sie tun?	Hello. How can I help you?
Was kann ich für Sie tun?	What can I do for you?
Kann ich sonst noch etwas für Sie tun?	Anything else I can do for you?
Wen wünschen Sie zu sprechen?	Who would you like to speak to?
In welcher Abteilung arbeitet er / sie?	Which department is he / she in?
Kann ich sonst noch etwas für Sie tun?	Can I assist you in any other way?

2. *Sagen Sie, wer Sie sind* – Tell them who you are

Hier ist Jack Brown. Guten Morgen.	Jack Brown here. Good morning.
Hier spricht Tom Smith von der Firma Ruver.	This is Tom Smith of Ruver speaking.
Spreche ich mit Herrn / Frau ...?	Hello? Is that Mr / Ms ...?

Let's start with a smile

Jim Turner has been trying for days to get through to Bill Gates. At last he got his secretary.

"My name is Jim Turner and I'm with the Human Resource Department at the Acme Company. I'm calling to check on a reference given to us by a job applicant. This applicant said that Mr Gates was a close personal friend. I'd like Mr Gates to get back to me about this individual and be so kind as to answer a few questions ..."

"Well, let's see," said the secretary and browsed through Mr Gates' agenda."I'll add your name to Mr Gates' list. You're right behind Steven Spielberg, Bill Clinton, Prince Charles and the Pope. And thank you for calling Microsoft."

(T) Etiquette on the phone: First and last words

When *receiving* an in-coming call a short 'Hello' and 'Goodbye' are not good enough. They could *damage* your company's image or even be the beginning and the end of a new business relationship. Remember, first *impressions* are the most powerful ones. Don't eat, drink or type while you are talking on the phone. And don't give the caller the impression that you are tired, overworked or under *time pressure*. Answer the phone in a warm and *relaxed voice*. Give the caller the impression that he is welcome. Remain natural and don't act. Here are some examples:

- This is how most receptionists answer the phone: "SATCO Company. Can I help you?" This opening is perfectly alright. But you would miss the *opportunity* of creating or strengthening the *relationship* to your potential customer.
- Here is a phrase that makes you appear more personal: "SATCO Company. Good morning. Anne Wilder speaking. What can I do for you?"
- Some receptionists let the *caller* know what line of business the company is in: PELC Company, your personal language consultant. Renny Bosy speaking. What can I do for you?"
- On the other hand, you shouldn't *overdo* it. Look at this example: "PELC Company, Germany's leading language consultant. Renny Bosy speaking. May I help you?"
- A simple "Goodbye" is not good enough, either. It should always be followed by "thank you for calling PELC" and "have a nice day."

annehmen
schaden
Eindruck
Zeitdruck
entspannt; Stimme
Gelegenheit
Beziehung
Anrufer
übertreiben

3. *Den Anrufer identifizieren* – Identifying the caller

Würden Sie mir bitte Ihren Namen nennen?	Could you give me your name, please?
Darf ich Ihren Namen erfahren?	Could I ask your name, please?
Dürfte ich um Ihren Namen bitten?	Could I have your name, please?
Wen darf ich bitte melden?	Who shall I say is calling?
Mit wem spreche ich, bitte?	Could I ask who I'm speaking to?
Entschuldigen Sie, ich habe Ihren Namen nicht richtig verstanden.	I'm sorry, sir. I didn't quite catch your name.
Entschuldigen Sie, wie, sagten Sie, ist Ihr Name?	I beg your pardon, what did you say your name was?
Bin ich mit ROBOTALOT in Bonn verbunden?	Is that ROBOTALOT in Bonn?
Spreche ich mit S.A.T. in Bonn?	Am I speaking to S.A.T in Bonn?
Möchten Sie Ihren Namen und Ihre Adresse hinterlassen?	Would you like to leave me your name and address?
Von wo rufen Sie an?	Where are you calling from?
Wären Sie so freundlich, mir auch Ihre Privatnummer zu geben?	Would you be kind enough to give me your home number, too?
Darf ich um Ihren Namen bitten?	May I ask who is calling?
Könnten Sie das bitte buchstabieren?	Could you spell that, please?
Schreiben Sie Brian mit 'i' oder 'y'?	Do you spell Brian with an 'i' or a 'y'?
Schreibt sich Dunbar mit Doppel-n?	Dunbar, is that with double N?
Herr Brain ... von welcher Firma, bitte?	Mr Brain ... from which company, please?
Und wie ist bitte Ihre Adresse?	And what's the address, please?
Könnten Sie mir bitte auch die Postleitzahl geben?	Could you let me have the post code as well, please?

Ⓟ Master your phrases

Task 1: Answering the phone

Which phrase is wrong?

1. May I assist you somehow other?
2. How can I help you?
3. Can I assist you in any other way?

Task 2: Typical German!

Please correct!

1. What can I for you do?
2. Who like you to speak?
3. I'd like to speak to your husband, if it goes.

Task 3: Identifying the caller

Spot the grammar mistake.

1. Could I ask who I speak to?
2. I'm sorry, sir. I haven't quite caught your name.
3. Do I speak to ROBOTALOT in Bonn?
4. Are you spelling Brian with an 'i' or a 'y'?

Time for a smile

Today I dialled a wrong number. The other person said, "Hello" and I said, "Hello, could I speak to Joey?"
He said, "Ugh ... I don't think so ... he's only two months old."
I said, "I'll wait."

4. *Wen wünschen Sie zu sprechen?* Who do you want to speak to?

Geben Sie mir bitte Ihre Verkaufsabteilung.	Could you put me through to your sales department, please?
Wären Sie so freundlich, mich mit Herrn Brain zu verbinden?	Would you be so kind as to put me through to Mr Brain?
Geben Sie mir bitte Apparat 344.	Could I have extension 344, please?
Grüß Gott. Ist Herr Jones da? Ich würde gerne mit ihm sprechen.	Hello, is Mr Jones there? I'd like to speak to him.
Ich würde gerne Herrn B. sprechen, wenn das möglich ist.	I'd like to speak to Mr Brain, if possible.
Ich würde gerne Herrn B. sprechen, wenn es geht.	I'd like to speak to Mr Brain, if I may.
Könnte ich Herrn B. sprechen, wenn das möglich ist?	Could I possibly speak to Mr B., please?
Wäre es möglich, mit Frau Child zu sprechen, falls sie da ist?	Could I possibly speak to Ms Child, if she's in?
Könnte ich Herrn Brain kurz sprechen?	Could I have a quick word with Mr Brain?
Könnte ich ihn kurz sprechen?	Could I just have a word with him?
Verbinden Sie mich bitte mit Tim Jones.	Put me through to Tim Jones, please.
Ob Sie mich wohl mit Herrn Smith verbinden könnten?	I wonder if you could put me through to Mr Smith.
Ist Mr Brain über das Autotelefon erreichbar?	Can Mr Brain be reached by car phone?
Hat Herr Brain einen Piepser bei sich?	Has Mr Brain got a pager?
Könnten Sie bitte versuchen, ihn anzupiepsen?	Could you please try to get him on the pager?
Könnten Sie ihn bitte anpiepsen?	Could you please page him? Could you try paging him?
Verbinden Sie mich bitte mit Herrn ...	Please put me through to Mr ...
Tut mir leid, sein Name ist mir entfallen.	Sorry, his name has my slipped mind.

Ich muß dringend mit dem Direktor sprechen. Es ist dringend. — I really need to speak to the director. It's urgent.

Es ist sehr wichtig, daß ich mit ihm spreche. — It's very important that I get into contact with him.

Geben Sie mir bitte Herrn Slicer. Es ist ein Notfall. — Please put me through to Mr Slicer. It's an emergency.

5. *Fragen, um was es geht* – Asking what it's about

Time for a smile

It was two o'clock in the morning when Fred phoned Joe. The phone rang for half an hour before it was picked up and Joe's sleepy voice said, "Hello." – "Sorry to get you out of bed at this time of night," said Fred. "That's all right," said Joe, "I had to get up anyway to answer the phone."

Würden Sie mir bitte den Grund Ihres Anrufs nennen? — Would you mind telling me what you are calling about?

Darf ich nach dem Grund Ihres Anrufs fragen? — May I ask the purpose of you call?

Was ist der Grund Ihres Anrufs? — What's the reason for your call?

Darf ich fragen, um was es geht? — May I ask what it is concerned with?

Um was geht es, bitte? — What's it in connection with?

Und was betrifft es, bitte? — And what does it concern, please?

Darf ich fragen, um was es geht? — May I ask what it's about?

Kennt Frau Child den Grund Ihres Anrufs? — Will Ms Child know what you are calling about?

Time for a smile

I got up one morning and couldn't find my socks, so I called Information. She said, "Information. Can I help you?" I said, "I can't find my socks." She said, "They're behind the couch." And they were!

6. *Der Grund des Anrufs* – The reason for the call

Es geht um Ihr Angebot.	It's about your quotation.
Ich rufe wegen des Zeitungsinserats an.	I'm ringing about your advert.
Es handelt sich um Ihre Anzeige.	It's in connection with your advert.
Ich rufe im Zusammenhang mit ... an.	I'm calling in connection with ...
Ich rufe wegen der freien Stelle an.	I'm phoning concerning the vacancy.
Ich rufe wegen einer Reklamation an.	I'm calling to make a complaint.
Ich rufe für Dr. Brain an.	I'm ringing for Dr Brain.
Ich rufe im Auftrag von Dr. Brain an.	I'm calling on behalf of Dr Brain.
Ich rufe an, um Ihre Reservierung zu bestätigen.	I'm phoning to confirm your reservation.
Ich rufe an, um Ihnen die Einzelheiten über ... mitzuteilen.	I'm ringing to let you know the details about ...
Der Grund meines Anrufs ist ...	The reason I'm calling is ...
Ich würde Dr. Brain gerne geschäftlich sprechen.	I'd like to speak to Dr Brian on business.
Ich möchte Dr. Brain in einer Privatangelegenheit sprechen.	I'd like to speak to Dr Brain about a private matter.
Ich glaube, es ist besser, ich spreche mit ihm persönlich.	I think I'd better speak to him personally.
Es ist vertraulich.	It's confidential.
Es ist etwas Privates.	It's a private matter.

Time for a smile

Secretary: "Excuse me, Mr Onion, but I think that somebody wants to talk to you on the phone."

Bob Onion: "You think ...? Now what on earth does that mean, young woman? Listen, does somebody want to speak to me or not?"

Secretary: "Well, Mr Onion, all I can say is that the caller asked if the 'senile old fool' was in the office, so I wasn't sure if you wanted to take it."

P Master your phrases

Task 4: Who do you want to speak to?

Fill in the gaps.

1. Could you .... me .... to your sales department, please?
2. Could I have .... 344, please?
3. Could I have a quick .... with Mr Brain?
4. I really .... to speak to the director. It's ....

Task 5: The reason for the call

Complete the dialogue.

1. May I ask what it is .... with?
2. And what does it ...., please?
3. What's it in .... with?

1. I'd like to speak to Dr Brian .... business.
2. I'm phoning .... the vacancy.
3. I'd like to speak to Dr Brain .... a private ....

Identifying the caller

The phone rang in the maternity ward:
Nurse: "St Joseph's hospital. Nurse Cassandra speaking."
Man: "I'm bringing my wife – she' s going to have a baby. It's urgent."
Nurse: "Is this her first baby?"
Man: "No, no. This is her husband!"

7. *Den Anrufer verbinden* – Putting the caller through

Können Sie mich bitte mit ... verbinden?	Can you transfer me to ..., please?
Verbinden Sie mich bitte mit Fred Niemec.	Please connect me with Fred Niemec.
Könnten Sie mich mit Herrn X verbinden?	Could you put me through to Mr X, please?

Könnten Sie mich bitte mit Frau Child verbinden?	Could you put me in contact with Ms Child, please?
Ich stelle Sie durch.	I'm putting you through.
Bleiben Sie bitte am Apparat!	Hold on, please.
Bleiben Sie bitte dran!	Hold the line, please.
Bleiben Sie am Apparat. Sie werden verbunden!	Hold the line. You are being connected now.
Sind Sie noch am Apparat?	Are you still holding?
Legen Sie nicht auf. Ich verbinde.	Don't hang up. I'll put you through.
Augenblick. Ich stelle Sie durch.	Just a moment, please. Putting you through.
Ich verbinde Sie mit der Kundendienstabteilung.	I'll pass you over to Customer Service.
Sie müssen vermutlich mit Herrn Brodie sprechen.	You'll need to speak to Mr Brodie.
Ich verbinde Sie mit seiner Abteilung.	I'm transferring you to his department.
Ich versuche Sie zu verbinden. Bleiben Sie bitte am Apparat.	Trying to connect you. Hold the line, please.
Tut mir leid, ich kann ihn nicht erreichen.	Sorry, I can't get his number.
Ich gebe Ihnen den Sachbearbeiter.	I'll transfer you to the person responsible.
Ich gebe das Gespräch zurück an die Rezeption.	I'll pass / hand you (back) to Reception.
Einen Augenblick. Sie werden verbunden.	Just one moment. It's ringing for you.
Dr. Brains Telefon läutet bereits.	Dr Brain's number is ringing.
Sie können sprechen / Sie sind verbunden.	You're through now.
Herr Brain kann Ihren Anruf entgegennehmen. Sprechen Sie bitte.	Go ahead, Mr Brain can take your call.
Herr Brown, Sie werden am Telefon gewünscht. Es ist Herr Black.	Mr Brown, you are wanted on the phone. It's Mr Black.

(T) Etiquette on the phone: Ten commandments

Using the telephone professionally is more than knowing the correct phrases. Here are the ten *commandments* for operators, receptionists, secretaries and, last but not least, bosses, some of whom have never been trained on how to use a phone and need these rules most.	*Gebote*
1. Don't connect anybody *on suspicion.* Don't *waste* their time and money.	*auf Verdacht* *verschwenden*
2. *Make sure* that they remember numbers and names correctly. Ask if you should repeat the information you have given him.	*sichergehen*
3. Don't give the client an *extension* number without knowing if his or her *contact* is *available.*	*Nebenstelle* *die gewünschte Person;* *erreichbar*
4. Don't keep the *caller* waiting when you cannot put him through.	*Anrufer*
5. Don't *bounce* him *back* to the *operator.* Connect him personally.	*zurückvermitteln;* *Vermittlung*
6. Make sure that the *relevant person* is there and tell the caller what the call is about.	*die betreffende Person*
7. If it *takes time* to get through to the relevant person, don't park the caller; get back to him in *intervals* of 20 seconds and tell him why you have to make him wait.	*Zeit brauchen* *Abstände*
8. *Offer* to call back, if you can't put the caller through.	*anbieten*
9. Don't put the *client* through without having *apologised* for having *kept* him *waiting.*	*Kunde* *sich entschuldigen;*
10. Thank him for his or her *patience.*	*warten lassen; Geduld*

8. *Wartezeiten überbrücken*
Getting through the waiting periods

Time for a smile

The telephone will ring when you are having a shower. You will reach it just in time to hear the click of the caller hanging up.

Tut mir leid, daß ich Sie habe warten lassen.	Sorry to have kept you waiting.
Tut mir leid, aber ich bekomme keine Verbindung.	Sorry, but I can't get this number.
Bedaure, ich kann diese Nummer nicht erreichen.	Sorry, I can't reach this number.
Frau Potter spricht gerade auf einer anderen Leitung.	Ms Potter is speaking on another line.
Ich versuche immer noch, Sie zu verbinden.	I'm still trying to connect you.
Die Leitung ist leider belegt.	I'm afraid the line is engaged.
Tut mir sehr leid, aber es wird gerade gesprochen.	I'm awfully sorry, but the line is busy.
Die Nebenstelle / der Apparat meldet sich nicht. Soll ich es noch mal versuchen?	There's no reply from the extension. Shall I try again?
Können Sie dranbleiben? Ich versuche es weiter.	Can you hold? I'm still trying to connect you.
Wenn Sie einen Moment am Apparat bleiben, versuche ich es noch einmal.	If you hold a moment, I'll try again.
Möchten Sie warten?	Would you like to hold?
Ich melde mich gleich wieder.	I'll be back to you in a minute.
Wir rufen Sie zurück.	We will call you back.
Frau Potter ist jetzt frei.	Ms Potter is available now.

Time for a smile

A telephone cord only hangs freely with no kinks in television shows.

Master your phrases

Task 6: Which words fit these requests?

switch / transfer / link / put / connect / contact

1. Can you .... me to the R&D department, please?
2. Please .... me with Fred Niemec.
3. Could you .... me through to Mr Brain?
4. Could you put me in .... with Ms. Child, please?

Task 7: Add an expression with the same meaning

1. I'm afraid the line is *engaged* / ....
2. Sorry, I can't *reach* / ....this number.
3. I'll be *with you* / ....you in a minute.

9. *Ungeduldig werden* – Getting impatient

Dies ist ein Ferngespräch. Ich kann nicht länger warten.	This is a long-distance call. I can't hold on any longer.
Vermittlung, ich warte nun schon eine Ewigkeit.	Operator, I've been holding for ages.
Ich werde jedesmal unterbrochen, wenn ich Herrn Brains Nummer wähle.	I get cut off every time I dial Mr Brain's number.
Dies ist nun schon das zweite Mal, daß Sie mich mit der falschen Abteilung verbinden.	This is the second time you have put me through to the wrong department.
Sie haben mir schon wieder den falschen Apparat gegeben.	You've given me the wrong extension again.
Ich möchte Ihren Chef persönlich sprechen.	I want to speak to your boss personally.
Es ist in seinem, nicht in meinem Interesse.	It's in his interest, not mine.
Herr Brain wird sehr ärgerlich sein, wenn Sie mich nicht sofort mit ihm verbinden.	Mr Brain will be very angry, if you don't put me through to him immediately.

Ich weiß, daß Herr Brain da ist. Ich habe vor fünf Minuten mit ihm telefoniert.	I know that Mr Brain is in. I was on the phone to him five minutes ago.
Ich rate Ihnen, mich jetzt zu verbinden, oder ich storniere den Auftrag für Ihre Firma.	I advise you to put me though now or I'll cancel the contract with your company.
Haben Sie Geduld. Es dauert nicht lange.	Please be patient. It won't take long.
Bitte beruhigen Sie sich. Ich tue mein Bestes.	Please calm down. I'm doing my best.

Time for a smile

When you dial the wrong number, you never get a busy signal.

10. *Ein Gespräch annehmen* – Taking a call

Nehmen Sie das Gespräch an?	Are you going to take the call?
Da ist ein Herr Smith für Sie am Apparat.	There's a Mr Smith for you on the phone.
Soll ich das Gespräch auf Ihren Apparat legen?	Shall I transfer him to your extension?
Ist es Ihnen recht, wenn ich das Gespräch auf Ihren Apparat lege?	Is it okay if I put the call through to your extension?
Würden Sie bitte ans Telefon gehen?	Would you please answer the phone?
Apparat von Herrn Dr. Brain. Sie sprechen mit Frau Child.	Dr Brain's phone, Ms Child speaking.
Natürlich nehme ich das Gespräch an.	Of course, I'll take it.

Time for a smile

"Why don't you answer the phone?"
"Because it's not ringing."
"Why must you leave everything until the last minute?"

11. *Keine Verbindung* – No connection

Tut mir leid, Frau Child ist nicht an ihrem Platz.	Sorry, Ms Child is not at her desk.
Ich sehe nach, wo sie ist.	I'll check where she is.
Tut mir leid. Dr. Brain ist im Augenblick nicht im Büro.	I'm sorry, Dr Brain is out of the office at the moment.
Er ist im Augenblick nicht hier.	He isn't here at the moment.
Ich glaube, Frau Child ist wohl in der Mittagspause.	I think Ms Child might be on her lunch break.
Und Herr Smith zum Mittagessen.	And Mr Smith is out for lunch.
Tut mir leid, er ist nicht da.	Sorry, he isn't in.
Kann ich etwas ausrichten?	Can I take a message?
Er spricht gerade auf der anderen Leitung.	He's on another line at the moment.
Sie sind leider wieder unterbrochen worden. Ich versuche es noch einmal.	I'm afraid you've been cut off. I'll try again.
Es nimmt niemand ab. Versuchen Sie es bitte später noch einmal.	There's no reply. Please try again later.
Der Teilnehmer meldet sich nicht. Soll ich etwas ausrichten?	There's no answer. Shall I take a message?
Herr Brain ist im Augenblick leider nicht erreichbar.	I'm afraid Mr Brain is not available at the moment.
Tut mir leid, aber Herr Brain hat diese Woche Urlaub.	I'm sorry, but Mr Brain is on holiday this week.
Ich höre, daß er heute außer Hause ist.	I've just been told he's out today.
Herr Brain ist geschäftlich unterwegs.	Mr Brain is away on business.
Bedaure, Herr Brain ist in einer Besprechung.	I'm sorry, Mr Brain is at a meeting.
Tut mir leid, Herr Brain ist augenblicklich nicht im Büro.	I'm afraid, he's out of the office at the moment.
Er ist mitten in einem Vorstellungsgespräch.	He's in the middle of an interview for a job.
Er hat gerade einen wichtigen Besucher.	He has got an important visitor just now.
Dr. Brain wird in Kürze zurück sein.	Dr Brain is expected back shortly.

Kann ich Ihnen irgendwie helfen?	Is there anything I can do for you?
Könnte Ihnen vielleicht seine Sekretärin weiterhelfen?	Could his secretary help you?
Möchten Sie mit jemand anderem sprechen?	Would you like to speak to someone else?
Um wieviel Uhr erwarten Sie Dr. Brain zurück?	At what time is Dr Brain expected back?
Können Sie mir sagen, wann ich ihn am ehesten antreffe?	Can you tell me when I am most likely to find him in?

Time for a smile

A caller who dials the wrong number will call a second time as soon as you have returned to your living room and made yourself comfortable.

12. *Eine Nachricht hinterlassen* – Leaving a message

Wären Sie so freundlich, Frau Child etwas auszurichten?	Would you be so kind as to pass a message on to Ms Child?
Könnte ich eine Nachricht hinterlassen?	Could I leave a message, please?
Wäre es möglich, eine Nachricht zu hinterlassen?	Would it be possible to leave a message?
Würden Sie John etwas von mir ausrichten?	Would you give John a message for me?
Kann ich ihm ein paar Zeilen hinterlassen?	Can I leave a note for him?
Würden Sie ihm bitte ausrichten, daß Bob Marley angerufen hat?	Would you please tell him that Bob Marley called?
Könnten Sie ihm sagen, daß ich angerufen habe?	Could you please tell him I phoned?
Könnten Sie ihn bitte fragen, ob ...?	Would you please ask him, if ...?
Könnten Sie Dr. Brain bitten, mich zurückzurufen?	Could you ask Dr Brain to call me back?
Teilen Sie ihm bitte mit, daß ich heute keine Zeit habe.	Could you let him know that I won't be free today?

Ⓣ Etiquette on the phone: 'Can you spell your name?'

When taking messages it's most important that you get the caller's name right. However, some names are very strange indeed; especially *foreign* names can have the most impossible combinations of *vowels* and consonants. Take, for example, Abenazor Montegue or Basil Skiskibowsky. Now, what do you do in a case like this?

You might *be tempted* to ask them "Could you spell your name, please?" Don't! Of course, they can spell their names. If there is one word of all they are able to spell, it's their own name. So don't make people spell it. It's not *polite.* Do it yourself. Here's an example.

"Excuse me Mr Kleinschroth, I just want to make sure I got your name right. Does it have a 'th' at the end? Excuse me, Dr Moos, may I just spell your name to check *whether* I've got it right? M, double O, S?"

They will like it. If there is one word most people like to hear it's is their own name – pronounced correctly and in a friendly tone. If a name is very complicated or if the line is bad, use the international alphabet to spell a word (see page 163).

Don't show that you've been to a German Gymnasium. Avoid making *remarks* on the origin or meaning of a name, even if you happen to know that Hamilkar della Barka actually means 'little hammer of the *barge.*' Don't compare names to animals or *tools.* "And how do you spell your name, Mr Spade? Like the spade in my garden? OK, *let's call a spade a spade* then."

foreign – *ausländisch*
vowels – *Vokale*
be tempted – *versucht sein*
polite – *polite?*
whether – *ob*
remarks – *Bemerkungen*
barge – *Barke*
tools – *Werkzeug*
let's call a spade a spade – *Nennen wir die Dinge beim Namen*

13. *Nachrichten entgegennehmen* – Taking messages

Kann ich Herrn Brain etwas ausrichten?	Can I take a message for Mr Brain?
Kann ich Herrn Brain etwas ausrichten?	Can I pass on a message to Mr Brain?
Möchten Sie ihm eine Nachricht hinterlassen?	Would you like to leave a message for him?
Soll ich das aufschreiben?	Shall I note that down?
Ich werde dafür sorgen, daß er Ihre Nachricht erhält.	I'll make sure that he gets your message.
Ich kümmere mich darum, daß Frau Child Ihre Nachricht erhält.	I'll see that Ms Child gets your message.
Ich gebe das an Frau Child weiter.	I'll pass that on to Ms Child.
Soll ich sie bitten, Sie zurückzurufen?	Shall I ask her to call you back?
Hat sie Ihre Nummer?	Does she have your number?
Haben Sie eine Nummer, unter der wir Sie erreichen können?	Do you have a telephone number at which we can contact you?
Ich gebe Ihnen Namen und Adresse. Brian Brain aus London.	I'll just let you have my name and address. It's Brian Brain from London.
Meine Privatnummer ist 833 324.	My home / private number is 833 324.
Im Büro erreichen Sie mich unter 787 996.	In the office you reach me on 787 996.
Während der Arbeitszeit erreichen Sie mich unter 330 404.	My number at work is 330 404.
Die Nummer meiner Firma ist 330 404.	My company number is double three o four o four.
Ich habe Apparat Nummer ...	My extension is ...
Die Vorwahlnummer ist ...	The area code is ...
Die Vorwahlnummer von London ist 01.	The dialling code for London is 01.
Die Vorwahlnummer von Deutschland ist 0049.	The country code for Germany is 0049.
Und wann wäre es für Sie günstig, daß Tom Sie anruft?	When would it be a good time for Tom to call you back?

Wann würde es Ihnen passen?	When would it be convenient for you?
Wann würde es Ihnen passen?	When would it suit you?
Würde Ihnen Dienstag um neun Uhr passen?	Would Tuesday at nine o'clock be a convenient time?
Sie hören von Herrn Brain am späteren Vormittag.	You will be hearing from Mr Brain later in the morning.
Hat jemand für mich angerufen?	Have there been any calls for me?

Time for a smile

McNab, a real Scotsman, decided to get married. So one morning he sent telegrams to three of his girlfriends proposing marriage. Two phoned to say 'yes' immediately, and the third phoned that night to say the same. He married the third girl saying, "The girl for me is the one who waits for the night rates."

14. *Mißverständnisse ausschließen*
Eliminating misunderstandings

Einen Augenblick bitte. Ich möchte mir die Einzelheiten aufschreiben.	Just a moment please. I would like to take the details down.
Haben Sie das?	Have you got that?
Soll ich es wiederholen?	Shall I repeat that?
Können Sie das bitte noch einmal vorlesen?	Can you read that back to me, please?
Darf ich Ihnen alle Punkte noch einmal vorlesen, um sicherzugehen?	May I just read back the details to you to make sure?
Vielleicht habe ich Sie nicht richtig verstanden. Könnten Sie das bitte wiederholen?	Perhaps I didn't understand you right. Could you say it again, please?
Ich bin mir nicht sicher, ob ich das richtig mitbekommen habe. Ich wiederhole.	I'm not sure whether I got that right. I'll repeat it.

Ich möchte sichergehen, daß ich alles richtig verstanden habe. — I would like to make sure that I've understood that correctly.

Darf ich Ihren Nachnamen buchstabieren, nur um sicherzugehen? — May I spell your surname, just to be sure?

Möchten Sie, daß ich alles noch einmal durchgehe? — Would you like me to go over it all again?

P Master your phrases

Task 8: Why they can't answer the phone

Fill in the prepositions.

1. I'm sorry, Dr Brain is .... of the office .... the moment.
2. He's .... another line .... the moment.
3. He's .... the middle .... an interview .... a job.
4. Could you pass .... a message .... me?

Task 9: What can you do with messages?

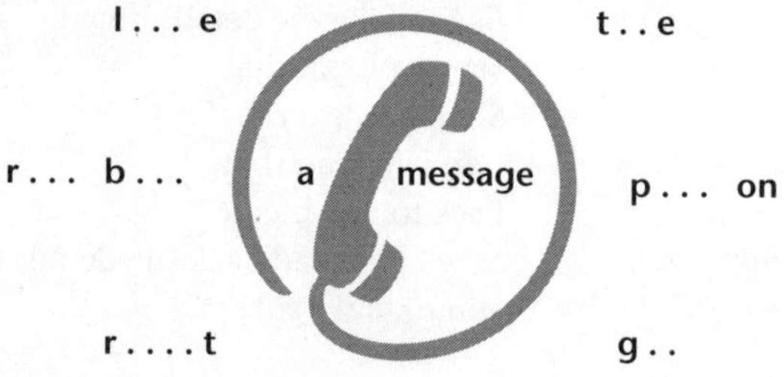

15. *Um einen Rückruf bitten* – Asking to be called back

Könnten Sie Frau Child bitten, Bob Marley anzurufen?	Could you ask Ms Child to call Bob Marley, please?
Könnten Sie Tom veranlassen, mich zurückzurufen?	Could you get Tom to ring me back?
Könnten Sie ihn bitten, mich unter meiner Privatnummer zurückzurufen?	Could you ask him to phone me back on my private number?
Sagen Sie ihm bitte, daß er sich mit mir in Verbindung setzen möchte.	Please tell him to get in touch with me?
Ich bin bis drei Uhr Ihrer Zeit zu erreichen.	I'll be available till 3 p.m. your time.
Haben Sie eine Nummer, unter der wir Sie erreichen können?	Do you have a telephone number we can contact you on?
Sie können mich unter folgender Nummer erreichen.	You can reach / call me at this number.
Er ruft Sie an, sobald er zurück ist.	He will get back to you as soon as he arrives.
Wann würde es Ihnen passen?	When would it be convenient for you?
Würde Ihnen Dienstag um neun Uhr passen?	Would Tuesday, at nine o'clock be a convenient time?
Sie können mich über das Autotelefon erreichen.	You can contact me by car phone.
Sie rufen mich doch an, wenn er zurückkommt?	You'll give me a ring when he gets back, won't you?

16. *Den Rückruf vereinbaren* – Arranging the return call

Wann kann ich Dr. Brain erreichen?	When can I reach Dr Brain?
Wann kann ich mit ihm sprechen?	When can I contact him?
Wie kann ich ihn erreichen?	How can I get hold ofhim?
Können Sie mir sagen, wann sie da ist?	Can you tell me when she'll be in?
Könnten Sie mir bitte sagen, wann sie wieder zurück ist?	Could you please tell me when she will be back?

Kann ich sie unter einer anderen Nummer erreichen?	Is there a number where I can reach her?
Wann wäre es günstig, es noch einmal zu versuchen?	When would it be a good time to try again?
Wann ist es am günstigsten, zurückzurufen?	When's the best time to ring back?
Können Sie mir sagen, wann ich ihn am ehesten antreffe?	Can you tell me when I am most likely to find him in?
Wäre neun Uhr eine gute Zeit, um Tom zu erreichen?	Would nine o'clock be a good time to get hold of Tom?
Ich versuche es dann morgen noch einmal.	I'll try tomorrow then.
Ich rufe sie gleich morgen früh an.	I'll call her first thing in the morning.

17. *Jemanden zurückrufen* – Calling someone back

Hier ist Fred Niemec. Ich sollte Herrn Slicer zurückrufen.	This is Fred Niemec returning Mr Slicer's call.
Tut mir leid, daß ich Ihren Anruf verpaßt habe.	I'm sorry, I missed your call.
Tut mir leid, daß Sie mich nicht erreicht haben.	Sorry, you didn't get me.
Hier spricht Brain. Man hat mir ausgerichtet, ich solle Sie zurückrufen	Brain here. I got a message asking me to call you back.
Sie haben mir eine Nachricht hinterlassen, daß ich Sie zurückrufen soll.	You left a message asking me to call you back.
Ich bin froh, daß ich Sie erreiche.	I'm glad I've got hold of you.
Ich freue mich, daß es mir gelungen ist, Sie zu sprechen.	I'm pleased I managed to get in touch with you.

18. *Sich für einen Rückruf bedanken* Thank someone for calling back

Ich bin froh, daß Sie so schnell zurückgerufen haben.	I'm glad you called back so soon.
Vielen Dank, daß Sie mich zurückrufen.	Thank you for returning my call.
Vielen Dank für Ihren Rückruf.	Thanks for calling me back.
Danke, daß Sie zurückgerufen haben.	Thanks for getting back to me.
Ich weiß das zu schätzen.	I appreciate it.
Wir haben Ihren Anruf erwartet.	We've been expecting your call.
Ich habe mich auf Ihren Anruf gefreut.	I've been looking forward to your call.

Ⓟ Master your phrases

Task 10: Beef up your word power

Mr Brain "erreichen"

r . . . .

get . . . . of

get . . . . . . with

c . . . . . .

Task 11: Scrambled sentences

Rearange the words.

1. when / I / can / Dr Brain/ reach?
2. how / of / him / can / I / hold / get?
3. reach / where / is / number / there / a / I / him / can?
4. back / when's / best / ring / the / time / to?

19. *Falsch verbunden* – Wrong number

Kein Anschluß unter dieser Nummer.	Number unobtainable.
Tut mir leid. Sie haben falsch gewählt.	Sorry, you've dialled the wrong number.
Man hat Sie falsch verbunden.	You've got through to the wrong number.
Tut mir leid, dies ist die falsche Nebenstelle.	Sorry, this is the wrong extension.
Entschuldigen Sie bitte, ich muß mich wohl verwählt haben.	I beg your pardon, I must have dialled the wrong number.
Tut mir leid, aber dies ist nicht die richtige Abteilung.	I'm sorry, but this is not the right department.
Seine Rufnummer hat sich geändert.	His number has been changed.
Die neue Nummer ist ...	The new number is ...
Diese Abteilung hat damit nichts zu tun.	This department doesn't deal with that.
Welche Nummer versuchen Sie zu erreichen?	What number are you trying to get /reach?
Welche Nummer haben Sie gewählt?	What number did you dial?
Wen, sagten Sie, wollten Sie sprechen?	Who did you say you wanted to speak to?
Niemand dieses Namens arbeitet hier.	Nobody by this name works here.
Aber ich sollte unter dieser Nummer anrufen.	Well, this is the number I was asked to ring.
Sie können ihn direkt anrufen.	You can dial him direct.
Haben Sie seine Durchwahl?	Have you got his extension?
Entschuldigen Sie bitte die Störung.	Sorry to have troubled you.

Time for a smile

Andrew Dobson called the television studio the other day.
"Excuse me sir, do you think that the pop group playing in your live show would fulfil a wish of one of your most loyal spectators?"
"With pleasure, sir. What would you like?"
"Well, tell them to play table tennis for a change."

20. *Höfliches am Telefon* – Polite noises on the phone

Spreche ich mit Herrn Brain?	Am I speaking to Mr Brain?
Habe ich das Vergnügen, mit Herrn Brain zu sprechen?	Do I have the pleasure of speaking to Mr Brain?
Guten Morgen. Dr. Brain am Apparat.	Good morning, this is Dr Brain.
Erinnern Sie sich an mich?	Do you remember me?
Ich habe gedacht, ich rufe Sie mal an.	I thought I'd give you a call.
Ah, Herr Brain, das ist aber eine unerwartete Freude.	Ah, Mr Brain. This is an unexpected pleasure.
Was für eine angenehme Überraschung!	What a pleasant surprise!
Nett, von Ihnen zu hören.	How nice to hear from you.
Es ist schön, wieder etwas von Ihnen zu hören.	It's good to hear from you again.
Nett, Ihre Stimme wieder zu hören.	Nice to hear your voice again.
Ich habe schon eine ganze Weile versucht, mich mit Ihnen in Verbindung zu setzen.	I've been trying to get into contact with you for some time.
Hätten Sie vielleicht einen Moment Zeit für mich?	I wonder / I was wondering if you could spare me a minute.
Oder soll ich später noch einmal anrufen?	Or shall I call back later?
Ich hoffe, ich störe nicht.	I hope I'm not disturbing you.
Keineswegs. / Nicht im geringsten.	Not at all.
Tut mir leid, wenn ich Sie belästige.	Sorry to trouble you.
Habe eine Ewigkeit nichts mehr von dir gehört.	Haven't heard from you for ages.
Vielen Dank für Ihren Rückruf.	Thanks for calling me back.
Es war nicht einfach, Sie an das Telefon zu bekommen.	It's been difficult getting hold of you.
Hallo, Tom. Wie geht es dir so?	Hello Tom. How are you keeping?
Wie schön, daß ich dich erreiche.	I'm pleased to have got hold of you.
Wie geht es dir so?	How are you doing?
Wie geht's, wie steht's? – Nicht schlecht.	How are things? – Not so bad.

21. *Die Leitung ist schlecht* – The line is bad

Time for a smile

McGregor was short of money, so he rang up his friend McTavish and asked for a loan of five pounds.
"Sorry," said McTavish, "you've got to speak up, I can't hear a word you're saying."
"Can you lend me five pounds?" screamed McGregor into the phone.
"Look," said McTavish, "the line is terrible. You must try it some other time."
At this stage the operator chipped in and said, "There's nothing wrong with the line, I can hear the caller distinctly."
"In that case, you lend him the money," retorted McTavish angrily.

Die Leitung ist leider schlecht.	I'm afraid the line is bad.
Ich verstehe Sie nicht gut.	I can't hear you very well.
Ich kann Ihre Stimme kaum hören.	I can hardly hear your voice.
Es hört sich an, als wären Sie meilenweit weg.	It's as if you' re miles away.
Tut mir leid, das habe ich nicht mitbekommen.	Sorry, I didn't quite catch that.
Können Sie mich gut hören?	Can you hear me all right?
Ich kann Sie kaum verstehen.	I can hardly hear you.
Könnten Sie bitte lauter sprechen?	Could you speak up, please?
Hier ist ein fürchterlicher Lärm.	There's an awful noise here.
Wir haben eine schlechte Leitung / Verbindung.	We've got a bad connection.
Die Verbindung ist furchtbar schlecht.	The connection / line is terrible.
Ich hoffe, Sie können mich jetzt besser verstehen.	I hope you can hear me a bit better now.
Sie klingen sehr leise.	You sound very faint.
Ich kann nicht verstehen, was Sie sagen.	I can't make out what you're saying.
Das ist jemand in der Leitung.	We've got a crossed line.

Leider ist die Leitung schlecht. Könnten Sie das wohl wiederholen?	I'm afraid the line is bad. Would you mind repeating that, please?
Da ist ein schreckliches Nebengeräusch.	There's terrible interference.
Sind Sie noch dran?	Are you still there?
Mein Gespräch ist weg.	I've lost my caller.
Die Leitung ist tot.	The line's dead.

22. *Verständigungsschwierigkeiten*
Communication problems

Ich fürchte, mein Englisch ist nicht sehr gut.	I'm afraid my English isn't very good.
Entschuldigen Sie, aber ich spreche nicht gut Englisch.	Excuse me, but I don't speak English very well.
Könnten Sie das bitte wiederholen?	Could you repeat that please?
Könnten Sie das wiederholen?	Could you say that again, please?
Dürfte ich Sie bitten, das zu wiederholen?	I wonder if you could say that again, please.
Könnten Sie bitte langsamer sprechen?	Could you speak more slowly, please?
Entschuldigen Sie bitte, aber das habe ich nicht mitbekommen.	I beg your pardon, but I missed that.
Ich weiß nicht, ob ich das richtig verstanden habe. Ich wiederhole.	I' m not sure whether I got that right. Let me repeat it.
Meinen Sie November oder September?	Do you mean November or September?
Sagten Sie Hoover oder Moover?	Did you say Hoover or Mover?
Könnten Sie das buchstabieren?	Could you spell that for me?

(P) Master your phrases

Task 12: How to be polite

Fit in the missing words.

1. I wonder if you could .... me a minute.
2. I hope I'm not .... you.
3. It's .... to hear from you again.

Task 13: What to say when the connection is bad

Fit in the missing words.

1. I can hardly .... you.
2. We've got a .... line.
3. The .... is terrible.
4. There's terrible ....

Time for a smile

Andrew Goodman was more than annoyed when his neighbour phoned him at 4 a.m. and said, "Your dog is barking so loudly that I can't sleep." Before Andrew could say anything, the neighbour had hung up.The following morning, at the same time Andrew phoned his neighbour and said, "I haven't got a dog."

23. *Unter Zeitdruck stehen* – To be under time pressure

Ich muß leider zum Schluß kommen. Ich stehe unter Termindruck.	I'm afraid I'll have to cut this short. I'm hard pressed for time.
Ich habe sehr wenig Zeit.	I'm very short of time.
Ich muß unser Gespräch in ungefähr fünf Minuten beenden.	I've got to leave you in about five minutes.
Ich muß nun aufhören. Ich habe in fünf Minuten eine Besprechung.	I have to go now. I have a meeting in five minutes.

Ich muß mich nun verabschieden.	Well, I'll have to say goodbye now.
Ich bin gerade in einer Besprechung.	I'm in a meeting at the moment.
Ich habe gleich einen Termin.	I have an appointment in a few minutes
Tut mir leid. Ich kann jetzt nicht sprechen. Ich bin mitten in einer Verhandlung.	Sorry, I can't talk to you now. I'm in the middle of a nego-tiation.
Entschuldigen Sie, aber ich muß unser Gespräch jetzt beenden. Mein Besucher ist eingetroffen.	Sorry, but I have to finish this discussion now. My visitor has arrived.
Ich kann im Augenblick nicht sprechen. Ich habe Besuch.	Sorry, I can't talk now. I've got a visitor.
Tut mir leid, Fred, aber ich hab's eilig. Ich muß jetzt Schluß machen.	Sorry, Fred, but I'm in hurry. I have to hang up now.
Kann ich Sie zurückrufen, wenn ich etwas Ruhe habe?	Can I phone you back when it's quieter?
Könnte ich Sie zurückrufen, wenn ich mehr Zeit habe?	Could I phone you back when I've more time?
Wann würde es Ihnen passen?	When would it be convenient for you?

Time for a smile

A rich banker who had made a fortune on the stock exchange phoned his new mistress:
"Darling, I sent you a birthday present: a Picasso and a Ferrari. Did you get them alright?" "Yes darling, they are wonderful. But could you please tell me which is the Picasso and which is the Ferrari?"

24. *Das Telefongespräch beenden* – Ending the call

Ich störe Sie nun nicht mehr länger in Ihrer Arbeit.	I'd better let you get on with your work.
Es war nett, mit Ihnen zu sprechen.	It's been nice talking to you.
Ich würde mich freuen, wieder von Ihnen zu hören.	I'm looking forward to hearing from you.

Ich bin Ihnen sehr verbunden. – Keine Ursache.	I'm much obliged to you. – Not at all.
Kann ich sonst noch etwas für Sie tun?	Anything else I can do for you?
Gibt es sonst noch etwas (zu besprechen)?	Will there be anything else?
Ich glaube, das wär's einstweilen.	I think that's it for now.
Ich glaube, das wäre im Moment alles.	Well, I guess that's all for now.
Vielen Dank für Ihren Anruf.	Thank you for calling. / Thank you for the call.
Sie hören von mir (am Dienstag).	You'll be hearing from me (on Tuesday).
Sie hören bald wieder von mir.	I'll get back to you soon.
Mach's gut.	Take care.
Lassen Sie was von sich hören.	Keep in touch.
Auf Wiederhören.	Goodbye.

Time for a smile

When the Vatican had got into financial trouble after the Ambrosio bank scandal, a rich Italian producer of wine thought that his day had come. He phoned the Pope.
"You Holiness, I'm calling to offer you a good bargain. I'll balance your budget, if your Holiness would modify one line in the Lord's Prayer."
"Which line are you referring to, my son?" asked the Pope.
"Well, actually it's only one word. Couldn't you replace bread with wine: 'And give us our daily wine today' instead of bread?"
The Pope consulted his secretaries, they checked all the old documents, then after a week the Pope called back.
"I'm afraid, my son, we'll have to wait a little. Our contracts with the Roman bakers only expire in the year 2222."

(T) Strategies for secretaries: Screening off the boss

Managers have one problem *in common*, they *lose* a lot of time on the phone – and time is money. It's their secretaries' job to take care that this time is not *wasted*. They *screen* their bosses from *unnecessary* incoming phone calls. Most of them follow this strategy:

gemeinsam
verlieren
verschwendet; abschirmen; unnötig

1. They ask
   - for the caller's name,
   - where he is calling from
   - what the *purpose of the call* is.
2. Then they *decide* if they should
   - *deal with* the caller themselves,
   - *transfer* the caller to another department
   - put the caller through to their boss.

Zweck des Anrufs
entscheiden
übernehmen
weitergeben

They *distinguish* three different types of callers:

unterscheiden

1. important callers the boss wants to talk to: those who *place orders*, those who have the power to ruin the company or those who are a *valuable source* of information. They are put through *immediately.*
2. callers who the secretary is not able to *place*: She is not sure whether to screen her boss or put them through. *Since* they might be important, she *promises* a return the call.
3. unimportant callers, salesmen, for example: Secretaries have *instructions* not to put them through.

Bestellungen machen
wertvolle Quelle
sofort
einordnen
da
versprechen
Anweisung

For each of these three types of callers, the secretary has a different strategy. What might she say to type 1, the important caller, if she can't connect him because her boss is at a meeting?

"Good morning, Mr Knot. Unfortunately Dr Brain is at a meeting. He told me to *arrange a return call* with you. When would be a good time for him to call you back?"

einen Rückruf vereinbaren

What could she say to type 2, the unknown caller?
"Mr Brain is not *available* at the moment. Can I help you? May I ask *the purpose of your call*? Dr. Brain will call you back as soon as possible."

erreichbar
Zweck Ihres Anrufs

And this is how she *gets rid of* type 3, the salesman who offers a computer:
"I believe that your computers are high quality, but we are *fully satisfied* with our supplier. And my boss has given *strict instructions* not to put through any *sales offers.*"

loswerden
völlig zufrieden
strenge Anweisung
Verkaufsangebote

You see, it is not easy to *get past* a well-trained receptionist or an *efficient* secretary.

vorbeikommen
gut, tüchtig

Time for a smile

Ronny (to his secretary): Did you phone my wife as I told you?
Secretary: Yes, sir, I told her that you would be late home from the office because of an unexpected conference.
Ronny: How did she react?
Secretary: She asked if she could rely on it.

25. *Den Chef abschirmen* – Screening off the boss

Ein Herr Smith ist am Telefon. Soll ich das Gespräch durchstellen?	There's a Mr Smith for you on the phone. Shall I put him through?
Ich habe einen Herrn Smarty am Apparat, der Sie unbedingt sprechen will.	I've got a Mr Smarty on the phone who seems to be very keen on speaking to you.
Es ist ein Vertreter. Nehmen Sie das Gespräch an?	It' s a salesman. Will you take the call?
Sagen Sie, ich rufe später zurück.	Tell him I'll call back later.
Ich kann dieses Gespräch nicht entgegennehmen. Ich habe Besuch.	I can't take that call. I've got a visitor.
Fragen Sie ihn, wann ich ihn zurückrufen kann.	Ask him when he would like me to call back.
Könnten Sie das Gespräch für mich annehmen. Ich habe zu tun.	Could you please answer the phone for me? I'm busy.
Ich stecke bis über beide Ohren in Arbeit. Vertrösten Sie ihn bitte auf später.	I'm up to my neck in work at the moment. Could you please put him off until later.
Ein Herr Smith möchte Sie sprechen. Soll ich das Gespräch auf Ihren Apparat legen?	There's a Mr Smith for you on the phone. Shall I put him through to your extension?
Frau Child ist leider nicht zu sprechen.	I'm afraid Ms Child is not available.
Herr Brain hat strenge Anweisung gegeben, nicht gestört zu werden.	Mr Brain left strict instructions that he was not to be disturbed.
Ich schlage vor, Sie versuchen es morgen noch einmal.	I suggest you try again tomorrow.
Kann ich Ihnen vielleicht weiterhelfen?	Maybe I can help you?
Könnte Ihnen vielleicht seine Sekretärin weiterhelfen?	Could his secretary help you?
Möchten Sie mit jemand anderem sprechen?	Would you like to speak to someone else?

Ⓟ Master your phrases

Task 14: What to say when you are busy

1. I'm hard .... for time.
2. I'm very .... of time.
3. I'm in a ....

Task 15: Guided translation

1. Well, I guess (*das wär's einstweilen*).
2. I'm afraid I (*ich muß es kurz machen*).
3. I'll (*muß mich nun verabschieden*).

Task 16: The perfect secretary

Fragen Sie Ihren Chef, ob

1. er das Gespräch annehmen will.
2. Sie das Gespräch durchstellen sollen.

Sagen Sie dem Anrufer, daß

3. Ihr Chef ausdrücklich gesagt hat, er wolle nicht gestört werden.
4. Ihr Chef nicht zu sprechen ist.

Task 17: Complete the dialogue

Boss to secretary	**Secretary to caller**
Tell him I'll call back later.	Mr Brain .... later.
Ask him when he would like me to call back.	When .... you back?
Could you please put him off until tomorrow?	Could you ....?

26. *Anrufbeantworter* – Answering machines

Time for a smile

People are getting used to answering machines. I called and got a real person last week and neither one of us spoke.
We were both waiting for the beep.

Hier ist der automatische Anrufbeantworter der Firma PELC.	This is the automatic answering machine of PELC.
Dies ist eine Bandaufnahme.	This is a recorded message.
Unsere Rufnummer hat sich geändert.	Our telephone number has been changed.
Sie erreichen uns unter 334 454.	You can phone us on 334 454.
Dieser Apparat ist im Augenblick nicht besetzt.	There's nobody here at the moment.
Wir sind im Augenblick leider nicht erreichbar.	Sorry, we can't be reached at the moment.
Sie rufen außerhalb unserer Bürozeiten an.	You have phoned outside office hours.
Bitte hinterlassen Sie eine Nachricht.	Please, leave a message.
Wir rufen Sie baldmöglichst zurück.	We'll ring you back as soon as possible.
Wir sind im Augenblick nicht erreichbar. Hinterlassen Sie Ihren Namen, Telefonnummer und eine Nachricht. Wir rufen Sie so schnell wie möglich zurück.	Sorry, we are out. But leave your name, number and message and we'll get back to you as soon as possible.
Sprechen Sie bitte nach dem Signalton.	Please speak after the tone.
Sie sind mit PELC verbunden. Unser Büro ist geöffnet von Montag bis Freitag zwischen 9 Uhr und 16 Uhr. Vielen Dank für Ihren Anruf.	You are speaking to PELC. Our office is open from Monday to Friday from 9 a.m. to 4 p.m. Thank you for calling.
Die gewählte Rufnummer hat sich geändert.	The number you have dialled has been changed.

Wählen Sie bitte 232 323.	Please call 232 323.
Die gewählte Rufnummer hat sich geändert. Die neue Nummer ist …	The number you have dialed has been changed. The new number is …
Kein Anschluß unter dieser Nummer.	Number unobtainable.
Ihr Anruf kann nicht ausgeführt werden. Bitte versuchen Sie es später noch einmal.	Your call cannot be put through. Please try again later.
Überprüfen Sie die Rufnummer, und versuchen Sie es noch einmal.	Please check the number and dial again.

Time for a smile

I climbed a mountain and hollered "Helloooo!" A voice came back that said, "The echo is busy at the moment. Leave a message at the beep, and we'll get back to you as soon as possible."

27. *Piepsen und Faxen* – Beeping and faxing

Ich piepse ihn an.	I'll beep him.
Ich piepse ihn an / lasse ihn ausrufen.	I'll page him.
Ich faxe Ihnen die Liste mit den neuen Preisen.	I'll fax you the list with the new prices.
Wir bestätigen den Termin per Fax	We'll confirm the appointment by fax.
Faxen Sie mir bitte Ihre Preisliste zu.	Please fax me your price list.

Food for thought

The US Presidency is a Tudor monarchy with telephones.
Anthony Burgess

28. *Nummern buchstabieren* – Spelling numbers

3022	three – O – double two
01-4 587 665	O – one- four – five – eight – seven – double six – five

29. The British Telephone Alphabet

A – Alfred	H – Harry	O – Oliver	V – Victor
B – Benjamin	I – Isaac	P – Peter	W – William
C – Charles	J – Jack	Q – Queen	X – X-ray
D – David	K – King	R – Robert	Y – Yellow
E – Edward	L – London	S – Samuel	Z – Zebra
F – Frederick	M – Mary	T – Tommy	
G – George	N – Nellie	U – Uncle	

Time for a smile

In my house there's this light switch that doesn't do anything. Every so often I would flick it on and off just to check. Yesterday, I got a call from a woman in Germany. She said, "Stop it."

C Crossword power

Across

1. This is the ✎ answering machine of PELC 7. Am I speaking ✎ Mr Brain? 9. Insert your money in the ✎ 11. I'm afraid the line is ✎ 12. sorry, Ms. Child is not at her ✎ . 15. Can I ✎ a message? 16. Thank you for returning my. ✎ 17. When's the ✎ time to ring back? 18. Sorry to ✎ you waiting. 20. Can you read that ✎ to me, please? 21. Could you ✎ that please?

Down

1. I' m ringing ✎ your advert. 2. Please speak after the ✎ 3. Can I take a ✎ for Mr Brain? 4. I can't ✎ that call 5. First dial the international ✎ 6. You have phoned ✎ office hours. 8. First lift the ✎ 10. Can I ✎ a message for him? 11. ✎ calls, dial 999! 13. May I ✎ your surname, just to be sure? 14. Could you please ✎ him off until later? 15. Who would you ✎ to speak to? 16. I didn't quite ✎ your name. 19. Anything ✎ I can do for you? 20. We'll confirm the appointment ✎ fax.

PERFEKT PRÄSENTIEREN

PERFECT PRESENTATIONS[1]

If you work in industry, the day will come when they ask you to make a presentation. Don't start shaking. No need to be nervous! Select the right phrases from our lists. They'll get you the response you deserve.

1 Zu diesem Teil empfehlen wir Ihnen *Get through at Meetings. Business English für Konferenzen und Präsentationen*, rororo 60292 (mit Audio-CD oder Kassette).

1. *Den Redner vorstellen* – Introducing the presenter

In Namen unserer Firma heiße ich Sie alle willkommen, um ...	On behalf of our company I'd like to welcome you all here to ...
Es ist mir eine große Freude, Ihnen Herrn X vorstellen zu dürfen.	I have the great pleasure of introducing Mr X.
Wir haben die Ehre, Herrn X aus Y zum Thema Umweltbelastung zu hören.	We have the honour of being addressed by Mr X from Y on the theme of pollution.
Wir freuen uns alle auf Ihre Präsentation.	We're all looking forward to your presentation.
Mr X wird nun zu Ihnen über das Problem ... sprechen.	Mr X, will now speak to you about the problem of ...

How to thank the host (1)

Thank you for that kind introduction. It seems that I shall now have to say two prayers for forgiveness: the first for my introducer for telling so many lies in praising me; the second for myself – for enjoying it so much.

2. *Stellen Sie sich vor* – Introduce yourself

How to introduce yourself (1)

Before I get to the work at hand, let me say that to be chosen as a presenter is more than an honour. We had to draw lots to see who would be the presenter. I lost!

Ich bin Otto Daimler.	I'm Otto Daimler.
Ich war drei Jahre als Berater für ... tätig.	I was a consultant to ... for three years.
Ich kenne Ihre Probleme, da ich wie die meisten von Ihnen Verkaufsmanager gewesen bin.	I know your problems since I was a sales manager like most of you.

Ich bin auf diesem Gebiet auch nicht mehr Fachmann als Sie. — I'm no more expert in this field than you are.

Creating a friendly atmosphere

I see we've got a very polite audience here tonight – they cover their mouths when they yawn.

3. *Freundliches Klima schaffen*
Creating a friendly atmosphere

Ich freue mich, daß ich die Gelegenheit habe, zu Ihnen über ... zu sprechen. — I'm glad to have the chance to speak to you on the subject of ...

Vielen Dank, daß Sie mich zum Thema ... eingeladen haben. — Thank you for asking me to tell you about ...

Ich bin dankbar, daß man mir Gelegenheit gibt, Ihnen unsere Produktpalette vorzustellen. — I'm grateful for having been offered the opportunity to present our product range.

Ich bin Ihnen dankbar, daß Sie eine Stunde Ihrer wertvollen Zeit opfern, um mir zuzuhören. — I appreciate that you're sacrificing one hour of your valuable time to listen to me.

Bitte unterbrechen Sie mich, falls irgend etwas nicht klar sein sollte. — Please stop me if anything isn't clear.

Zögern Sie nicht, mich zu unterbrechen, wenn Sie eine Frage haben. — Don't hesitate to interrupt me when you have a question.

Introducing yourself (2)

My purpose is not to bore you, but to introduce people who will.

(T) Advice to presenters: Overcoming nervousness

For all but the most extrovert, an invitation to make a presentation is something to be *dreaded*. But it needn't be, particularly if you are in business. As a businessman you have some *advantages* when it comes to making public speeches. One of the main *obstacles* to success is the fear of *failure*. Very often speakers just *put off* preparing their presentation until the last moment, and that's a *recipe* for *disaster*. So begin by putting your energy into preparing your talk. By the way, learning your presentation *by heart* is almost as bad as reading it to the audience. Another point to remember is that it's not *advisable* to use your invitation to speak as a platform for your own *views*. You may well hold strong *opinions* on important subjects, but you should not *pontificate* when your job is to inform. As a businessman you are versed in the art of *persuasion*; you know how to *assess* customers, weigh up situations and respond appropriately. All these skills are directly *applicable* when it comes to making a presentation. As a business person you have a lot to talk about. Who doesn't have a funny story to tell about their *subordinates*, colleagues or bosses? And who hasn't experienced the pleasures and problems of office life? When you have to stand up to make a presentation you can be sure that most of the people in your audience will be able to identify with you.

- *fürchten*
- *Vorteile*
- *Hindernis; Versagen*
- *aufschieben*
- *Rezept*
- *Katastrophe*
- *auswendig*
- *ratsam*
- *Ansichten*
- *Meinungen*
- *predigen*
- *Überredungskunst*
- *einschätzen*
- *anwendbar*
- *Untergebene*

4. *Das Thema ankündigen* – Announcing the subject

How to win the attention of the audience

I am hear to speak to you, you are here to listen to me.
If you finish first, please let me know.

Darf ich um Ihre Aufmerksamkeit bitten?	Can I have your attention, everyone?
Wie Sie wissen, bin ich hier, um Ihnen ... vorzustellen.	As you know, I'm here to present ... to you.
Ich möchte Ihnen einen kurzen Überblick über ... geben.	I'd like to give you a brief breakdown of ...
Sie sind heute hier zusammengekommen, um etwas über unsere Vorstellungen über ... zu hören.	Now, you've met here today to hear something about our ideas on ...
Gegenstand dieser Präsentation ist ...	The topic of this presentation is ...
Das Thema der heutigen Präsentation ist ...	The subject of today's presentation is ...
In meiner Präsentation werde ich unser neues Projekt erläutern.	In my presentation I'll be explaining our new project.
Heute nachmittag will ich Ihnen die Probleme im Zusammenhang mit ... erklären.	What I'm going to explain this afternoon are the problems involved in ...
Heute früh will ich einen Rückblick auf das letzte Geschäftsjahr geben.	This morning I'd like to look back at the past fiscal year.
Ich versuche Ihnen einen Überblick über die Aktivitäten unserer Firma in Asien zu geben.	I'm trying to give you an overview of our company's activities in Asia.

How to break the ice

Before I begin my speech, I'd like to warn you that I'm suffering from a severe handicap – I'm sober.

5. *Tischvorlagen ansprechen* – Referring to hand-outs

Darf ich Ihre Aufmerksamkeit auf die Tischvorlage vor Ihnen lenken?	May I draw your attention to the handout in front of you?
In den Tischvorlagen, die ich herumgehen lasse, finden Sie ...	In the handout which I'll be passing round, you'll find ...
In dem Ordner, den ich austeile, finden Sie die Kopien der Overheadfolien.	In the folder which I'll be distributing, you'll find the copies of the OHP transparencies.
Ich habe eine detaillierte Kostenaufstellung vorbereitet, die ich gleich verteile.	I've prepared a detailed cost breakdown, which I'll be handing round now.
Wie Sie alle Ihren Unterlagen entnommen haben, die Sie vorab erhalten haben, ...	As you all know from your pre-conference handouts ...

How to thank the presenter for the handouts

Many thanks for your documentation.
I'll lose no time in reading it.

6. *Einen Überblick geben* – Giving an overview

Meine Präsentation gliedert sich in drei Teile.	My presentation will be in three parts.
Ich werde drei Hauptbereiche behandeln.	I'll be covering three main areas.
Ich werde Ihnen die wichtigsten Stufen unseres Projekts schildern.	I'll be developing the major stages of our project.
Im ersten Teil meiner Präsentation werde ich	In the first part of my presentation I'll ...
Im zweiten Teil unserer Besprechung ist Zeit für Diskussion und Fragen.	Then, in the second part of the meeting, there will be a period for free discussion and question time.
Zuerst würde ich gerne ... Zweitens könnten wir ... Und ich werde schließen mit ...	Firstly, I'd like to ... Secondly, we could ... And I'll finish with ...
Zuerst gebe ich Ihnen einen Überblick	First, I'll give you an overview of ...

über ... Dann werde ich ... Schließlich ...	Then I'll ... Finally ...
Damit ist mein Überblick abgeschlossen.	That completes my overview.
Alles in allem wird das ungefähr ... Minuten in Anspruch nehmen.	Altogether this will take about ... minutes.
Ich stehe Ihnen am Schluß gerne für Fragen zur Verfügung.	I'll be happy to answer any questions at the end.

How to thank the host (2)

After such a warm reception I can hardly wait to hear myself speak.

7. Strukturieren Sie Ihre Präsentation
Structure your presentation

Fangen wir mit ... an.	Let's start with ...
Lassen Sie mich einleitend sagen ...	To begin with, let me say ...
Ich beginne mit ...	I'll start off by dealing with ...
Betrachten wir zuerst die Vorteile.	Let us first consider the advantages.
Zuerst möchte ich ... erklären.	First of all I'd like to explain ...
Ich möchte zuerst etwas über ... sagen.	I'd like to start by saying something about ...
Wir könnten unsere Diskussion beginnen mit ...	We could begin by discussing ...
Ich möchte Ihnen zuerst eine allgemeine Vorstellung von ... geben.	First, I'd like to give you a general idea / picture of ...
Ich beginne mit einer Zusammenfassung der Probleme, die wir mit ... haben.	I'll begin by summarising the problems we're having with ...
Ich würde meiner Präsentation gerne einen Überblick über das Projekt voranstellen.	I'd like to begin my presentation by giving you an overview of the project.
Bevor wir zu ... kommen, könnten wir vielleicht zuerst ...?	Before we move on to ..., could we perhaps first ...?
Wie Sie wissen, ...	As you know ...

Hinzu kommt, daß ...	In addition ...
Im Gegensatz dazu ...	In contrast ...
Einerseits ... / Andererseits ...	On the one hand ... / On the other hand ...
Das hat zur Folge, daß ...	The effect of this is that ...
Daraus resultiert ...	As a result ...
Bevor ich fortfahre, wollen wir einmal ... betrachten,	Before we go on let's just consider ...
So viel zu den Kosten.	Right. So much for the costs.
Und nun zum Gewinn.	Now for the profits.

8. *Den nächsten Schritt ankündigen* Announcing the next step

Als nächstes will ich mich auf ... konzentrieren.	Next, I'd like to concentrate on ...
Der nächste Punkt, den ich behandeln möchte, ist ...	The next point I wish to deal with is ...
Wenn wir uns nun ... zuwenden.	If I could now turn to ...
Wenn es dazu keine weiteren Fragen gibt, würde ich gerne ...	If there are no further questions at this point, I'd like to ...
Gut. Nun zu unserem nächsten Punkt.	Right. Now to our next point.
Ich würde gerne zu meinem nächste(n) Thema / Punkt / Frage / Problem kommen.	I'd like to move on to my next subject / point / item / issue / problem.
Das nächste Dia erklärt ...	The next slide will clarify ...
Wie Sie dem folgenden Diagramm entnehmen ...	As you can see in the following chart ...
Könnten wir nun zum wichtigsten Grund für ... kommen?	Perhaps we could move on to the main reason for ...
Kommen wir zu der Frage, warum ...	Let's move on to the question why ...
Das ist also die gegenwärtige Situation. Betrachten wir nun ...	So that's the present situation. Now let's look at ...
Lassen Sie mich nun auf die anderen Funktionen zu sprechen kommen.	Let me now come to the other functions.

Ⓟ Master your phrases

Task 1: Tense and aspect

Can you get the verb forms right?

1. Mr X (*speak*) to you about marketing on the Internet.
2. I (*be*) a consultant to IBM for three years.
3. I (*try*) to give you an overview of our activities.
4. In the handout I (*pass*) round, you (*find*) all the figures.

Task 2: Those tricky little words

Fill in the prepositions.

1. I'm no more expert .... this field than you are.
2. This morning I'd like to look back .... the past fiscal year.
3. .... behalf of the Board I'd like to welcome you all to ...
4. So much .... the costs.

Task 3: Spot the mistake

1. I know your problems since I was sales manager like you.
2. I'm no more expert in this field then you are.
3. How you know, I'm here to present our products to you.

Task 4: Odd phrase out

Which phrase has a different meaning? Why?

1. I'm glad
2. I appreciate
3. I'm grateful

} that you're sacrificing one hour of your valuable timeto listen to me.

How to evaluate the presenter

Excellent:	He talks like a god.
Good:	He talks like an angel.
Average:	He talks to himself.
Unsatisfactory:	He argues with himself.
Hopeless:	He loses the argument.

9. *Zum Mitdenken aktivieren*
Motivating them to think along with you

Wo liegt nun genau das Problem?	Now, where exactly is the problem?
Beachten Sie den Unterschied zwischen ...	Observe the difference between ...
Gibt es eine einfache Lösung zu diesem Problem?	Is there a simple solution to the problem?
Welche Erklärung gibt es dafür?	What's the explanation for this?
Wie können wir dies erklären?	How can we explain this?
Was können wir dagegen tun?	What can we do about this?
Inwieweit betrifft dies uns?	How will this affect us?
Was sind die Folgen für die Firma?	What are the implications for the company?
Wie können wir von dieser Entwicklung profitieren?	How can we benefit from this development?
Welchen Nutzen ziehen wir aus dieser Situation?	What are the benefits from this situation?
Wo liegen also die Vorteile?	Now, what about the advantages?
Welche Wirkung hat dies nun?	What effect does this have?
Wir sollten nicht übersehen, daß ...	We should not overlook / ignore the fact that ...
Was können wir daraus schließen?	What conclusions can we draw from this?
Wie Sie später sehen werden ...	As you will see later ...

Why presentations go wrong

If you explain so clearly
that nobody can misunderstand,
somebody will.

Ⓣ Advice to presenters: Overcoming disasters

What to say when things go wrong during your presentation? The best way of handling minor catastrophes is a joke or a witty quotation. In the case of the first *disaster*, I usually quote one of Murphy's Laws: "If anything can go wrong, it will." And when I *fumble* for an OHP transparency that has mysteriously *disappeared* I quote: "Nothing is as easy as it looks, and everything takes longer than you think."

In the rare *event* of a *chain* of disasters – the flipchart falls over and the table *collapses* so that coffee is spilled over the director's jacket – you'll win the audience over with: "Left to themselves things tend to go from bad to worse" or in the case of the director: "Matter will be damaged in direct proportion to its *value*."

The real catastrophe is when you can hear their impatient *shuffles* or see them yawning. There's not a lot you can do, but provoke them by saying: "I see we've got a very polite audience here today – they cover their mouths when they *yawn*."

A presentation normally ends with question time or a discussion and it is always a bit *awkward* if nobody is *bold* enough to make a *contribution*. *Encourage* them by saying: "It is not necessary to understand things in order to *argue* about them."

Unglück
fummeln
verschwinden
Fall; Kette
zusammenbrechen
Wert
Scharren mit den Füßen
gähnen
peinlich
kühn; Beitrag
ermutigen
streiten

What are presentations all about?

The purpose of a presentation is to transfer resources away from accomplishing objectives and concentrate them on explaining how well you're doing.

10. *Gründe und Lösungen anbieten* Offering reasons and solutions

Es gibt zwei Gründe dafür. Erstens ... Zweitens ...	There are two reasons for this. First ... Second ...
Ein Grund dafür ist ...	One reason for this is ...
Ein weiterer Grund ist ...	Another reason is ...
Zwei Faktoren sind dafür verantwortlich. Erstens ... Zweitens ...	This is due to two factors. Firstly ... Secondly ...
Der wichtigste Grund dafür ist ...	The main reason for this is ...
Ein spezieller Grund dafür ist ...	A particular reason for this is ...
Das Schlüsselproblem ist ...	The key problem is ...
Das Hauptproblem ist ...	The basic problem is that ...
Der wichtigste Punkt ist ...	The main point is ...
Die grundlegende Idee ist ...	The basic idea is ...
Das bedeutet, daß ...	This means that ...
Ein wichtiger Faktor / Umstand, an den wir denken müssen, ist ...	An essential factor to bear in mind is ...
Deshalb müssen wir ...	Therefore we have to ...
Wir haben zwei Möglichkeiten zur Auswahl.	We have two options.
Wir würden empfehlen ...	We would recommend ...
Aus unserer Sicht wäre es am besten ...	In our view, the best course would be to ...
Ich schlage vor ...	I recommend ...
Eine Möglichkeit, das Problem zu lösen, ist ...	One way to solve the problem is ...
Deswegen ...	Because of this ...
Darum ... Also	As a result ...
Folglich ...	Consequently ...

Advice from the expert

The best audience is one that is intelligent,
well-educated and a little drunk.
Alben Barkley

11. *Alternativen aufzeigen* – Showing alternatives

Betrachten wir die Alternativen.	Let's consider the options.
Die erste Möglichkeit ist ...	The first option is to ...
Gehen wir die Möglichkeiten durch ...	Let's go through the possibilities ...
Welche Alternativen haben wir noch?	What alternatives have we got?
Einerseits könnten wir ...	On one hand we could ...
Andererseits könnte man versuchen, zu ...	On the other hand, one could try to ...
Jedoch gibt es noch eine weitere Alternative.	However, there is another alternative.
Eine Möglichkeit, das Problem zu lösen, ist ...	One way to solve the problem is to ...
Aber wie steht es mit der zweiten Alternative?	But what about the second option?
Betrachten wir nun die dritte Möglichkeit.	Now let's look at a third option.
Betrachten wir zuerst die Vorteile.	Let's first look at the benefits.
Es gibt jedoch auch Nachteile.	There are, however, disadvantages.

How to thank the presenter

Thank you, Mr Smith, you have presented a series of good, new ideas. Unfortunately the good ideas weren't new and the new ideas weren't any good.

12. *Beispiele anführen* – Introducing examples

Lassen Sie mich ein Beispiel geben.	Let me give you an example.
Nehmen wir zum Beispiel ...	Consider for example ...
Als Beispiel möchte ich anführen ...	Let me take / cite as an example ...
Lassen Sie mich das veranschaulichen.	Let me illustrate this.
Um diese Zahlen anschaulich zu machen ...	To illustrate these figures ...
Ein typisches Beispiel ist Spanien.	A case in point is Spain.

Ich glaube, das folgende Beispiel veranschaulicht diesen Punkt.	I think the following example illustrates this point.
Ich bin sicher, Sie erinnern sich an den Fall, als ...	I'm sure you remember the case when ...
Nehmen wir zum Beispiel die Schweiz.	Consider, for instance, Switzerland.
Betrachten wir doch einmal den Fall ...	Let's look at the case of ...
Die Erfahrung hat gezeigt, daß ...	Experience has shown that ...
Wie Sie alle wissen ...	As you all know ...
Sie werden sich erinnern, daß ...	As you remember ...
Um dieses Argument zu veranschaulichen, würde ich Ihnen gerne ein Modell zeigen.	To illustrate this point I'd like to show you a model.
Sie sind alle vertraut mit ...	You are all familiar with ...
Die Unterlagen / Belege zeigen deutlich, daß ...	The evidence clearly shows that ...
Es ist eine erwiesene Tatsache, daß ...	It's a proven fact that ...

Advice from the expert

A good speech is like a well-kept lawn:
short and neat.

13. *Anschauungsmaterial einsetzen* Using visual material

Bevor ich beginne, können alle die Leinwand sehen?	Well, before I start, can everybody see the screen?
Wenn Sie vielleicht Ihre Stühle ein bißchen verrücken würden.	If you would move your chairs a little.
Zuerst würde ich Ihnen gerne eine Folie zeigen, um die technischen Details zu klären.	First, I'd like to show you an OHP sheet to explain the technical details.
Das nächste Dia zeigt ...	The next slide shows ...
Wie Sie dem ersten Bild / Diagramm entnehmen können ...	As you can see in picture one / in diagram one ...

Ich meine, dieses Dia spricht für sich selbst.	I think that this slide is self-explanatory.
Diese Kurve zeigt / stellt ... dar.	This curve represents ....
Betrachten wir uns nun die Zahlen für ...	Let's now look at the figures for ...
Das Interessante daran ist ...	The interesting thing here is ...
Wenn wir diese beiden Kurven vergleichen, dann ...	If we compare these two curves then ...
den Höchststand erreichen	to reach the peak
die Talsohle erreichen	hit rock bottom / reach the lowest point
Beobachten Sie den Unterschied zwischen ...	Notice the difference between ...
Es ist interessant zu sehen, daß ...	It is interesting to notice that ...
Wenn wir X genauer betrachten ...	If we look more closely at X ...
Schauen Sie nun auf die obere rechte Ecke der Grafik.	Please, look at the upper right-hand corner of the graphic.
Der obere Teil des Dias zeigt das Innere des Behälters.	The upper part of the slide shows the interior of the container.
Dieses Diagramm vergleicht die Umsätze in den beiden Ländern.	This chart compares turnover in the two countries.
Wie Sie bemerken ...	As you have noticed, ...
Sie werden sicherlich sofort erkennen, daß ...	So you will, no doubt, see instantly that ...
Sie können hier die Entwicklung in den letzten beiden Jahren verfolgen.	You can see here the development over the past two years.

14. *Um Fragen und Kommentare bitten*
Inviting questions and comments

Wenn Sie Fragen haben, will ich sie so gut, wie ich kann, beantworten.	If you have any questions I'll do my best to answer them.
Und nun beantworte ich gerne alle Ihre Fragen.	Now I'd be happy to answer any questions you may have.
Ich beantworte gerne jede Ihrer Fragen.	I'd be happy to answer any of your questions.

Ich würde mich über jeden Kommentar freuen.	I'd welcome any comments.
Haben Sie irgendwelche Fragen?	Are there any questions?
Wenn Sie irgendwelche Fragen haben, würde ich sie jetzt gerne beantworten.	If you've any questions, I'd be pleased to answer them now.
Wenn Sie Fragen haben, zögern Sie nicht, sie zu stellen.	If you have any questions, please don't hesitate to ask.
Beantwortet das Ihre Frage?	Does that answer your question?
Habe ich mich klar genug ausgedrückt?	Have I expressed myself clearly?
Kann ich fortfahren?	Can I continue / go on?

Why presentations go wrong

It is not necessary to understand things
in order to argue about them.

15. *Um Wiederholung bitten* – Asking for repetition

Ich fürchte, ich verstehe nicht ganz, was Sie meinen.	I'm afraid I don't quite understand what you mean.
Leider konnten wir akustisch nicht verstehen, was Sie sagten.	I'm afraid we weren't quite able to catch what you were saying.
Ich konnte leider nicht ganz folgen, was Sie über ... sagten.	I'm afraid I didn't quite follow what you said about ...
Ich fürchte, mir ist nicht ganz klar, was Sie damit meinen.	I'm afraid I'm not quite clear what you mean by that.
Ich habe Ihren letzten Punkt leider nicht ganz verstanden.	I'm afraid I didn't get your last point.
Könnten Sie das wiederholen?	Could you go over it again, please? / Would you mind going over your last point again?
Könnten wir bitte die letzte Folie noch einmal sehen?	Could we see that last transparency again, please?

Advice from the expert

A speech does not have to be eternal to be immortal.

16. *Um Zusatzinformationen bitten*
Asking for additional information

Könnten Sie das etwas genauer ausführen?	Could you be a little more precise / specific / explicit?
Könnten Sie das noch etwas weiter ausführen?	Perhaps you could expand on that?
Würden Sie dies bitte etwas ausführlicher beschreiben?	Would you care to elaborate on that?
Könnten Sie uns noch mehr Einzelheiten über ... geben?	Could you give us some more details about ...?
Könnten Sie etwas mehr in die Einzelheiten gehen?	Could you explain in a little more detail?
Ich würde gerne noch etwas mehr erfahren über ...	I'd be interested to know / learn / hear a little more about ...
Könnten Sie ein paar Beispiele nennen, die das verdeutlichen?	Could you offer us some examples to make this clearer?

(T) Advice to presenters: The OHP and the seven deadly sins

1. Don't sit – stand
2. But don't stand in front of the screen.
3. And don't turn your back on the audience.
4. Use a transparent pointer or a biro. Don't point with your hand.
5. Place the pointer on the foil, otherwise the trembling of your hand will be amplified. A small movement becomes a big and hectic movement on the screen.
6. Don't tap on the transparency with your pencil or your pointer.
7. Don't talk to your transparency, the screen or to the OHP – talk to the audience.

Ⓟ Master your phrases

Task 5: Beef up your word power

Use a phrase that has almost the same meaning and fill the gap.

We should not *overlook* fact that ...	We should not .... the fact that ...
I'd like to *move on* to my next issue.	I'd like to .... to my next item.
Can I *continue*?	May I ....?
In 1996 profits *reached the lowest point.*	In 1996 profits ....

Task 6: Visual aids for presentations

What are they in English?

Dia	Folie
Tischvorlage	Diagramm
Leinwand	Grafik

Task 7: Word builder's corner

Say it with a verb.

What's the *explanation* for this?	How can we .... this?
What are the *benefits* from this situation?	How can we .... from this situation?
What are the *implications*?	What does this ....?

What you should not say to the presenter

Your presentation has been most entertaining.
Are there any hard facts to follow?

17. *Fragen stellen* – Asking questions

Vielen Dank für Ihre interessante Präsentation.	Thank you for an interesting presentation.
Gestatten Sie eine Frage?	Would you mind me asking a question?
Ich hätte zunächst die Frage, warum ...	Perhaps I could start by asking why ...
Wenn ich Sie richtig verstanden habe ...	If I understood you correctly ...
Als Sie ... erwähnten, meinten Sie damit ...?	When you said ... did you mean ...?
Ich weiß nicht, ob ich Sie richtig verstanden habe, aber ...	I was wondering if I understood correctly, but ...
Darf ich Sie etwas zu Ihrem ersten Punkt fragen?	I was wondering if I could ask something about your first point.
Darf ich fragen, wie / ob / warum / was ...?	May I ask how / if / why / what ...?
Würden Sie mir nicht zustimmen, daß ...	Wouldn't you agree that ...

18. *Wie Sie Einwände behandeln*
How to deal with objections

Ich bin froh, daß Sie mich das fragen.	I'm glad you asked me that question.
Ich habe diese Frage erwartet.	I was expecting that question.
Ich dachte mir, daß mich jemand dazu etwas fragen würde.	I thought someone would ask me about that.
Sie haben da einen wichtigen Punkt angesprochen.	You've raised an important point there.
Danke, daß Sie mich daran erinnern.	Thank you for reminding me of that.
Lassen Sie es mich anders ausdrücken.	Let me put it another way / in other words / differently.
Beantwortet dies Ihre Frage?	Does that answer your question?
Ich fürchte, ich habe mich nicht deutlich ausgedrückt. Lassen Sie es mich so sagen.	I'm afraid I didn't express myself clearly. Let me put it this way.

Ich habe mich vielleicht unklar ausgedrückt.	Perhaps I haven't made myself clear.
Dies hören wir natürlich nicht zum ersten Mal von unseren Kunden.	Of course, this is not the first time we have heard this from our customers.
Ich teile Ihre Besorgnis und versichere Ihnen, daß ...	I share your concern about ... and I assure you that ...
Ich verstehe Ihre Befürchtung. Aber sie ist unbegründet.	I understand your apprehensions. But they are unfounded.
Was ich versuche, Ihnen zu sagen, ist folgendes: ...	What I'm trying to say is this: ...
Ja, ich verstehe schon, was Sie meinen. Jedoch werden Sie zugeben, daß ...	Yes, I quite see your point. However, you'll admit that ...
Ja, das ist etwas, worüber wir auch viel nachgedacht haben, aber ...	Yes, it's something we've thought about a lot, too, but ...
Das ist eine richtige Beobachtung. Andererseits, wenn wir berücksichtigen, daß ...	That's an accurate observation. On the other hand, if we consider that ...
Ich weiß, es ist schwer, dies zu akzeptieren, aber die Beweise liegen auf der Hand.	I know it's difficult to accept this, but the evidence is there.
Ich glaube, wir verlieren unser Ziel aus dem Auge.	I feel we're losing sight of our objective.
Ich glaube, wir kommen vom Thema ab.	I feel we're getting away from the subject.
Wir scheinen aneinander vorbeizureden.	We seem to be talking at cross-purposes.
Leider gibt es darauf bis jetzt noch keine Antwort.	I'm afraid we don't have an answer to that yet.

Siehe auch *Discussing the clever way*, Seite 274 ff.

(T) Advice to presenters: The presenter as an entertainer

Presentations are not *lectures*. The professional presenter is sometimes *closer* to an entertainer than to a teacher. Know the difference between a lecture and a presentation. Start with a *witty* remark. You have been invited to give a presentation. After the chairman has introduced you and made a few *flattering* remarks about your background, you could begin by saying: "After such a warm *reception* I can hardly wait to hear myself speak."
Tell them for how long you are going to speak. "I'm here to speak to you for about 30 minutes. You are here to listen to me. *In case* you finish first, please let me know."
But what if it's going badly? For example when you stand in front of the OHP while you are using it and the audience is *annoyed*. ('Could you move to the side, please. We can't see anything. Your body's in the way.') Well, make a joke *at your own expense* ('Oh, I'm sorry, of course. I know I'm a bit big – temporarily at least. But I'm already on a diet, you know').
However, don't *overdo* it. A joke is not funny until it is laughed at. If it is not laughed at, it is a *major disaster.*
Not everybody has the *confidence* or the technique to go for laughs. But there are other ways of catching the attention of your audience. I once *attended* a presentation where the speaker distributed *candy* to the audience. He told them to let it *melt* under their tongues. He would try to be finished before the candy had melted in their mouths. This had an unforgettable effect on all of us. Everybody was waiting to see if the presenter was able to *keep his promise.*

Vorlesung
näher
geistreich
schmeichelhaft
Empfang
falls
verärgert
auf eigene Kosten
übertreiben
eine größere Katastrophe
Selbstvertrauen
beiwohnen
Bonbon
zergehen
Wort halten

19. *So gewinnen Sie Zeit* – How to play for time

Entschuldigen Sie, könnten Sie Ihre Frage bitte wiederholen?	I'm sorry, could you please repeat your question?
Sie fragen also, warum wir ...	So, what you're asking is why we ...
Wenn ich Ihre Frage richtig verstehe, wollen Sie wissen ...	If I understand your question correctly, you would like to know ...
Wenn Sie sagen ..., meinen Sie damit ...?	When you say ... do you mean ...?
Darauf würde ich gerne später zurückkommen, wenn Sie nichts dagegen haben.	I'd like to come back to this later, if you don't mind.
Ich würde diese Frage gerne für später aufheben, wenn es recht ist.	I'd like to leave this question until later, if you don't mind.
Könnten wir das verschieben bis nach der Demonstration?	Could we postpone this until after the demonstration?
Ich glaube, wenn wir diesen Punkt zurückstellen, kann ich Ihnen zeigen, daß ...	If we leave this point until later, I think I can show you that ...
Können wir diese Frage offenlassen, bis wir ...?	Could we leave this issue open until we ...?
Ich möchte meine Firma in dieser Sache nicht festlegen.	I wouldn't like to commit my company in this matter.
Ich habe leider nicht die genauen Daten bei mir.	I'm afraid I don't have the exact data / information with me.
Würden Sie das bitte wiederholen?	Would you mind going over that again / repeating that?
Ich bin nicht sicher, daß ich Sie richtig verstanden habe.	I'm not sure I've fully understood you.

How to be aggressive

Excuse me, Mr Smith, but who wrote this nonsense into your manuscript?

20. *Einer Frage ausweichen* – Avoiding a question

Ich fürchte, ich bin nicht die richtige Person, um diese Frage zu beantworten.	I'm afraid I'm not the right person to answer that.
Dr. Hill ist kompetenter als ich und kann diese Frage besser beantworten.	Dr Hill is a much better person to answer that.
Ich fürchte, wir haben nicht genug Zeit, um auf jedes Detail einzugehen.	I'm afraid there isn't enough time to go into every detail.
Ich fürchte, wir können hier nicht auf alle Aspekte des Problems eingehen.	I'm afraid we can't cover all the aspects of the problem here.
Ich meine, wir können dieses Problem im Augenblick beiseite lassen. Die eigentliche Frage ist ...	I think we can leave this problem aside for the moment. The real question is ...
Nun, es ist zum jetzigen Zeitpunkt schwer zu sagen ...	Well, it's rather difficult to say at present ...
Mir stehen leider nicht genügend Informationen zur Verfügung, um dies zu beantworten.	I'm afraid I don't have enough information at my disposal to answer that.
Ich weiß nicht, ob hier der richtige Ort ist, diese spezielle Frage zu diskutieren.	I'm not sure this is the right place to discuss this particular question.
Ich muß zugeben, ich habe keine Antwort darauf, wenn es überhaupt eine geben sollte.	I must admit that I don't know the answer, if there is one.

Advice to public speakers

Stand up, speak up, shut up.

21. *Das Ende ankündigen* – Announcing the end

Damit komme ich mit meinem Beitrag zum Schluß.	Well, that completes my side of things.
Lassen Sie mich abschließend sagen ...	Let me conclude by saying ...
Lassen Sie mich mit den Worten schließen ...	Let me end by saying that ...

Ich möchte mit der Feststellung schließen, daß ...	I'd like to conclude by stating that ...

Siehe auch *Discussing the clever way: Concluding the contribution*, Seite 283.

22. *Zusammenfassen* – Summarising

Kurz gesagt ...	So, in short ...
Kurz und gut, ...	In brief / In short, ...
In einem Wort ...	To put it in a nutshell ...
Wenn ich zusammenfassen darf ...	If I may summarise ...
Lassen Sie mich wiederholen.	Let me recapitulate / recap.
Ich möchte die wichtigsten Punkte wiederholen.	I'd like to repeat the main points.
Lassen Sie mich die Hauptargumente zusammenfassen.	Let me run through the main arguments again ...
Schauen wir uns noch einmal die wichtigsten Punkte an.	Let us go over the main points again.
Wie wir heute in dieser Präsentation gesehen haben ...	So, as we've seen in this presentation today ...
Zusammenfassend können wir also sagen, daß ...	So, to summarise we can say that ...
Zusammenfassend kann man sagen, ...	To sum up we can say that ...
Im großen Ganzen gesehen ...	On the whole ...
Alles in allem können wir sagen, ...	All in all we could say that ...
Abschließend möchte ich sagen, daß ...	I'd like to round off by saying ...

Advice from the expert

There are two things that are more difficult than making a good presentation: climbing a wall which is leaning towards you and kissing a girl who is leaning away from you.

Ⓣ Advice to presenters: Use spoken English instead of written English

Most people prepare their presentation in writing. The result is, more often than not, a written paper and not a presentation. Don't forget that your audience is doing you a favour by listening to you. They want to be talked to, so don't read them a paper. Here are some rules you should observe.

- When preparing your presentation, don't copy from catalogues or specifications. They are written English.
- Learning your presentation by heart is almost as bad as reading it to the audience.
- Use your own words and have them checked by one of the native speakers in your company or an English trainer.

Here are a few examples:

Avoid written style	Use spoken English
A, B, C	**A and B and C**
The Intelligent Robot is two metres tall, weighs 200 KGs, has a new generation of brains, the gift of speech.	Our Intelligent Robot is two metres tall **and** weighs 200 KGs, **and** he has a new generation of brains **and** most important of all he has the gift of speech.
third person: He, they	**first or second person: I, you**
Participants of meetings will have experienced of how tiring it is to listen to a presentation that is read by the presenter.	**You** are in a meeting and the presenter doesn't talk to **you**. He reads his paper. And what happens? **You** doze off after a few minutes. **I** think you all know what **I** mean.
avoid abstract phrases	**call a spade a spade**
The user of the traditional domestic equipment will have encountered disagreeable **failures.**	I suppose **you** know that sort of unpleasant surprise. You bought a **cheap vacuum cleaner** and when you tried it at home it started **blowing instead of sucking.**

23. *Sich verabschieden* – Saying good-bye

Sollten Sie noch irgendwelche Fragen haben, können Sie mich jederzeit anrufen.	If you have any further questions, feel free to phone me up at any time.
So, das war's für heute. Vielen Dank für Ihre Aufmerksamkeit	So that was it for today. Thank you for your attention.
Vielen Dank für Ihre Aufmerksamkeit, meine Damen und Herren.	Thank you for your attention, ladies and gentlemen.
Es war mir ein Vergnügen, zu Ihnen zu sprechen.	It's been a pleasure talking to you.
Ich hoffe, es hat Ihnen gefallen.	I hope you enjoyed it.
Danke, daß Sie gekommen sind.	Thank you for being here.

Time for a smile

At the end of a presentation, the chairman rose and said, "Your presentation has not left me any the wiser." The presenter retorted, "Perhaps not wiser, sir, but better informed."

P Master your phrases

Task 8: Wrong word order

1. If I you correctly understood prefer you plan C.
2. I can't myself yet commit.
3. Could we this issue open leave until later?
4. I hope it enjoyed you.

Task 9: Scrambled letters

Can you repair these words?

1. I understand your *paperhinonses.*
2. We seem to be talking at cross-*supposer.*
3. It's difficult to accept this, but the *dencieve* is there.
4. I feel we're losing sight of our *vetibejoc.*

C Crossword power

Across

1. Thank you for ✎ your valuable time to listen to me. 5. I'm grateful for having the ✎ to present our product range. 8. Are there ✎ questions? 9. A ✎ in point is Japan. 10. One way to ✎ the financial problem is to reduce our staff. 13. Could you explain in a little ✎ detail? 15. There is no simple ✎ to the problem. 17. The ✎ problem in Germany is unemployment.

Down

2. I ✎ that you're sacrificing one hour of your time to listen to me. 3. Let's not ✎ the fact that our products are too expensive. 4. First, I'd like to give you a general ✎ of the project. 5. I'm trying to give you an ✎ of our company's activities. 6. You've ✎ an important point there. 7. English for 'Folie' 11. I appreciate that you're sacrificing one hour of your ✎ time. 12. A case in ✎ is the success of Microsoft. 13. Excuse me, would you ✎ me asking a question? 14. Let me ✎ it another way. 16. Thank you for reminding me ✎ this problem.

ERFOLGREICH VERKAUFEN

SELLING SUCCESSFULLY[1]

This part of the book guides you through the most important stages of the selling process. The individual steps reflect the strategy a successful salesman will follow. And there is also a lot of psychology involved. To give you a few examples: A good salesman avoids words like 'pay', 'buy' or 'spend money'. These words are 'losers' because they remind the customer that he will lose money. The smart rep uses 'winners': 'investment' instead of payment, 'own' instead of buy. But see for yourself.

1 Alles über Business English für höhere Umsätze finden Sie in *Sell like Hell. Business English für Verkaufsgespräche*, rororo 60722.

1. *Am Telefon* On the phone

Let's start with a smile

Selling is the most exciting thing you can do with your clothes on.
John Fenton

Telefonische Anfragen – Queries over the phone

SATCO. Guten Morgen. Sie wünschen?	SATCO. Good afternoon. Can I be of help?
Was kann ich für Sie tun?	What can I do for you?
Ich rufe wegen des Zeitungsinserats an.	I'm ringing about your advert in the paper.
Darf ich fragen, wo Sie von uns gehört haben?	May I ask where you heard about us?
Sind Sie an unserer neuen Kollektion interessiert?	Are you interested in our new collection?
Ich interessiere mich für Motoren für Modellhubschrauber.	I'm interested in engines for model helicopters.
Sie sind an der richtigen Adresse.	You've come to the right place.
Ich mache mir ein paar Notizen.	I'll take a few notes. May I have
Dürfte ich Ihre Adresse und Telefonnummer haben?	your telephone number and address?
Wir haben mehrere Produkte, die für Sie geeignet sind.	We've got several products that would suit you.
Wieviel möchten Sie investieren?	How much are you intending to invest?
Wenn ich Sie richtig verstehe, brauchen Sie etwas Robustes.	If I've understood correctly, you need something robust.
Um sicherzugehen, daß ich alles verstanden habe, Sie suchen …	To make sure I've understood everything, you're looking for …

Ⓣ Sales tactics: Getting through to the Purchasing Manager

Getting through to the manager who is responsible for *purchases* is not always easy. There is the receptionist and the secretary whose task it is to *screen* their bosses from you and your *competitors.* Don't ask to be put through "to the person who *runs purchasing department.*" They would *immediately* know that you are one of those "unwanted" *reps.* You would only be put through to the following ritual:

Einkäufe
abschirmen; Konkurrenten
leiten; Einkaufsabteilung; sofort
Vertreter

You: I want to speak to the managing director.
Rec.: Will he know who you are and why you are calling?
You: My name is Ronny Smarty. I've an interesting *range* of *copiers* to offer to your company.
Rec.: I'll just check where he is. Please hold the line.
(Music will be piped into your ears and then:)
Rec.: Hello? I'm sorry. *I'm told* he's out today.

Palette; Kopierer
Wie ich höre

So don't give the *impression* that you want to sell anything or to *waste* anybody's time with sales talk. Secretaries are told not to put through unknown sales representatives. But they are not trained to *distinguish* between "important" and "unwanted" information. So don't sell products – offer information.

Eindruck machen
verschwenden
unterscheiden

Rec.: SATCO, Jane Smith speaking. Good morning, how can I help you?
You: This is Ronny Smarty speaking from XOREX Copiers. I'd like to send the person in charge of the purchasing department a few

brochures, but I don't know is name. Who would that be, please?	*Prospekte*
Rec.: That will be Mr Knot.	
You: Thank you very much. Oh *by the way*, you wouldn't *happen to know* his first name?	*übrigens* *zufällig wissen*
Rec.: It's Robert, Robert Knot.	
You: Thanks a lot. You've been most helpful.	
Rec.: *You're welcome*. Good bye.	*Keine Ursache*
The next time you ask to be put through to Mr Knot or his secretary directly. *In the meantime* Mr Knot will have *received* your brochures.	*Inzwischen* *erhalten*
Honesty is a good policy, but sometimes you have to *fall back* on a *white lie*.	*Ehrlichkeit* *zurückgreifen; Notlüge*
You: I met your head buyer *the other day* and he asked me to send him our *quotations* for photocopiers. *Unfortunately* I've a bad memory for names. I wonder if you can help me.	*neulich* *Angebote* *leider*
Rec.: Yes, of course. His name is Knot, Robert Knot.	
You: Thank you very much. You've been most helpful. By the way, what's your name?	
Rec.: Jane Smith.	
Don't forget to ask the receptionist's name. You will use it, when you make your second call. And send Mr Robert Knot your brochures before you make the next call. Now you have got the name of both the manager and the receptionist, and you will use them *to your advantage*. You will no longer *sound* like an unwanted person. You also have a reason to call and you can *refer to* the brochures which might already be in the hands of Mr Knot.	*zu Ihrem Vorteil* *klingen* *sich beziehen auf*

You: Good morning, Ms Smith. This is Ronny Smarty from XOREX. Could you put me through to Robert Knot, please?

Rec.: Will Mr. Knot know what the reason of your call is?

You: It's about the documents we sent him last week.

Rec.: Hold the line, please. I'm putting you through.

Sich an der Sekretärin vorbeimogeln
Getting round the secretary

Guten Morgen. Mein Name ist Bright. Ob Sie mir wohl weiterhelfen könnten?	Good afternoon. My name is Bright. I wonder if you can you help me?
Darf ich nach dem Grund Ihres Anrufs fragen?	May I ask the purpose of your call?
Um was geht es bitte?	What's it in connection with?
Ich würde Ihrem Einkaufsleiter gerne die Prospekte schicken, die er angefordert hat.	I'd like to send your purchasing manager the brochures he has asked for.
Leider habe ich seine Karte verlegt. Könnten Sie mir weiterhelfen?	Unfortunately I've misplaced his business card. Can you help me?
Übrigens, wie ist seine Durchwahlnummer?	By the way, what's his extension?
Wissen Sie zufällig, wer seinen Terminkalender führt?	Do you happen to know who keeps his schedule?
Könnten Sie mich mit Frau Grappner verbinden? Sie erwartet meinen Anruf.	Could you put me in contact with Ms Grappner? She's expecting my call.
Könnten Sie mich bitte zu Herrn Caponini durchstellen? Danke.	Could you put me through to Mr Caponini? Thank you.
Um was geht es bitte?	What is it concerned with?
Er sagte, ich solle ihn anrufen, wenn ich in der Stadt bin.	He said I should give him a ring when I'm in town.

Es betrifft die Dokumente, die wir ihm letzte Woche geschickt haben. It's about the documents we sent him last week.

Wann ist es am günstigsten zurückzurufen? When would be the best time for me to call back?

Siehe auch *Telephoning effectively*, Seite 132ff.

Ⓣ Sales tactics: How to get round the secretary

First call:

- Don't ask to be put through to the boss the first time.
- Don't tell them that you have a product to sell.
- Don't sound like a salesman.
- Get the name from the receptionist or the secretary.
- Pretend to know the person you want to contact.
- Don't offer your product, offer information.
- Tell them that the boss is "expecting" information from you.
- Ask for the secretary's name.

Second call:

- Send your brochures before you make the second call.
- Address the secretary by her name.
- Ask to be put through to the boss.
- Tell the secretary it is about the documents you sent him.
- Tell her it is about a highly technical or financial subject.

Ⓟ Master your phrases

Task 1: Guided translation

1. You've come (*an die richtige Adresse*).
2. If I've (*richtig verstanden*), you need something reliable.
3. We've got several products (*die für Sie geeignet wären*).
4. (*Wissen Sie zufällig*) who keeps his (*Terminkalender*)?

Task 2: A question of cleverness

What would the 'salesman of the year' have said?

A = bad; B =good; C = best

❒ Mr Brown is expecting me.
❒ I'd like to speak to Mr Brown.
❒ Mr Brown asked me to call at 10 a.m.

❒ When would be a good time for Mr Brown to call me back?
❒ When would be a good time to call Mr Brown back?
❒ Could you please ask Mr Brown to call me back?

The USP – the unique selling proposition

A door-to-door salesman knocked at the door of a typical suburban house in Wimbledon.
“Good morning,“ he said. “Would you care to buy a copy of 'Five Hundred Excuses To Give Your Wife For Staying Out Late'?“
“Why on earth would I want a book like that?“ said the lady.
“Because,“ replied the salesman, “I sold a copy to your husband at his office this morning.“

2. *Kundenfang*
Canvassing

How to canvass effectively

One door-to-door salesman does very well by using the opening line: "Can I interest you in something your neighbour said you couldn't possibly afford?"

Stellen Sie sich erneut vor – Reintroduce yourself

Hallo, Herr Schmidt. Bright von L.M.A. am Apparat. Wenn Sie sich erinnern, wir haben uns im Flugzeug getroffen.	Hello, Mr Smith, it's Bright here from L.M.A. If you recall, we met on the plane.
Mein Name ist Smith von X. Sie erinnern sich bestimmt noch an unser Gespräch über ...	My name's Smith from X. I'm sure you remember our discussion about ...
Ich weiß nicht, ob Sie sich an mich erinnern. Wir sind uns auf der Messe in Glasgow begegnet.	I'm not sure whether you remember me. We met at the trade fair in Glasgow.
Darf ich Sie kurz an unser Gespräch in X erinnern?	Could I just remind you of our conversation in X?
Letzte Woche haben wir am Telefon über Ihre Anforderungen gesprochen.	On the phone last week we talked about your requirements.

Modern Times

I hate those answering machines which advise me in a thirty second pre-recorded speech that I will have ten seconds to talk when I hear the beep in five seconds.

Sam Levenson

Verweisen Sie auf Ihre Broschüren – Refer to your brochures

Ich weiß nicht, ob Sie sich daran erinnern, daß Sie von uns einen Katalog erhalten haben.	I don't know whether you remember getting our catalogue.
In der Zwischenzeit dürften Sie unsere Informationen über … bekommen haben.	In the meantime you should have received our brochures about …
Seit unserem Treffen müßten Sie unsere Informationsmappe erhalten haben.	Since we met you should have received our information pack.
Unsere Informationsmappe sagt alles über uns.	Our information pack explains all about us.

The difficulty of door-to-door selling

"Dad, there's a man at the door with a moustache."
"Tell him I've got one already."

Vereinbaren Sie einen Termin – Make an appointment

Ich hätte lieber einen Termin, als es am Telefon zu besprechen, wenn Ihnen das recht ist.	Rather than discussing it on the phone, I'd prefer to meet you, if that's convenient for you.
Herr Schmidt, ich glaube, wir sollten uns wegen … treffen.	Mr Smith, I really feel we should get together concerning …
Sollten wir das nicht lieber in der Praxis überprüfen?	Wouldn't it be better to check everything out in practice?
Ich beanspruche nicht mehr von Ihrer Zeit als absolut nötig.	I won't take up any more of your time than is absolutely necessary.
Wann können wir uns treffen?	When can we get together?
Wann würde es Ihnen passen?	When would it suit you?
Wann wäre es für Sie günstig?	When would be a good time for you?
Einverstanden. Sagen wir also Montag.	Okay. Let's make it Monday then.

Würde Ihnen 17 Uhr passen?	Would 5 p.m. be alright?
Leider nein. Ich habe schon einen Termin um 17 Uhr.	Sorry, I've got a previous appointment at 5 p.m.
Könnten Sie etwas später?	Could you make it a bit later?
Sagen wir, um 19 Uhr.	Let's say at 7 p.m.
Wir könnten uns zu einem Arbeitsessen treffen.	We could meet for a working lunch.
Ich muß den Termin leider absagen.	I'm afraid I've got to cancel the appointment.

Siehe auch *Business people on the move: Making an appointment*, Seite 20 ff.

3. *Ankunft beim Kunden*
Arriving at the customer

Austausch von Höflichkeiten – Exchanging polite noises

Mr Shark läßt jetzt bitten.	Mr Shark will see you now.
Guten Tag. Mein Name ist Bright.	How do you do? My name's Bright.
Freut mich, Sie kennenzulernen, Herr Bright.	Pleased to meet you, Mr Bright.
Ganz meinerseits.	The pleasure is mine.
Wie geht es Ihnen. Mein Name ist Shark.	How are you? Shark's my name.
Ich weiß, daß Sie eine sehr beschäftigte Frau sind.	I appreciate that you're a very busy woman.
Ich bin dankbar, daß Sie für mich Zeit gefunden haben.	I'm grateful you found time to see me.
Danke für Ihre Einladung.	Thank you for your invitation.
Danke, daß Sie uns etwas von Ihrer wertvollen Zeit widmen.	Thank you for sparing us your valuable time.
Ich werde Sie wirklich nicht lange aufhalten.	I really won't take too much of your time.
Ich bin sehr froh, daß wir Gelegenheit haben, diese Angelegenheit zu besprechen.	I'm so glad that we have the opportunity to discuss this matter.

Knüpfen Sie an Vorgespräche an – Refer to preparatory talks

Zuerst würde ich gerne auf ein paar Punkte zurückkommen, die Sie mir neulich genannt haben.	First, I'd like to go back over a couple of points you mentioned to me the other day.
Ich habe die Anforderungen durchgesehen, die Sie mir letzte Woche geschildert haben.	I've been checking through the requirements you described to me last week.
Sie erwähnten, daß Sie zehn XL-Kopierer brauchen könnten.	You mentioned that you might need about ten XL copiers.
Wenn Sie gestatten, fasse ich zusammen, was wir am Telefon vereinbart haben.	If you allow me, sir, I'll just recap what we agreed on the phone.
Vergewissern wir uns, daß wir Ihren Bedarf richtig erkannt haben.	Let's make sure that we're right on target for your needs.

(T)

Sales tactics: Creating the sales climate

The Meet-Formula

- Meet them on common ground
- *Extract* a first 'yes' answer:
- Exchange *memories*
- *Top* it with *testimonials*

hier: auslösen
Erinnerungen
hier: abschließen
Referenzen

Meet them on *common ground*: Build bridges between you and customers. Find out what you *have in common*. This is part of the preparation. "We seem to be both interested in remote-controlled aircraft."

gemeinsamer Boden
gemeinsam haben

Extract first 'yes' answers: Make them *confirm* that they have received your brochures. "I sent you some information as we agreed. I hope it's arrived." Even if they haven't, they wouldn't admit it. *Avoid* 'no' answers. Don't ask whether they have read your brochures. In most cases they haven't. Just ask whether they have got them. If they say no, don't be upset. Guide them to the next step: "Good, I'll come back to that in a moment."

bestätigen
vermeiden

Exchange memories: Talking about hobbies, university etc. opens people up. You will notice that their voices change, that they wake up and relax. "By the way, sir, Newcastle is a favourite city of mine, I used to do a lot of athletics there." – "Oh really, I used to *compete* myself."

an Wettkämpfen teilnehmen

Top it with testimonials, consumer reports or customer records. "As far as reliability is concerned we've been *rated* 'best on the British market for engine technology'. I guess that speaks for itself."

beurteilen

Ⓟ Master your phrases

Task 3: Get your tenses right

1. I'm not sure whether you remember me. We (*treffen*) at the trade fair in Glasgow.
2. In the meantime you should (*erhalten*) our brochures about ...
3. You said I (*soll*) give you a ring when I'm in town.

Task 4: Which words do not fit the context?

1. When can we get / come / meet / go together?
2. Sorry, I've got a previous / former / earlier appointment at 5 p.m.
3. If you memorise / recall / remember we met on the plane.

Task 5: Let's go *woggling* again

1. I'd prefer to meet you, if that's *woggle* for you.
2. When would it *woggle* you?
3. We could meet for a *woggling* lunch.
4. Thank you for *woggling* us your valuable time

Food for thought

Never simply say: “Sorry, we don't have what you are looking for.“
Always say: “Too bad, I just sold the last one today.“
Robert Skole

(T) Sales tactics: What selling is all about

Here is an overview of six main aspects of the selling process. After you have *acquired* a good knowledge of your products, their strengths and weaknesses, you should do the same for your competitors' products. | *erwerben*

Then follow our ICARUS-FORMULA.

Identify customer: Find the right potential buyer for what you're selling. When you're selling yourself into a new job, it means finding the right *employer*. | *Arbeitgeber*

Contact customers: You've been invited to visit a potential customer. Remember, you never get a second chance to make a good first impression.

Ask the right questions: Ask for *permission* to take notes. Find out about interests, personal and company goals, their experiences with your *competitors*. | *Erlaubnis*; *Konkurrent*

Representing your product *requires* the most preparation. Practise your answers to questions with a family member or friends. Make a list of your strongest qualities. | *erfordern*

Use the information you obtained to meet any *concerns* your client may have. *Counterbalance* them with the *benefits* of your product. Find out how important *objections* are and suggest a solution. | *Befürchtungen*; *aufwiegen*; *Kundenvorteil*; *Einwand*

Sell: Don't press for a *contract*! Closing the sale should follow smoothly after *addressing* concerns. | *Vertrag*; *ansprechen*

4. *Auf den Kundentyp eingehen*
Handling various customer types

Tasten Sie den Kunden ab – Sound the customer out

Was für Produktgattungen halten Sie auf Lager?	What sort of lines do you stock?
Sie brauchen vermutlich ziemlich viel Büromaterial?	You must need a fair amount of stationery, mustn't you?
Auf welche Artikel wollen wir uns konzentrieren?	What products would you like to focus / concentrate on?
Welche Produktreihe interessiert Sie am meisten?	Which line is of most interest to you?
Sie erwähnten Kameras. Welche beabsichtigen Sie anzubieten?	You mentioned cameras. Which one do you intend to offer?
Warum bevorzugen Sie Digitalkameras?	Why do you prefer to use digital cameras?
Uns würden Ihre Gründe dafür interessieren.	We would be interested to know your reasons for this.
Fällt Ihnen noch etwas ein, das Sie regelmäßig bestellen?	Can you think of anything else you order regularly?
Könnten Sie uns vielleicht sagen, warum Ihr Ingenieur gerade diesen Typ angegeben hat?	Could you possibly tell us why your engineer has specified this particular type?

Der hektische Kunde – The hectic customer

Wir wissen, daß Sie ein vielbeschäftigter Mann sind.	We appreciate that you're a very busy man.
Deshalb werden wir uns kurz fassen.	So we will be brief.
Wir beschränken uns auf die wichtigen Punkte, um so wenig von Ihrer Zeit wie möglich zu beanspruchen.	We will stick to the essential points so as to take up a minimum of your time.
Sie werden unsere Besprechung	You won't think our meeting has

nicht für Zeitverschwendung halten, wenn Sie unsere Argumente gehört haben.	been a waste of time after you have heard our arguments.
Kommen wir gleich zur Sache.	Let's come straight to the point.
Seien Sie versichert, daß wir Ihre Anforderung genau ermittelt haben.	I'd like to assure you that we're right on target for your needs.
Lassen Sie mich kurz erklären ...	Let me explain briefly...

Der harte, faktenbewußte Kunde – The hard, factual customer

Ich sehe, Sie sind ein Freund von harten Fakten und Zahlen.	I can see you are a man who appreciates hard facts and figures.
Wir würden gerne gleich zu Fakten und Zahlen kommen.	We'd like to get straight down to some facts and figures.
Wir wollen Ihre Zeit nicht mit Zahlen verschwenden, die wir nicht belegen können.	We don't want to waste your time with figures we cannot substantiate.
Hier sind einige Zahlen, die Sie sicher überzeugen werden.	So here are some figures we are sure you will find convincing.
Sie werden sicher beeindruckt von den Informationen sein, die wir für Sie mitgebracht haben.	You will be impressed by the information that we have brought along for you.

Der aggressive Kunde – The aggressive customer

Ich verstehe Ihre Skepsis voll und ganz.	I can fully understand your scepticism.
Würden Sie unser Angebot lieber mit Ihren Ingenieuren besprechen?	Would you prefer to discuss our offer with your engineers?
Sie brauchen sich nicht sofort zu entscheiden.	Please don't feel you have to come to an immediate decision.
Wir wissen, daß man unser Angebot genau prüfen muß, um alle Vorteile zu würdigen.	We know our offer needs careful study in order to appreciate its advantages to the full.
Ich verstehe Ihre Zurückhaltung,	I understand your reluctance, but

aber Sie werden zustimmen, daß dies weitaus das beste Angebot ist.	you'll agree that it is by far the best offer for you.
Ich bin sicher, Sie werden die Vorteile erkennen.	I'm certain you'll see the advantages.
Ich bin überzeugt, Sie werden die Vorzüge sehen, wenn Sie sich unser Angebot in Ruhe betrachten.	I'm convinced that, if you take time to consider our offer, you'll see its benefits.
Ich bin sicher, Sie werden nach sorgfältiger Prüfung zugeben, daß unser Angebot das meiste für Ihr Geld bietet.	I'm sure that, after careful consideration, you will admit that our offer represents the best value for money.

Der ausweichende Kunde – The evasive customer

Ich verstehe, was Sie sagen wollen, aber einige Details sind mir leider noch nicht ganz klar.	I think I see your general meaning, but I'm afraid some of the details are not quite clear.
Könnten Sie das vielleicht ein bißchen präzisieren?	Could you possibly be a little more precise on this point?
Ich bin mir nicht ganz sicher, ob ich Ihre Ausführungen richtig verstanden habe.	I'm not quite sure I follow your line of thought here.
Könnten Sie mir bitte näher erläutern, was Sie meinen?	Could you please clarify exactly what you mean?
Ich kann verstehen, daß Sie sich noch nicht sofort festlegen wollen, aber wir glauben, unser Angebot verdient es, ernsthaft in Betracht gezogen zu werden.	We can fully understand that you don't want to come to an immediate decision, but we feel our offer merits serious consideration.

Der voreingenommene Kunde – The prejudiced customer

Ist es nicht möglich, daß Ihr Händler Ihnen nicht mehr die modernste Technologie liefert?	Isn't it possible that your supplier may no longer be offering you the most modern technology?
Sind Sie so sicher, daß Ihr Lieferant	Are you so certain that your

heute immer noch der beste auf diesem Gebiet ist?	supplier is still the best in this field today?
Sie sollten nicht die beachtlichen Vorteile übersehen, die wir Ihnen bieten können.	You should not overlook the considerable advantages we can offer you.
Würden Sie unser Angebot in Betracht ziehen, wenn wir Ihnen einen besseren Preis bieten?	If we can offer you a better price, would you be ready to consider our offer?
Wenn ich Ihnen besseren Service anbiete, wäre es nicht in Ihrem Interesse, es einmal mit uns zu versuchen?	If I offer better service, wouldn't it be in your interest to give us a try?
Schließen Sie nicht unser Angebot aus, bevor Sie die Fakten unparteiisch geprüft haben?	Don't you think you are ruling out our offer before taking an impartial look at the facts?

P Master your phrases

Task 6: Is it *what, which* or both?

1. .... sort of lines do you stock?
2. .... line is of most interest to you?
3. .... products would you like to focus on?
4. .... do you think is best suited for my needs?
5. .... discount would you offer on an order for 100 items?
6. You mentioned cameras. .... do you intend to offer?

Task 7: Word order: Where do these adverbs go?

exactly; possibly; correctly; fully

1. I can understand your scepticism.
2. Could you be a little more precise on this point?
3. Could you please clarify what you mean?
4. If I've understood, you need something reliable.

Task 8: Fit in these tricky little words

by; back; over; along; back; over; to; through

1. I'd like to go .... a couple of points you mentioned to me the other day.
2. I've been checking .... the requirements you described to me last week.
3. We will stick .... the essential points so as to take .... a minimum of your time.
4. You will be impressed .... the information that we have brought .... for you.

Task 9: Say it the sales way!

We have helped you a little with the vowels.

wissen; in Anspruch nehmen; versichern; genau ermitteln; zusammen-fassen; zur Sache kommen

1. I *a. . . e . i a . e* that you're a very busy man.
2. I won't *. a . e* up too much of your time.
3. Let's come *. . . ai . . .* to the point.
4. I *a . . u .e* you, we're exactly *o . . a . .e .* for your needs.
5. If you allow me, sir, I'll just *. e . a .* what we said.

Ⓒ Crossword power

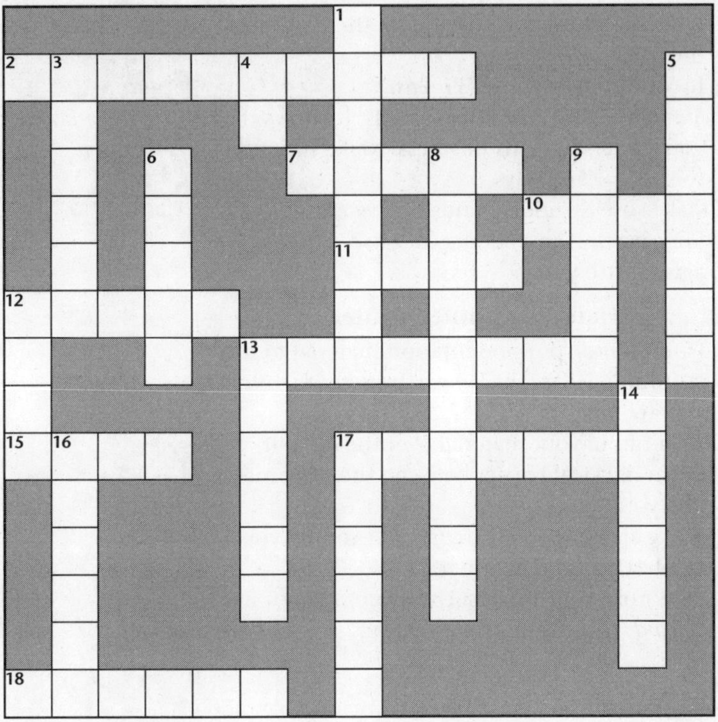

Across

2. English for *'Büromaterial'* 7. I'll just ✎ what we agreed on the phone. 10. English for *'Anruf'* 11. He has a lot to do, he is very ✎ . 12. What sort of lines do you ✎ ? 13. Another word for *'buy'* 15. ✎ a few notes 17. May I ask the ✎ of your call? 18. short for *'advertisement'*

Down

1. I'm not sure whether you ✎ me. 3. Let's make sure that we're on ✎ for your needs. 4. I'm here ✎ business. 5. German for *'the other day'* 6. Let's ✎ it out in practice. 8. German for *'screen'* someone off 9. Repair the word product *'nager'* 12. We've got several products that would ✎ you. 13. Why do you ✎ to use digital cameras? 14. another word for *'remember'* 16. I'll just recap what we ✎ on the phone. 17. I'd like to go back over some ✎ you mentioned the other day.

(T) Sales tactics: Preparing product presentations

Before you start

1. Your presentation should *solve* the customer's problem. *lösen*
2. Identify the customer's *needs*. *Bedarf*
3. *Summarise* the customer's needs. It shows that you understand his business. Make him *agree* to it. *zusammenfassen* / *zustimmen*
4. Make sure he understands the *benefits*. *Vorteile*
5. Summarise the benefits and ask whether he agrees with you.

Handling printed matter

1. Don't hand your presentation material to the customer. He might *browse* through it while you are talking. *durchlesen*
2. Don't hold your material over the desk. It creates a physical barrier between the customer and you.
3. Move alongside to the customer so that you can both view it together.
4. Don't use your fingers. Use a pen or a pointer to *guide* the customer's attention. *lenken*

Using the OHP

1. The verbal *sheet* is a killer. Use memorable pictures to which the audience will react emotionally. *Folie*
2. Don't put more words on *foils* than you would put on a T-shirt. *Folie*
3. Keep it simple. Don't overload. Don't use more foils than you have fingers on one hand.
4. Is the OHP plugged in? Is it in focus? Do you have enough space to move around?
5. Don't sit – stand, but not in front of the screen.
6. Use a pointer. Don't *tap* on the foil with it. *klopfen*
7. Don't talk to your foil – talk to the audience.

5. *Präsentieren Sie Ihr Produkt* Present your product

How best to prepare your presentation

To help a new salesman become familiar with the company's product, the sales manager suggested he demonstrate it to his wife. The next morning the manager asked, "How did the presentation go?" "I did what you told me," said the salesman, "and when I finished, I asked my wife, 'Would you buy it?' She said, 'Yes'! When I asked her why, she replied, 'Because I love you'!"

Beschreiben Sie die Eigenschaften – Describe the features

Lassen Sie mich Ihnen eine allgemeine Vorstellung von dem System geben.	Let me give you a general idea of the system.
Was das System macht, ist grundsätzlich dies: ...	Basically, what the system does, is ...
Dieses System kommt hauptsächlich in / für ... zum Einsatz.	The fundamental application of this system is in / for...
Das System wird hauptsächlich in / für ... verwendet.	This system is mainly used in / for ...
Dies ist ein ganz besonderes Produkt, weil ...	This product is very special because ...
Ein typisches Merkmal unserer Dienstleistung ist ...	A typical feature of our service is ...
Eine seiner herausragenden Eigenschaften ist ...	One of its outstanding features is ...
Die wichtigsten Eigenschaften unseres Service sind Schnelligkeit und Zuverlässigkeit.	The primary characteristics of our service are rapidity and reliability.
Es hat mehrere neue Eigenschaften.	It has several new features.
Dieses Modell weist drei Neuerungen auf.	This model features three innovations.

Diese Produktfamilie ist besonders interessant, weil ...	This product line is of special interest because ...
Werfen wir einen kurzen Blick auf die technischen Daten.	Let's have a quick look at the specifications.
Nun würde ich Ihnen gerne die neuen Funktionen beschreiben.	Now, I'd just like to describe the new functions.
Alle Bauteile sind auf dem neuesten Stand der Technik.	All the components are state of the art.
Unsere neuen Produkte sind auf einem hohen Stand der Technik.	Our new products are highly sophisticated.
Dieses Produkt ist Testsieger in drei Verbraucherzeitschriften.	This product has been rated best in three consumer magazines.
Es hat sich in vielen Tests bewährt.	It has been proven in many tests.
Dieses Auto hat sogar den Elchtest bestanden.	This car has even passed the Elk test.
Es hat alle Vergleichstests mit den Konkurrenzprodukten bestanden.	It has passed all the benchmarking tests.
Wir haben es unter extremen Bedingungen geprüft und getestet.	We have tried and tested it under extreme conditions.
Der Verschleiß ist unerheblich.	The wear and tear is negligible.
Es ist widerstandsfähig und zuverlässig.	It is tough and reliable.
Dies ist das neueste Design.	This is the latest design.
Die Konkurrenzprodukte sind veraltet / nicht mehr auf dem neuesten Stand.	Our competitors' products are obsolete / out of date / no longer up to date.
Es ist kostensparend.	It's cost efficient.

Setzen Sie Ihre Unterlagen ein – Use your documents

Dürfte ich diese Folien auf den Projektor legen?	I'll just put these transparencies on the O.H.P., if I might.
Hier sind einige Referenzen unserer Stammkunden.	Here are a few testimonials from our regular customers.
Alle diese Firmen gehören zu unserem Kundenstamm.	These companies are all part of our customer base.

Bevor wir ..., könnten wir noch die Produktmappe durchsehen?	Before we ... could we just look through the portfolio?
Vielleicht werfen Sie einen Blick in meine Produktmappe.	Perhaps you could look into my portfolio.
Hier sehen Sie unsere ganze Hubschrauberfamilie.	There you can see our entire range of helicopters.
Darf ich Ihre Aufmerksamkeit auf dieses Diagramm lenken?	Could I just draw your attention to this diagram?
Dieses Bild gibt Ihnen eine ungefähre Vorstellung.	This picture gives you a rough idea.

Führen Sie Ihr Produkt vor – Give a live demonstration

Könnte ich dieses System einmal in Aktion sehen?	Could I see this system in action?
Entschuldigen Sie, haben Sie einen Vorführraum?	Excuse me, do you have a presentation room?
Testen wir es einmal in der Praxis.	Let's test it out in practice.
Prüfen wir das System auf Herz und Nieren.	Let's put the system through its paces.
Wie Sie sehen, ist es leicht zu montieren, zu bedienen und zu warten.	As you can see, it's easy to assemble, handle and maintain.
Darf ich Ihnen zeigen, wie man es startet?	If I might just show you how to start it.
Darauf komme ich später zurück, wenn Sie einverstanden sind.	I'll come back to that later, if you don't mind, sir.
Wie Sie sehen, sind hier mehrere Meßinstrumente.	Here, as you can see, are several meters.
Funktioniert es nicht fabelhaft?	Doesn't it perform admirably?
Der Motor summt wie eine Biene.	The motor's humming like a bee.
Beachten Sie, wie ruhig der Motor läuft.	Notice how smoothly it runs.

Siehe auch *Perfect presentations*, Seite 165 ff.

6. *Kundenvorteile ansprechen* Addressing benefits

Time for a smile

Salesman: Believe me, this sewing machine will pay for itself in no time.
Customer: Good. When it does, send it to me.

Kundenvorteile hervorheben – Highlighting customer benefits

Ich bin sicher, unser neues Modell wird Sie interessieren.	I feel sure our new model will be of interest to you.
Ich glaube, wir haben genau die Produkte, die Ihren Anforderungen entsprechen.	I think we've got just the products to cover your requirements.
Wir haben genau die Produktpalette, die Ihren Bedürfnissen entspricht.	We've got just the range of products to cover your needs.
Unser System hat drei wichtige Vorteile im Vergleich zu den Systemen, die auf dem Markt sind.	Our system has three main advantages compared to the systems on the market.
Der wesentliche Vorteil unseres Systems ist ...	The basic advantage of our system is ...
Sie werden sicher von unserer neuen Fernbedienung gehört haben.	Of course, you'll have heard of our new remote control.
Ich brauche Ihnen nicht die Vorteile des ABS-Systems aufzuzählen.	I don't need to tell you the advantages of the ABS system.
Sie stimmen sicher mit mir überein, daß Airbags heute unverzichtbar sind.	No doubt you would agree that airbags are a must nowadays.
Der größte Vorteil dieses Systems ist, daß man keine Sicherungen benötigt.	The main advantage of this system is that no fuses are necessary.
Unser Produkt gefällt dem jungen unternehmungslustigen Kunden.	Our product appeals to the young enterprising customer.
Dies ist ein starker Kaufanreiz für Ihre Kunden.	This gives your customers a big incentive to buy.

Ich bin sicher, Sie erkennen die Vorteile.	I'm certain you'll see the benefit of that.
Aber noch wichtiger sind die Vorteile, die Ihnen die speziellen Funktionen bieten.	But more important are the advantages you get from the special functions.
Unser System ist Testsieger auf dem britischen Markt für Maschinenbau.	Our system has been rated best on the British market for engine technology.
Ich glaube, das spricht für sich.	I guess that speaks for itself.
Das System ist kompatibel mit allen früheren Systemen.	This system is compatible with all previous systems.
Die Technologie ist hoch entwickelt.	The technology is highly advanced.
Hier ist noch ein Beispiel dafür, was Ihre Kunden dabei gewinnen.	Here's another example of how your customers will profit from it.
Wir haben die Erfahrung gemacht, daß ...	Our experience is that ...
Die Erfahrung hat gezeigt, daß ...	Experience has shown that ...
Nach unserer Erfahrung ...	In our experience ...
Wären Sie nicht gerne stolzer Besitzer dieses Schiffs?	Wouldn't you like to be the proud owner of this ship?
Ich bin sicher, daß dieser Bausatz XY Ihren Anforderungen genügen wird.	I feel sure this kit XY will meet your requirements.
Ich bin absolut sicher, daß wir Ihren Bedarf decken können.	I'm absolutely certain we can cover your needs.
Und wenn Sie besondere ... brauchen, können wir das einrichten.	And if you need special ..., we can arrange this for you.
Das ist richtig. Und deshalb haben wir für Sie dieses Gerät entwickelt.	That's correct! And so we've developed this device for you.
Und deshalb haben wir für Sie diese Änderung vorgenommen.	And so we did this special modification for you.

Kundenbedürfnisse zusammenfassen – Summarising customer needs

Wenn ich kurz wiederholen darf, was Sie mir am Telephon gesagt haben.	If I could repeat what you told me on the phone.
Darf ich kurz wiederholen, was Ihre Firma brauchen könnte?	Could I just recap what your company might be needing?
Sie brauchen also einen Lieferanten, der garantiert, daß ...	So you need a supplier who can guarantee that ...
Wenn ich richtig verstanden habe, benötigen Sie am dringendsten ...	If I've understood correctly what your most urgent need is ...
Sie benötigen eine moderne Kollektion mit einem starken Kaufanreiz für Ihre Kunden, nicht wahr?	You require a modern collection which gives your customers a big incentive to buy, don't you?
Kurz und gut, Sie sind interessiert an ...	To get to the bottom line, you're interested in ...
Also, letztendlich stellen Sie drei Bedingungen.	So at the end of the day, you have three conditions.
Ich glaube, wir haben das Wichtigste besprochen.	I think that covers the main points.

Paying them back in their own coin

I ordered a remote controlled helicopter for my son's birthday. It arrived in a kit which contained 123 pieces. The instructions said that it could be assembled in one hour. After a week, just in time for the birthday, I managed to fit the pieces together. I wrote a check, tore it into 123 pieces, and sent it to the company.

P Master your phrases

Task 10: Highlight your USPs (Unique Selling Points)

1. A typical *f . . . . . e* of this device is reliability.
2. The primary *c. . . . . c* of our service is rapidity.
3. I don't need to tell you the *a . . . . s* of the ABS system.
4. I'd just like to describe the new *f . . . . s* of this gadget.

Task 11: Would you buy this product?

Fit in the verbs. The first has been done for you.

1. It has *failed* all the benchmarking tests.
2. It has been .... 'unsatisfactory' in a consumer magazine.
3. It hasn't .... the 'Elk Test'.
4. It doesn't .... your requirements.

Task 12: Or would you rather buy this article?

1. It gives your customers a big (*Kaufanreiz*) to buy.
2. It is the (*neueste*) generation of our helicopters.
3. Its technology is highly (*fortgeschritten*).
4. It is (*auf dem Stand der Technik*).

7. *Den Auftrag an Land ziehen*
Landing the contract

Preisauskünfte einholen – Inquiries about prices

Ich habe Ihre Anzeige gelesen und hätte gerne Preise und Zahlungsbedingungen.	I've seen your advertisement and I'd like to know your prices and terms.
Wie teuer ist die neue Druckmaschine, die Sie anbieten?	What's the price of the new printing press you're offering?
Können Sie mir ein Preisangebot für ... machen?	Could you quote me a price for ... / Can you give me a quotation for ...
Könnten Sie uns ein verbindliches Angebot machen?	Could you make us a firm offer?
Wieviel Rabatt können Sie uns bei einer Bestellung von 100 Stück geben?	What discount would you offer on an order for 100 items?

Siehe auch *Negotiating professionally: Negotiating prices*, Seite 236.

Den Auftrag geben – Placing the order

Ihr Angebot ist in Ordnung. Wir können gleich bestellen.	That offer you sent us was fine. We're ready to order now.
Ich möchte 20 Kopierer in Auftrag geben.	I'd like to place an order for 20 copiers.
Ich notiere mir Ihre Bestellung.	I'll take that order down then, sir.
Kann ich bitte Ihren Namen und Ihre Adresse haben?	Could I have your name and address, please?
Und wie wollen Sie zahlen? Mit Scheck oder Kreditkarte?	And how would you like to pay, sir? By cheque or by credit card?
Können wir den Auftrag stornieren?	Can we cancel the order?

Lieferbedingungen absprechen – Agreeing on delivery terms

Können Sie uns die Geräte ab Lager liefern?	Can you supply us with the equipment from stock?
Wohin soll die Ware gehen?	Where will the goods be delivered?
Wir benötigen das Gerät dringend.	We do need the device urgently.
Können Sie es umgehend zusenden?	Can you dispatch it straight away?
Wir werden es umgehend abschicken.	We'll dispatch it immediately.
Wir können Ihnen die Lieferung noch vor Monatsende schicken.	We'll be able to send your consignment before the end of the month.
Tut mir leid, wir haben eine Lieferfrist von drei Wochen.	Sorry, there's a three week delivery period.
Wie hätten Sie die Lieferung gerne? Per Bahn, Straße oder per Luftfracht?	How would you like delivery to be made: by rail, road transport or air freight?
Wann wird die Ware bei uns sein?	When will the goods reach us?
Die Lieferung ist heute früh zusammengestellt worden. Sie sollte bis Donnerstag bei Ihnen sein.	The consignment was collected this morning. It should reach you by Thursday.
Wir können die Bauteile umgehend versenden.	We can dispatch the components immediately.
Wir schicken die Artikel per Luftfracht, wenn es Ihnen recht ist.	We'll send the articles by air freight, shall we?
Sie wünschen sofortige Lieferung, nicht wahr?	That's for immediate delivery, is it?
Je eher Sie die Geräte schicken, desto besser.	The sooner you can send the devices, the better.

Ⓣ Sales tactics: Overcoming objections

Ten steps to overcome *objections*

1. Be prepared. *Anticipate* concerns. Have a solution ready before the customer *raises an objection.*
2. If you haven't talked about customer benefits, *shelve* the objections: "Can I come back to that later?"
3. Don't interrupt. Listen *patiently.*
4. Pause and look thoughtful as if you're giving careful *consideration* to his or her objection. You gain more thinking time.
5. Feed the objection back to the customer. "So you think it costs too much. Today most things do, don't they."
6. Find out if the objection is a priority. "Can you tell me *how much too much* you think it is?" "So your *hesitation* is just this £300, isn't it?" Price is not a priority if the customer wants the product.
7. Ask whether the customer has other objections before you answer them one by one.
8. Use the FEEL-FELT-FOUND ANSWER: "I understand how you **feel** ... By the way, other clients also **felt** that ... then they **found** that they received good *value* for money from that product for about five years."
9. *Counterbalance* worries with benefits.
10. Ask the closing 'If-question'. "If I can satisfy you regarding the price (delivery etc.), would you be ready to *place an order*?"

Einwand
vorwegnehmen
Einwand erheben
(auf später) verschieben
geduldig
Betrachtung, Überlegung
um wieviel zu teuer
Zögern
Gegenwert
gegenüberstellen
Auftrag geben

8. *Reklamationen* Complaints

Gründe für Reklamationen – Reasons for complaints

Fehler	defects, flaws	*Lieferbarkeit*	availability
Nachlässigkeit	negligence	*Verpackung*	packaging
Lieferung	delivery	*Zuverlässigkeit*	reliability
Beschädigung	damage	*Lastenheft*	specifications

Das Problem ist ...	The problem / the trouble is ...
Die Lieferung ist nicht eingetroffen.	The shipment has not arrived.
Die Lieferung ist unvollständig.	The shipment is not complete.
Folgende Artikel fehlen.	The following items are missing.
Diese Artikel entsprechen nicht den Mustern, die wir erhalten haben.	These items are not like the samples we got.
Die Qualität ist einfach nicht gut genug.	The quality just isn't good enough.
Waren sind beschädigt worden.	Goods have been damaged.
Die Artikel haben Fehler.	The articles are defective.
Der Preis entspricht nicht dem Angebot.	The price isn't the same as your offer.
Die Teile entsprechen nicht der Spezifikation.	The components are not up to specs.
Ich fürchte, da hat jemand einen Fehler gemacht und mir das falsche Modell geschickt.	I'm afraid someone has made a mistake and sent me the wrong model.
Sie haben den Liefertermin nicht eingehalten.	You didn't meet the delivery date.
Sie haben unseren Vertrag nicht eingehalten.	You didn't fulfil our contract.
Es scheint, daß etwas mit der Zollerklärung nicht in Ordnung war.	There's something wrong with the declaration, it seems.
Ich wünschte, Sie würden die vereinbarten Lieferfristen einhalten.	I wish you'd keep to the deadlines we've fixed.

Die Teile, die ich letzte Woche bestellt habe, sind immer noch nicht eingetroffen.	The parts I ordered for last week still haven't arrived.
Solche Verzögerungen wirken sich schlecht auf meinen Umsatz aus.	These delays can have a bad effect on my sales.
Wir haben die Rechnung schon zum dritten Mal angemahnt.	We have sent three reminders to you.

Wie Sie reklamieren – How to make a complaint

Ich bedaure, daß ich reklamieren muß, aber ...	I'm sorry to complain but ...
Ich bedaure, das sagen zu müssen, aber ...	I'm sorry to have to bring this up, but ...
Bei wem kann ich reklamieren?	To whom can I make a complaint?
Ihr Kundendienst entspricht leider nicht unseren Erwartungen.	I'm afraid the service hasn't met our expectations.
Ich muß leider sagen, daß die Qualität minderwertig ist.	I'm sorry to mention this, but the quality is below standard.
Ich beschwere mich normalerweise nicht, aber in diesem Fall ...	I don't normally complain, but in this case ...
Ich muß Ihnen leider eine größere Reklamation melden.	I'm afraid I have to register a serious complaint.
Ich habe eine schwerwiegende Reklamation.	I've a serious complaint to make.
Ich möchte mit allem Nachdruck reklamieren ...	I really want to complain most strongly ...
Sie halten mich vielleicht für einen Querulanten, aber ich kann so etwas nicht schon wieder akzeptieren.	You may think I'm a nuisance, but I really can't accept this kind of thing again.
Ich habe leider einige Probleme mit Ihren Bürorobotern.	I'm afraid I'm having problems with your office robots.
Ich bin ziemlich enttäuscht, daß ...	I'm rather disappointed that ...
Ich kann ... nicht akzeptieren.	I'm afraid I can't accept that ...
Ich bin bis jetzt völlig enttäuscht von Ihrem Kundendienst.	So far I've been totally dissatisfied with your customer service.

Ich möchte Ihnen sagen, daß ich unzufrieden bin mit ...	I really want to express my dissatisfaction with ...
Sie werden kein Geld bekommen, wenn ...	You will not be receiving payment if ...
Wann bekomme ich vollen Schadenersatz? Das ist es, was ich wissen möchte.	When am I going to get full compensation? That's what I want to know.

(P) Master your phrases

Task 13: Where do these verbs belong?

place; quote; cancel; deliver; dispatch; supply; collect; register

1. Could you .... me a price for this copier?
2. I'd like to .... an order for 20 copiers.
3. Can you .... us with the equipment from stock?
4. The consignment will be .... this morning.
5. Can you .... them at once?
6. How do you want us to .... the goods?
7. I'm afraid I have to .... a serious complaint.
8. Can we .... the order?

Task 14: Word lover's corner

Can you complete the table?

Verb	Noun	German
neglect	....	Nachlässigkeit
deliver	....	Lieferung
package	....	Verpackung
specify	....	Lastenheft
complain	....	Beschwerde

Task 15: Beef up your word power

Find a word that has almost the same meaning as the one in *italics.*

1. The following *items* are missing. *a* . . . .
2. Some of the *parts* are defective. *c* . . . .
3. I have to *make* a serious complaint *r* . . . .
4. You have not *kept* the deadline. *m* . . . .

Task 16: How would you like the delivery to be made?

- by *r . . .*
- by *r . . . t . . . .* or
- by *a . . f . . . . . .*?

Task 17: Say it the other way round

Use the opposite of the words in italics.
The first has been done for you.

1. The quality isn't *satisfactory.*
   The quality is *unsatisfactory.*
2. I can't *accept* this kind of thing again.
   This kind of thing is ....
3. The shipment is *not complete.*
   The shipment is ....
4. The printing press is *not reliable.*
   The printing press is ....
5. I've *not* been *satisfied* with your customer service.
   I am .... with your customer service.

(T) Sales tactics: Defusing the angry customer

A customer who complains is like a bomb that may explode. So handle him with care and *defuse* him: | *entschärfen*

1. *Take* each complaint *seriously.* Remember, the customer is always right. | *ernst nehmen*
2. Listen carefully and *take notes.* | *Notizen machen*
3. Don't *interrupt* the angry customer. | *unterbrechen*
4. Don't give him the feeling that he is too stupid to handle the product or unable to read the *instructions.* | *Gebrauchsanweisung*
5. Ask polite questions until you have fully understood the problem. Wait for the answer before asking the next question.
6. Summarise the complaint. That shows him that you take it seriously.
7. *Apologise,* but do not admit any fault unless it is *proven.* | *sich entschuldigen*, *bewiesen*
8. Never put the *blame* on another person or department in your company. | *die Schuld geben*
9. Regard a complaint as a chance to *improve* your product or services. | *verbessern*
10. Thank the customer for his criticism because he has helped you to save money in the future.
11. A customer who is complaining should never be told to call back. It' s your *duty* to return the call. | *Pflicht*
12. If the complaint turns out to be unjustified, give him the opportunity to save face: (I'm pleased we managed to sort it all out.)
13. If a customer becomes *offensive,* suggest that he should speak to your colleague or your boss. | *beleidigend*

9. *Was Sie dem verärgerten Kunden sagen* What to say to the angry customer

Zuhören und fragen – Listen and ask

Wo liegt das Problem?	What seems to be the trouble?
Was haben Sie für ein Problem?	May I ask what the problem is?
Würden Sie mir bitte Ihr Problem schildern?	Would you be so kind as to describe your problem?
Ich mache mir ein paar Notizen.	I'll make a few notes.
Ich schreibe mir das schnell auf.	I'm just taking this down.

Zeigen Sie Verständnis – Show sympathy

Dies tut mir furchtbar leid.	I'm awfully sorry to hear that.
Das ist wirklich ärgerlich.	That's really a nuisance.
Ich verstehe Ihr Problem.	I can see your problem.
Ich kann Ihre Unzufriedenheit verstehen.	I understand your dissatisfaction.
Ich verstehe den Grund Ihrer Reklamation.	I do understand the reason for your complaint.
Ich verstehe Ihren Standpunkt.	I understand your point of view.
Es tut mir sehr leid, daß wir Ihnen Unannehmlichkeiten bereiten.	I'm very sorry for the inconvenience.
Ich kann mir Ihre Enttäuschung vorstellen.	I can imagine your disappointment.
Ich bin sicher, Ihre Reklamation ist gerechtfertigt.	I'm sure your complaint is justified.
Wir nehmen die Reklamationen von Kunden sehr ernst.	We take customer complaints very seriously.
Ich sehe ein, daß Sie dies in ein schwierige Situation bringt.	I realise that this puts you in a difficult position.

Entschuldigen Sie sich, selbst wenn Sie recht haben **Apologise even if you are right**

Tut mir leid, daß uns ein Fehler unterlaufen ist.	Sorry about the mistake on our part.
Wir bedauern, daß wir Ihnen Unannehmlichkeiten bereitet haben.	We're very sorry you've been inconvenienced.
Wir bedauern, daß wir Ihre Bestellung übersehen haben.	Sorry, but we overlooked your order.
Es kann sein, daß bei uns im Haus ein Fehler unterlaufen ist.	Well, there may have been a slip at our end.
Die Unannehmlichkeiten, die Ihnen dadurch entstehen, tun mir außerordentlich leid.	I'm extremely sorry for any inconvenience this has caused you.
Es tut mir leid, daß die Ware Ihnen Schwierigkeiten macht.	I'm sorry the product is giving you problems.
Bitte akzeptieren Sie unsere Entschuldigung,	Please accept our apology.
Entschuldigen Sie bitte den Fehler unserer Rechnungsabteilung.	I do apologise for the error made by our accounts department.
Da ist offensichtlich etwas schiefgelaufen. Entschuldigen Sie bitte den Fehler.	Something has obviously gone wrong. Please accept our apology for this mistake.
Da ist offensichtlich ein Versehen passiert.	There's obviously been some sort of an oversight.
Da ist leider etwas durcheinandergeraten.	I'm afraid there's been a mix-up.
Wir müssen uns für die Verspätung entschuldigen, aber es war höhere Gewalt.	We owe you an apology for the delay, but it's due to circumstances beyond our control.

Bieten Sie Lösungen an – Offer solutions

Wie können wir Ihnen helfen?	How can we help you?
Wir klären das Problem und rufen Sie sofort zurück.	We'll check the problem and call you back immediately.
Und was genau ist mit der Lieferung nicht in Ordnung?	And what exactly is wrong with the delivery?
Wie können wir das wiedergutmachen?	How can we make up for the inconvenience?
Ich bin sicher, wir können das in Ordnung bringen.	I'm sure we can sort this out.
Ich werde mich sofort darum kümmern.	I'll see to it immediately.
Ich werde die Dinge so schnell wie möglich in die Wege leiten.	I'll get things moving as quickly as I can.
Ich rufe Sie sobald wie möglich zurück.	And I'll get back to you on this as soon as possible.
Was erwarten Sie von uns in diesem Fall?	What do you expect us to do in this case?
Sollen wir Ihnen unseren Fachmann schicken, um das zu reparieren?	Shall we send our specialist to fix it?
Wir ersetzen natürlich die Ware.	We'll of course replace the article.
Oder hätten Sie lieber Ihr Geld zurück?	Or would you like your money back?
Wir arbeiten daran.	We've been working on it.
Die Waren waren in einwandfreiem Zustand, als sie unser Haus verlassen haben, aber ...	The goods were in perfect condition when we sent them off, but ...
Wir leisten selbstverständlich Ersatz.	Of course, we'll replace it

Die letzten Worte – Last phrases

Vielen Dank für Ihre Verbesserungsvorschläge.	Thank you for your suggestions on improving our product.

Es freut mich, daß es uns gelungen ist, die Angelegenheit zu regeln. — I'm pleased we managed to sort it all out.
Ich bin froh, daß wir das Problem lösen konnten. — I'm relieved that we were able to solve your problem.
Zögern Sie nicht, wieder anzurufen, sollte es erneut Probleme geben. — Don't hesitate to call again should another problem crop up.

Beleidigenden Kunden begegnen – Handling rude customers

Ihre Reklamation ist völlig gerechtfertigt, aber darf ich Ihnen die Sache aus unserer Sicht erläutern? — Your complaint is perfectly justified, but may I explain the matter from our point of view?
Es tut mir leid, aber Sie sind beleidigend, und das hilft uns nicht weiter. — I'm sorry – you are being offensive, and that won't solve the problem.
Es tut mir leid, aber Sie werden beleidigend. — I'm sorry, but you are getting rude / insulting.
Ich werde meinen Chef bitten, Sie zurückzurufen. — I'll ask my boss to call you back.

A letter of complaint

Lord Richfield wrote to the director of the nuclear power plant near one of his farms:
Dear Sir,
I'm sorry to trouble you again, but this morning I found another of my prize chickens stiff and cold on the ground. Would you be kind enough to explain to me what the matter is?

After a some weeks he got the following reply:

Your Lordship,
I'm afraid, that chicken is dead, too.

Ⓒ Crossword power

Across

1. You need a phone to make it. 4. The meeting has been a ✎ of time. 6. This is good ✎ for money. 7. What lines do you ✎? 8. Why don't you give us a ✎? 9. We'll be ✎. 11. We're exactly ✎ target for your needs. 12. Our components are state of the ✎. 15. May I ask the ✎ of your call? 19. What is the typical ✎ of this product? 21. Repair the word in: What sort of *niles* do you stock? 22. What do you ✎ by that?

Down

1. We're able to (*abdecken*) your requirements. 2. Our offer represents the ✎ value for money. 3. May I ✎ a few notes? 4. The ✎ and tear is negligible. 5. Let's come straight to the ✎. 8. We met at a ✎ fair in Paris. 9. Author of this book. 10. Companies exhibit their products there. 13. We're right on ✎ for your needs. 14. I won't take ✎ too much of your time. 16. This car has _ _ o_ e _ itself in many tests. 17. Companies offer it. 18. Another word for *requirements*. 20. Let's get ✎ to some facts and figures.

PROFESSIONELL VERHANDELN

NEGOTIATING PROFESSIONALLY

This part of the book is mainly about negotiating prices, which is the most delicate part of the sales process. "What does it cost?" A typical first question asked by customers. Costs are what the customer is most concerned about. Sales people fear this question and try to put the answer off until the end of their sales talk after they have highlighted the special features of their product and customer benefits. We put the right phrases into your mouth.

1. *Ein Preisangebot machen* – Offering a price

Wir könnten Ihnen ... anbieten.	We'd be able to offer you ...
Das ist wirklich ein interessantes Angebot.	That's certainly a very interesting proposition.
Wir können Ihnen einen Rabatt von 12 % auf unseren Katalogpreis gewähren.	We can grant you a discount of 12 % on our catalogue prices.
Wir gewähren einen höheren Rabatt bei Auftragswiederholung.	We give a better discount on a repeat order.
Wir können Ihnen einen Rabatt von 10 % geben, wenn Ihr Auftrag bis 30. Oktober bei uns eingeht.	We can give you a 10 % discount if your order reaches us by October 30th.
Bei einem Auftrag von mehr als $10.000 können wir Sonderrabatte gewähren.	If your order's over $10,000 in value, we can allow a special discount.
Tut mir leid, aber dies sind die besten Bedingungen, die wir anbieten können.	Those are the best terms we can offer, I'm afraid.
Die Preise verstehen sich natürlich ab Werk.	Prices ex-works, of course.
Das Angebot versteht sich CIF München, im Preis sind also Fracht und Versicherung enthalten.	The quotation is CIF Munich, so the prices include freight and insurance.
Die Kosten belaufen sich auf $27.000 inklusive Fracht und Versicherung.	The cost will be $27,000 including freight and insurance.
Nun, ich kann Ihnen den Rabatt geben, den wir für Mengen über 200 gewähren. Das sind 7 %.	Well, I can give you the quantity discount that we allow for 200 or over. That's 7 %.
Bei Barzahlung gibt es 2 % Skonto.	There's a 2 % cash discount.

Ⓣ Advice to negotiators: Handling price and prospect

Disarm him

You will never be the cheapest. The price is the only *weapon* the customer has. The way to *disarm* him is to *convince* him that you are there not to cheat him out of his money, but to improve his business, offer solutions and create *opportunities.* The first thing to remember is not to present your price until after the customer has accepted your summary of his needs and understands the *benefits* he will be investing in. What do you say? "Let me tell you what you'll be getting first. Then carry on with the price" or "I'll leave you with the full price details at the end."

Waffe; entwaffnen
überzeugen
Gelegenheit
Vorteile

Balance it: price – benefit

Never mention the price without *balancing* it with a benefit:
"Is price your only *consideration*. Your investment of 50 marks a month will give you round the clock contact with your engineers."

aufwiegen
Überlegung

Sandwich it: benefit – price – benefit

"In order to *improve* the English of your sales people to win business and get results for your investment of 3000 marks, we also offer you a system to *measure* their improvement on a monthly basis."

verbessern

Go for the difference

You are trying to sell a motorbike. "£2000 is too expensive." This is an *objection* much *dreaded* by sales people. Ask them 'Too expensive compared to what?' He will tell you, '*Compared to* the £1800 a Japanese motorbike costs.' Then you go for the

Einwand; gefürchtet
verglichen mit

difference. "How much money are we talking about, only £200, isn't it?" The difference sounds less daunting than the full *amount*.

amount – *Betrag*

Reduce the difference

Now that you know what amount the customer is worried about (£200), help him to see how he can handle it and have what he really wants. Hand him a *calculator*. This is a good way to get him involved as you work out the finances. "Now the *life-span* of this motorcycle is about ten years, is that right? Well, £200, let's divide that by ten years, okay? We get £20, don't we? That's less than £2 a month, isn't?"

calculator – *Taschenrechner*
life-span – *Lebensdauer*

How to get the best price

The proprietor of a highly successful opticians was instructing his son. "Son," he said, "after you have fitted the glasses, and the customer asks what the charge will be, you say, 'The price is a hundred dollars.' Then pause and wait to see if he flinches. If he does not flinch you continue, '... for the frames. The lenses will be another hundred dollars.' Then you pause again, this time only slightly, and watch for the flinch. If the customer does not flinch this time, you add firmly ... each'."

2. *Preise aushandeln* – Negotiating prices

Wenn Ihre Bedingungen vernünftig sind, können wir schon bald bestellen.	If your terms are reasonable, we'll be able to place an order soon.
Bitte nennen Sie Ihren niedrigsten Preis für ...	Please let us have your best / lowest price for ...
Unser niedrigstes Preisangebot ist 60 Dollar das Dutzend.	Our lowest price is $60 a dozen.
Können Sie mir ein Angebot über 500 Stück machen?	Could you give me a quote for 500 items?

Ihre Preise erscheinen uns ein bißchen zu hoch.	Your prices seem to be on the high side.
Aber Sie können mir sicher ein besseres Angebot machen.	But surely you can quote me better terms than that.
Könnten Sie es nicht ein bißchen billiger machen?	Couldn't you make it a bit cheaper?
Immerhin müssen wir einer Ihrer besten Kunden sein.	After all, we must be one of your best customers.
Gewähren Sie einen Mengenrabatt für ...?	Is there a quantity / bulk discount for ...
Wir könnten Ihnen 8 % anbieten, wenn Sie Ihren Auftrag erhöhen.	We could make it 8 %, if you increased your order.
Geben Sie Skonto bei schneller Bezahlung?	Do you allow / grant / give a prompt payment discount?
Geben Sie Skonto bei Barzahlung?	Do you offer a cash discount?
Der Preis hängt von der Größe Ihres Auftrags ab.	The price depends on the size of the order you want to place.
Was würden Sie uns berechnen für / wenn ...	What would you charge us for / if...?
Ist das Ihr bestes Angebot? Ich dachte, die Preise würden sinken.	Is that your best quote? I thought prices would be coming down now.
Ist das Ihr letztes Angebot?	Is that your final offer?
Sie werden feststellen, daß dies Produkt sein Geld wert ist.	You'll realise that you receive good value for money from this product.
Weiter können wir leider nicht gehen.	I'm afraid that's as far as we can go.

How to read a brochure

A woman asks a beautician:
"How much is a chin massage?"
"£20."
The woman is outraged:
"But your brochure says £10."
"Well," the beautician explains,
"that is per chin."

3. *Zeit gewinnen* – Stalling for time

Ich glaube, eine Entscheidung zum jetzigen Zeitpunkt wäre verfrüht.	I feel a decision at this stage would be premature.
Bei einer so wichtigen Frage sollten wir nichts übereilen.	We shouldn't act in haste on such a key matter.
Klären wir doch zunächst die wichtigen Punkte.	Why don't we sort out the main points first?
Danach regeln wir die offenen Fragen.	Then we can come back and tie up the loose ends.
Lassen wir das zuerst einmal beiseite.	Let's leave that on one side for a moment. / Let's come back to that later.
Lassen Sie mich zuerst sagen, was Sie bekommen, und dann können wir vom Preis reden.	Let me first tell you what you'll be getting, then we can talk about the price.
Der Preis ist offensichtlich sehr wichtig für Sie.	Price is obviously very important for you.
Wenn der Preis stimmt, kommen wir dann ins Geschäft?	So if the price is right, can we do business together?
Ich möchte meine Firma in dieser Frage nicht festlegen.	I wouldn't like to commit my company in this matter.
Könnten wir eine halbe Stunde Pause machen?	Could we break for half an hour?
Ich brauche etwas Zeit, um das auszuarbeiten.	I need a bit of time to work that out.
Ich muß das mit meiner Firma abklären.	I'll have to clear that with my office.
Ich überprüfe das und komme dann wieder auf Sie zu.	I'll check that and get back to you.

Siehe auch *Perfect presentations: How to play for time*, Seite 186.

Food for thought

When money is at stake, never be the first to mention sums.

Sheik Ahmend Yamani

4. *Den Preis rechtfertigen* – Justifying the price

Preise sind, wie Sie wissen, relativ. Prices are very relative, as you know.

Haben Sie sich schon einmal bei unserer Konkurrenz umgeschaut? Have you checked with our competitors?

Sie werden feststellen, daß unsere Preise nicht zu unterbieten sind. You'll find our prices can't be beaten.

Sie sollten genau betrachten, was unser Preis alles beinhaltet. You should consider exactly what is included in our price.

Wann immer ein Kunde Einwände gegen unsere Preise hatte, hat sich herausgestellt, daß unser Angebot preiswerter war. Whenever a customer has objected to our prices, we have found that our offer represented better value for money.

Wenn eine Firma einen sehr niedrigen Preis anbietet, hat die Sache oft einen Haken. When a company offers a very low price then there is often a snag / catch / hitch in it.

Natürlich kann man einen niedrigen Preis machen, wenn man minderwertige Materialien verwendet. Of course it is possible to offer a low price by using inferior materials.

Wenn es um Qualität geht, machen wir keine Kompromisse. We refuse to compromise on quality.

Es würde uns überraschen, wenn Ihnen eine andere Firma ein preiswerteres Angebot machen konnte. We would be surprised if another company has been able to offer you better value than we have.

Time for a smile

A man calls his lawyer and asks, "How much would you charge me to answer three questions?"
"£400," the lawyer replies.
"Jesus," says the man. "that's a lot of money, isn't it?"
"I guess so," replies the lawyer. "What's your third question?"

5. *Einen Kompromiß vorschlagen* – Suggesting a compromise

Wir sind bereit, gewisse Zugeständnisse zu machen.	We are prepared to make certain concessions.
Wir wollen Ihnen auf halbem Weg entgegenkommen.	We are ready to meet you halfway.
Einigen wir uns auf einen Preis, der beiden Seiten gerecht wird.	Let's agree a fair price to both parties.
Schließen wir einen Kompromiß.	Let's strike a compromise.
Ich bin sicher, wir kommen zu einer Einigung.	I'm sure we can come to an agreement on that.
Ich bin sicher, wir finden einen Kompromiß.	I'm sure we'll be able to find a compromise.
Es scheint, daß wir uns insoweit einig sind, als ...	It seems we have established common ground in so far as ...
Kann ich davon ausgehen, daß wir uns in diesem Punkt einig sind?	Can I take it that we agree on this point?
Ein ausgewogener Kompromiß wäre ...	A balanced compromise would be ...
Ich hoffe, wir können uns auf folgender Basis einigen ...	I hope we can reach agreement along the following lines ...
Ich wäre bereit, darüber einen Kompromiß zu schließen.	I'd be willing to compromise on that.
Ich glaube, es ist immer noch möglich, einen Kompromiß zu finden.	I think it is still possible to strike a compromise.
Was wir brauchen, ist eine Kompromißlösung, mit der wir beide vom Tisch aufstehen können und etwas in der Hand haben.	What we need is a compromise solution where both of us walk away from this table with something in our hands.
Vielleicht sollten wir einen Kompromiß schließen, anstatt zu prozessieren.	Perhaps we should compromise rather than go to court.

Food for thought

Compromise makes a good umbrella but a poor roof.
James Russell Lowell

(P) Master your phrases

Task 1: Beef up your word power

1. We can { *a*.............. / *g*.............. / *g*.............. / *o*.............. } a discount of 12 % on our catalogue prices.

2. Customers expect { *c*.......... / *b*......... / .... / *p*.......... *p*.......... } discounts.

3. When a company offers a very low price there is often a { .... *h* / .... *g* / .... *h* } in it

Task 2: Phrase smith's workshop

1. *o . . . r* good value for money
2. *s . . . . e* a compromise
3. *m . . t* someone halfway
4. *p . . . .* an order

Food for thought

If you cannot catch a bird of paradise, better take a wet hen.
Nikita Khrushchev

6. *Kompromisse an Bedingungen knüpfen* Linking compromises to conditions

Das Problem ließe sich aus der Welt schaffen, wenn ...	We might be able to get round this problem, if ...
Ich denke, ich könnte dem Vorschlag zustimmen unter der Bedingung, daß ...	I think I could accept / go along with your proposal with the provision that ...

Wir sind bereit zu ...	We are willing to ...
unter dem Vorbehalt, daß ...	with the provision that ...
Wir wären bereit zu unterschreiben, vorausgesetzt, daß ...	We would be prepared to sign, provided that ...
Wir wären bereit, Ihnen einen Preisnachlaß zu gewähren, unter der Bedingung, daß ...	We would be prepared to give you a reduction on the condition that ...
Wir sind durchaus geneigt, bei Ihnen zu kaufen, wenn Sie bereit sind, zu ...	We are more than ready to buy from you as long as you are ready to ...
Wenn Sie bereit wären zu ..., wären wir einverstanden zu ...	If you would be prepared to ..., then we would be ready to ...
Wenn Sie bereit wären zu ..., dann könnten wir ...	If you would be willing to ... then we could ...
Wenn wir zustimmen, hoffen wir, daß Sie sich mit ... revanchieren werden.	If we agree, we hope you would reciprocate by ...
Wenn wir zustimmen, wäre das abhängig von ...	If we agree, it would be conditional on ...
Wir sehen keine Einwände, vorausgesetzt, Sie ...	We see no objection, provided that you ...
Ich glaube nicht, daß wir annehmen können, es sei denn ...	I don't think we could accept, unless ...

Time for a smile

"My son Tom is so forgetful," complained a sales manager to his secretary, "I asked him to get me a packet of cigarettes on his way back from lunch, but I'm not even sure he'll remember to come back himself."

A few minutes later Tom dashed into the office, shouting: "Dad! At lunch I met old man Kelly, who hasn't bought a penny's worth from us in five years and before we parted I talked him into a half-a-million-dollar order!"

"What did I tell you?" sighed the sales manager, "he forgot the cigarettes!"

7. *Zustimmung erbitten* – Asking for consent

Ist das annehmbar?	Is that acceptable?
Wäre das zufriedenstellend?	Would that be satisfactory?
Wäre das eine Basis für einen Kompromiß?	Would that be a basis for a compromise?
Wäre das eine annehmbare Kompromißlösung?	Would that be acceptable as a compromise solution?
Wir hoffen, daß dies verhandlungsfähig ist.	We hope that this will be negotiable.

8. *Dem Kompromiß zustimmen* Agreeing to the compromise

Das entspricht eher unseren Vorstellungen.	That sounds more like what we had in mind.
Damit könnten wir leben.	I think we could live with that.
Wir haben nichts dagegen einzuwenden.	We see no objection to that.
Ich glaube, das wäre annehmbar.	I think that would be acceptable.
Dies scheint ein vernünftiger Kompromiß zu sein.	That seems to be a reasonable compromise.
Ich glaube, wir können Ihrer Bedingung zustimmen.	I think we could agree to your condition.
Um einer Einigung nicht im Wege zu stehen, ...	To avoid standing in the way of an agreement ...
Wollen wir hoffen, daß wir es nicht zu bereuen haben.	Let's hope we don't live to regret it.
Wir haben also Einigung erzielt.	So we've reached an agreement.
Also, wir sind übereingekommen, daß ...	Right, we're agreed that ...

Food for thought

We know what happens to people who stay in the middle of the road. They get run over.

Aneurin Bevan

9. *Kompromisse ablehnen* – Rejecting compromises

Sie bringen uns in eine schwierige Lage.	You are placing us in a difficult position.
In diesem Fall müßten wir den Kompromiß schweren Herzens ablehnen.	In that case, we should very reluctantly have to reject the compromise.
Aus einer Reihe von Gründen fällt es mir schwer, Ihrem Vorschlag zuzustimmen.	For a variety of reasons I find it difficult to agree to your proposal.
Zu meinem Bedauern kann ich den Vertrag in der vorliegenden Fassung nicht unterschreiben.	I regret I cannot sign the contract as it stands.
Wir können es uns nicht leisten, den Vorschlag anzunehmen.	We cannot afford to accept this proposal.
Ich fürchte, wir müssen diesen Vorschlag ablehnen.	I'm afraid we are obliged to reject the proposal.
Sie lassen uns keinen anderen Ausweg, als diesen Kompromiß abzulehnen.	You leave us with little alternative but to reject the compromise.
Obwohl wir eine Pattsituation genauso sehr vermeiden wollen wie Sie, halten wir Ihren Vorschlag für unannehmbar.	Although we want to avoid a deadlock as much as you do, we find your suggestion unacceptable.
Wir sind nicht völlig davon überzeugt, daß dies eine dauerhafte Lösung ist.	We are not entirely convinced that this is a viable solution.
Sie verhandeln zu unnachgiebig. Wir können nicht anders, als Ihre Bedingungen abzulehnen.	You're driving a hard bargain. We can only reject your conditions.
Ich fürchte, es gibt keine Basis für eine Einigung.	I'm afraid there is no basis for an agreement.
Wir müssen neu verhandeln.	We'll have to renegotiate.

Advice from the expert

A verbal contract is not worth the paper it's written on.

Samuel Goldwyn

10. *Das Geschäft abschließen* – Closing the deal

Wenn ich Ihnen einen akzeptablen Preis mache, würden Sie dann den Auftrag geben?	If I can satisfy you regarding the price, would you be ready to place the order?
Können Sie jetzt, da Sie alle Informationen haben, den Auftrag geben?	Now that you've got all the information, are you able to place the order?
Über wie viele Einheiten sprechen wir?	How many units are we talking about?
Lassen Sie uns das Geschäft abschließen wie besprochen.	Let's do a deal on what we've discussed.
Also, abgemacht?	So it's a deal?
Ich glaube, wir sind miteinander im Geschäft.	I think we're in business!
Geben wir uns die Hand darauf / Schlagen Sie ein!	Let's shake (hands) on that.
Wenn Sie gestatten, fasse ich zusammen, was wir vereinbart haben.	If you'll allow me, sir, I'll just recap what we have agreed.
Fassen wir zusammen.	Let me recap what we've agreed.
Auf eine erfolgreiche Zusammenarbeit!	Here's to a successful partner ship!

Time for a smile

"Don't worry!" said a well-known lawyer to a businessman who was accused of tax fraud. "The judge is my cousin. Their chief witness goes with my secretary. And I'm planning to bribe four of the jurors. Meanwhile, try to escape!"

Ⓟ Master your phrases

Task 3: Guided translation

To offer you a helping hand, here are the little words you'll need.

up, down, with, out

1. Why don't we s............ .... the main points first?
2. Then we can t............ .... the loose ends.
3. I thought prices would be c............ .... now.
4. Have you c............ .... our competitors?

Task 4: Word lover's corner

Replace the verbs in *italics* with another verb plus one or two particles.

to, with, round, out, with, along

1. We might be able to *solve* this problem.
2. I think I could *accept* your proposal.
3. I'm sure we can *reach* an agreement on that.
4. Why don't we *discuss* the main points first?

Task 5: Three phrases for "vorausgesetzt, daß"

We are willing to sign { *with* .... / .... / *on* .... } that you give us a a reduction.

C Crossword power

Across

1. English for *'Versicherung'* 6. Your prices seem to be on the high ✎ . 8. Could you give me a ✎ for 500 items? 9. Let's come ✎ to that later. 10. Why don't we ✎ out the main points first? 12. I'm sure we'll be ✎ to find a compromise. 13. Do you allow a ✎ payment discount? 15. Is that your ✎ offer? 17. We'll be able to ✎ an order soon. 19. You'll find our prices can't be ✎ . 20. Do you ✎ a discount? 21. Is there a ✎ discount? 22. We are prepared to ✎ you half-way.

Down

1. Price is obviously very ✎ for you. 2. The price depends on the ✎ of your order. 3. We give a better discount on a ✎ order. 4. There's a 2 % discount for ✎ . 5. English for *'Menge'* 7. English for *'Rabatt'* 8. Repair the word *'toniquato'* 11. If your order's over $10,000 in value, we ✎ a special discount. 14. So it's a ✎ ? 15. Our prices include ✎ and insurance. 16. Could we ✎ for half an hour? 17. You ✎ us in a difficult position. 18. Can I ✎ it that we agree on this point?

6 PART

BESPRECHUNGEN MEISTERN

MASTER YOUR MEETINGS[1]

Meetings can be a horror show: Participants arrive late or are not prepared; nobody pays attention to the agenda; the minutes are not taken accurately, which means there will be arguments at the next meeting. But it is possible to manage meetings in a professional way, and to choose the right thing to say. Read on and good luck!

1 Meistern Sie Ihre Konferenzen und Präsentationen mit *Get Through at Meetings*, rororo 60262.

1. *Die Eröffnung* – The opening

Gut, laßt uns anfangen.	Right, shall we get started?
Kommen wir zur Sache.	Let's get down to business, shall we?
Ich glaube, wir sollten anfangen.	I think we should get under way.
Meine Damen und Herren, ich erkläre die Sitzung für eröffnet.	Ladies and Gentlemen, I declare the meeting open.
Ich habe die Ehre, die erste Sitzung des Komitees für ... eröffnen zu dürfen.	I have the honour to declare the first session of the committee on ... open.
Meine Damen und Herren, darf ich die Besprechung nun eröffnen?	Ladies and Gentlemen, may I open this meeting now?
Ich freue mich, Sie heute alle begrüßen zu dürfen.	I'm happy to welcome all of you today.
Vielen Dank, daß Sie heute gekommen sind.	Thank you for coming today.
Im Namen der Unternehmungsleitung darf ich Sie herzlich begrüßen.	On behalf of the management allow me to extend a warm welcome to you.
Ich freue mich, Sie anläßlich ... bei uns begrüßen zu können.	It's a pleasure / I'm glad to welcome you here on the occasion of ...
Ich hoffe, wir werden ein gutes Gespräch führen.	I hope we will be able to have a fruitful discussion.
Fred scheint wieder durch höhere Gewalt verhindert zu sein.	Fred seems to be held up by some act of God again.
Ich darf Direktor Blocks Verspätung entschuldigen.	May I apologise for the fact that Director Block is late?
Herr Brain ist in einer dringenden Angelegenheit verhindert.	Mr Brain has been held up by urgent business.

How to maintain discipline

"There are two sides to every question," said the new boss at the first meeting, "my side and the wrong side. And don't say 'yes' until I've finished."

Ⓣ

Meetings in Spain

The Spanish are a proud and *independent* nation. Theirs is not a meeting culture. Like the torero in the arena the senior executive takes his decisions on his own and uses the meeting to *communicate* his *instructions.*

Although most companies have introduced the American philosophy of how to run a company, the idea that a meeting can be used to decide on an action plan, *allocate responsibilities* and co-ordinate *implementation* is something that is not part of the Spanish mentality. Modern young executives who try to use meetings as a management tool *complain* that they are too long and ineffective. The necessary skills, strategies and the etiquette have still to be learnt.

Spaniards do not work well in a meeting because they see it as a forum to *defend* their opinions and *obtain* agreement to it rather than arrive at a decision. Unless the chairperson *pulls the subject back to the agenda,* if there is one, it will be rapidly *abandoned.* Consensus is most easily reached by getting everyone to agree with the chairperson rather than with each other. They feel that, in the end, it is the boss who is *responsible.*

Britons and Americans who are *used to* producing a result to which everyone has *contributed* something, and in which everyone will share the *responsibility*, will find this frustrating.

unabhängig
mitteilen
Anweisungen
obwohl
Verantwortung übertragen; Durchführung
sich beklagen
verteidigen
erreichen
zur Tagesordnung zurückführen
aufgeben
verantwortlich
daran gewöhnt
beitragen
Verantwortung

Adapted from John Mole *Mind Your Manners*.
Nicholas Brealy Publishing. London: 1995.

2. *Die Tagesordnung* – The agenda

Haben alle eine Kopie der Tagesordnung erhalten?	Has everyone received a copy of the agenda?
Gestatten Sie mir, folgendes zur Tagesordnung zu bemerken.	Please allow me to make the following remarks about the agenda.
Wir haben eine umfangreiche Tagesordnung.	We've got a full agenda.
Möchte jemand noch einen Punkt auf die Tagesordnung setzen?	Would anybody wish to add an item / point to the agenda?
Ich schlage vor, der Tagesordnung folgende Punkte hinzuzufügen:	I'd like to suggest / propose that we add the following items to the agenda:
Ich meine, wir sollten auch die Frage behandeln, ob wir ...	I think we should also take up / deal with the question about whether we ...
Diese Frage ist schon in Punkt 5 enthalten.	This question is already covered under item 5.
Die Frage der ... könnte unter "Sonstiges" behandelt werden.	The issue of ... might be considered under the item "Other business".
Könnten wir Punkt 3 der Tagesordnung streichen?	Could we delete item 3 from the agenda?
Ich kann dem Vorschlag, diese Frage zu streichen, nicht zustimmen.	I'm afraid I can't accept the proposal to remove this question.
Ich schlage vor, wir beschränken uns auf ...	I suggest we limit / confine ourselves to ...
Der erste Punkt der Tagesordnung ist ...	The first item on the agenda is ...
Lassen Sie uns mit dem ersten Punkt der Tagesordnung beginnen.	Let's start with the first item on the agenda (informal).

Why meetings fail

The last time I sat in at a meeting we were presented with a plan which had two alternatives. We therefore narrowed it down to eighteen possibilities for further discussion.

3. *Ein angenehmes Klima schaffen*
Creating a pleasant atmosphere

Machen Sie es sich gemütlich.	Make yourself at home.
Lassen wir die Förmlichkeiten beiseite.	Let's forget the formalities.
Ich weiß es zu schätzen, daß Sie uns eine Stunde Ihrer kostbaren Zeit opfern.	I appreciate that you are sacrificing an hour of your valuable time.
Ich möchte zu aller erst Bryan für ... danken.	I want to begin by thanking Bryan for ...
Ich möchte zu Beginn Tom zu seiner Leistung gratulieren.	I'd like to begin by congratulating Tom on his performance.

The ideal meeting

A meeting should consist of three men,
two of whom are absent.
Robert Copeland

P Master your phrases

Task 1: Scrambled letters

Can you repair the words in *italics*?

1. Ladies and Gentlemen, I *redecal* the meeting open.
2. I'm happy to *mewocle* all of you today.
3. On behalf of the Board *lowal* me to *dexten* a warm welcome to you.
4. May I *galoposie* for the fact that Director X is late?
5. I *perepataic* that you are sacrificing an hour of your valuable time.

Task 2: Prepositions

Fill in the missing prepositions.

1. I think we should also deal .... the question of overtime.
2. This question is already covered .... item 5.
3. Could we delete item 3 .... the agenda?
4. Let's get .... business, shall we?
5. Let's start .... the first item .... the agenda.
6. I'd like to begin .... congratulating Tom .... his performance.

Task 3: Beef up your word power

Add an expression that has a similar meaning

1. I suggest we *limit* / .... ourselves to the most important questions.
2. I'd like to *suggest* / .... that we add the following items to the agenda.
3. I think we should also *take up* / .... the question of whether we ...
4. Could we *delete* / .... item 3 from the agenda?

Food for thought

A committee is a group
that keeps the minutes
and loses the hours.
Milton Berle

(T) Meetings in Britain

1. The Staff meeting

In Britain the meeting is the most important and *time-consuming* management tool. It is considered a part of the work and not a *necessary evil.* Even unimportant decisions are discussed, voted on and *put into practice.*
An important meeting is *scheduled* well in advance and a detailed *agenda* is distributed to all participants. Not everybody will have read it or come to the meeting well-prepared. However, everybody is expected to make a *contribution*, if only by asking questions, giving ones opinion and listening patiently to the *views* of colleagues. It is considered fair play not to *influence* members beforehand in order bring about a decision with the help of a lobby. Of course, there may be some *exceptions* to the rule, especially in politics. After all, the lobby was invented in Britain.

zeitraubend
notwendiges Übel
verwirklichen
anberaumen
Tagesordnung
Beitrag
Ansichten
beeinflussen
Ausnahmen

Discussions may be controversial. But it is the chairperson's *concern* to *avoid clashes.* Loyalty to the boss and the company is stronger even than fundamental disagreement. It is usual first to listen to the arguments of the others and then *support a suggestion.*

Anliegen; Zusammenstöße vermeiden

Vorschlag unterstützen

2. International meetings

A staff meeting without some concrete result is regarded as a *failure.* This does not hold true for international meetings. Even in the absence of disagreement, British managers will rarely make a final *decision* at the first meeting. It is advisable to go for a long-term relationship – not for the quick deal. So don't *push* them to sign a contract, they don't like to be hurried. *Suggest* that a final decision should be taken at the next meeting. Bargaining is not the norm, but some concessions will *satisfy* the British negotiator's interest in economy.

The English feel *superior* to the rest of the world. At international meetings British members often give the *impression* that they are arrogant and that they have little to learn from members of more successful nations. They view the Irish as being wildly eccentric, the Welsh *dishonest,* the French insincere, the Germans easily led bullies, the Italians hysterical, the Spanish lazy and the Russians gloomy. And since most conferences are held in English, they easily win the *war of the words.* This adds to the picture of the arrogant British.

Americans, Germans and Scandinavians like to *come straight to the point.* The English are different. The majority of meetings begin and end with small talk.

Mißerfolg

Entscheidung

drängen

vorschlagen

zufriedenstellen

überlegen

Eindruck

unehrlich

Wortgefecht

gleich zur Sache kommen

4. *Das Protokoll* – The minutes

Haben alle eine Kopie des Protokolls der letzten Besprechung?	Has everybody got a copy of the minutes of our last meeting?
Haben alle das Protokoll eingesehen?	Has everybody seen the minutes?
Können wir das Protokoll als angenommen betrachten?	Can we take the minutes for / as read?
Wer führt heute das Protokoll?	Who is going to keep the minutes today?
Wer ist heute der Protokollant?	Who's today's minute-taker?
Tom hat sich wie üblich freiwillig für das Protokoll gemeldet. Danke Tom.	Tom has volunteered to keep the minutes, as usual. Thank you, Tom.

How not to explain the purpose of a meeting

The President of a big company opened a meeting of salesmen by announcing:
"Ladies and gentlemen, the purpose of this meeting is to fire you with enthusiasm. If it doesn't work I'm going to fire you – with enthusiasm."

5. *Den Zweck erläutern* – Explaining the purpose

Wie Sie der Tagesordnung entnehmen ...	As you can see from the agenda ...
Thema unserer Besprechung ist ...	The subject of our meeting is .....
Der Grund unseres Beisammenseins ist ...	The reason for our gathering / coming together is ...
Das Ziel der heutigen Tagung ist, eine Entscheidung über ... zu treffen.	The objective / purpose of our session is to take a decision on ...
Der Zweck der heutigen Besprechung ist ...	The purpose of today's meeting is ...
Womit wir uns heute befassen müssen, ist ...	What we need / have to deal with is ...
Was wir heute diskutieren / erörtern wollen ist ...	What we want to discuss / consider today is ...
Unsere Aufgabe ist es, Empfehlungen über ... zu erarbeiten.	The task before us is to come up with recommendations on ...

Wir sind heute zusammengekommen, um zu entscheiden, ob wir riskieren sollen, ...	We've come together today to decide if / whether we should risk ...
Diese Sitzung ist eine gute Gelegenheit, Ideen über eine neue Strategie für ... auszutauschen.	This meeting is / provides a good opportunity to exchange ideas on a new strategy for ...
Drei Probleme sollten heute gelöst werden.	There are three problems that should be solved today.
Heute müssen drei Entscheidungen gefällt werden.	There are three decisions to be taken today.
Meine Damen und Herren, sehen wir den Problemen ins Auge.	Ladies and Gentlemen, let's face the problems.
Wir haben ernste Schwierigkeiten bei / mit ...	We've run into serious problems concerning ...

6. *Einige typische Anlässe* – Some typical occasions

Nun, wie Sie alle wissen, sind wir hier, um ... zu / weil ... / wegen ...	Now, as you all know, we're here to ... / because ... / because of ...
Wir müssen unsere Etats beschließen.	We have to decide on our budgets.
Willkommen zu unserer wöchentlichen Produktionsbesprechung.	Welcome to our weekly production meeting.
Wie Sie alle wissen, befinden wir uns in einer tiefen Rezession.	As you all know we are in a deep recession.
Wir haben in letzter Zeit eine ganze Reihe Kundenbeschwerden gehabt.	We've been having quite a few customer complaints recently.
Unsere Forschungsabteilung hat ein neues Produkt entwickelt.	Our R&D department has come up with a new product.

The true nature of meetings

A meeting is a group of men who individually can do nothing, but together can decide that nothing can be done.

Fred Allen

Ⓟ Master your phrases

Task 4: People and functions

Fit in the missing letters.

ch _ _ r p _ r s _ n

g_ _st sp_ _k_r | pr_s_nt_r | m_n_t_-t_k_r | p_rt_c_p_nt

Task 5: Why meetings are held

Meetings should always have	*o. . . . . s*
	p. . . . . . s
	r. . . . ns
	r. . . . ts

What is a committee?

A group of the unwilling,
picked from the unfit,
to do the unnecessary.

(T)

Meetings in America

In the United States meetings are *primarily* a communication tool for *imparting* information. The attendee sees it as an *opportunity* to present his proposals, examine the suggestions of his colleagues and *support* or *reject* them. The object is not to make a decision but to test the presenter's competence, preparation and *depth* of *knowledge.*

Most decisions will have been lobbied beforehand and will be *approved* at the end of a meeting. A decision is not the result of a *consensus,* in the sense of collective *responsibility,* but for a commitment to a course of action. If anything goes wrong, the participants will not *share* the responsibility. It is their *superior* who alone will be held responsible.

The status of the executive has little to do with *seniority.* It is determined by how much power he has. Power is *measured* in how much of the business is under his direct control.

In dealing with colleagues at all *levels* it is important to demonstrate competence and professionalism. Bringing up a problem without a *suggested solution* or without the relevant data, in the expectation that a solution will be worked out with the participants during the meeting, is a sign of *weakness*. Americans *pursue* their personal and *corporate goals* with frankness, energy and sometimes with aggression. They often lose patience with the *participative* committee cultures of European companies. They may find their European colleagues *lacking in motivation* and commitment.

Adapted from John Mole *Mind Your Manners.*
Nicholas Brealy Publishing. London: 1995, p. 156 ff.

in erster Linie
vermitteln
Gelegenheit
unterstützen; verwerfen
Tiefe; Wissen
zustimmen
Übereinkunft
Verantwortung
teilen
Vorgesetzter
Dienstalter
messen
Ebene
Lösungsvorschlag
Schwäche; verfolgen
Firmenziele
Mitbestimmungs-
an Motivation fehlen lassen

7. *Tagesordnungspunkte* – Items on the agenda

Lassen Sie uns mit dem ersten Punkt der Tagesordnung beginnen.	Let's start with the first item on the agenda.
Zuerst gibt uns Herr X eine kurze Präsentation seiner neuesten Erfindung.	First Mr X is going to give us a short presentation of his latest invention.
Das erste Problem, das wir zu erörtern haben, ist ...	The first problem we have to consider is ...
Vielleicht sollten wir zuerst ... betrachten?	Perhaps we should first look at ...?
Machen wir zuerst ein kurzes Brainstorming.	Let us start with a short brainstorm.
Ich würde gerne mit einem kurzen Überblick über die Verkaufszahlen des letzten Quartals beginnen.	I should like to begin with a short overview of last quarter's sales figures.
Ich möchte Ihnen zu Beginn unseren neuen Prototyp vorstellen.	I wish to begin by presenting our new prototype.
Ich würde gerne kurz ... erwähnen.	I'd like to mention briefly ...
Ich möchte kurz auf ... eingehen.	I'd like to touch upon ...
Zuallererst würde ich gerne einige Bemerkungen zu ... machen.	First of all, I'd like to make a few remarks concerning ...
Ich würde gerne etwas zu dem Problem des / der ... sagen.	I'd like to comment on the problem of ...
Und nun, meine Freunde, weiter mit den Einzelheiten.	And now, my friends, on to the details.

Why meetings fail

A committee is twelve men
doing the work of one.

8. *Gäste vorstellen* – Introducing guests

Ich freue mich, Ihnen Herrn X vorstellen zu dürfen.	It's my pleasure to introduce Mr X.
Herr X, willkommen bei ISC in Heidelberg.	Mr X, welcome to ISC in Heidelberg.
Im Namen des Vorstands heiße ich unsere Partner aus Japan herzlich willkommen.	On behalf of the Board I extend a hearty welcome to our partners from Japan.
Wir haben die Ehre, Herrn X zum Thema Umweltbelastung zu hören.	We have the honour of being addressed by Mr X on the theme of pollution.
Wir freuen uns alle auf Ihre Präsentation.	We're all looking forward to your presentation.
Mr X wird nun zu Ihnen über das Problem ... sprechen.	Mr X will now speak to you about the problem of ...
Mr X, bitte sehr.	Mr X, over to you.
Mr X, Sie haben das Wort.	Mr X, the floor is yours.
Zunächst möchte ich Ihnen sagen, wie froh ich bin, an diesem Seminar teilnehmen zu können.	Let me say at the outset how happy I am to be able to attend this seminar.
Ich freue mich sehr, daß man mich zu diesem Kongreß eingeladen hat.	I'm delighted to have been invited to this congress.
Ich bin sicher, wir haben alle Ihren Vortrag sehr interessant gefunden.	I'm sure we all found your talk very interesting indeed.
Herr X, wir möchten Ihnen für die Informationen danken.	We'd like to thank you for the information, Mr X.

First words for guest speakers

Before I get to the work at hand, let me say that to be chosen as guest speaker for this occasion is more than an honour. We had to draw lots to see who would be the guest speaker – I lost!

(T)

Meetings in Japan

Time management

Japanese are very *punctual.* Otherwise time is fluid. A meeting will *carry on* until it is finished or interrupted by the *demands* of a senior person outside. You should not try to *rush things* or take control. Fast answers are not respected, and long *silences* are normal – they are thinking time.

pünktlich
andauern
Forderungen
drängen
Schweigen

Presentations

If you are making a presentation to Japanese managers, don't watch out for signs of *approval* or *disapproval.* Don't expect them to show their interest by interrupting you with questions. They won't laugh, frown or *cough.* Laughter is seen as a sign of *embarrassment.* They will observe and listen in silence. It is a sign of their respect for your ideas. And if they listen with their eyes closed, it is because they are concentrating on what you are saying.

Beifall
Ablehnung
husten; Verlegenheit

Negotiating

In Japan, the first meeting is usually for *preliminary* observation, a sort of Japanese shadow boxing. Personal *relations* are more important than contracts. *Lawyers* are considered an unnecessary *evil.* So don't bring your lawyers! They would think that you do not trust them. Experts, however, are highly respected.

vorläufig(e)
Beziehungen
Juristen; Übel

Decision-making

The Japanese negotiator represents a team. The *participants* at meetings may often change because decisions are made by consensus across many management levels – at the third or fourth meeting. But then, fast action is expected.

Teilnehmer

Contracts

They prefer *oral agreements* to written ones. By the way, a contract is an agreement between gentlemen. If market or other conditions change they think it natural to *renegotiate* the contract.

mündliche Vereinbarung
neu verhandeln

9. *Meinungen sammeln* – Collecting opinions

Darf ich um Reaktionen zu Susans Präsentation bitten?	May I ask for reactions to Susan's presentation?
Wie denkst du über ...?	What do you think of ...?
Was ist Ihre Meinung zu ...?	What's your opinion of ...?
Was ist Ihre Ansicht über ...?	What's your view on ...?
Was hältst du davon, Bob?	What's your feeling, Bob?
Wie ist dein Standpunkt dazu?	What's your point of view?
Wie stehst du zu ...?	What's your position on ...?
Wie sehen Sie das Problem?	How do you see the problem?
Ich würde gerne eure Meinungen zu ... hören.	I'd like to hear your views on ...
Möchtest du vielleicht etwas dazu sagen, Tina?	I wonder if you'd like to comment, Tina?
Und wie stehen Sie zu dieser Frage, Dr. Brain?	And where exactly do you stand on this issue, Dr Brain?
Ich würde gerne Professor Dosch bitten, uns seine Meinung zu sagen.	I'd like to ask Professor Dosch to give us his view.
Bob, hast du etwas (dazu) zu sagen?	Have you got anything to say, Bob?
Was ist dein Eindruck, Ron?	What's your feeling Ron?
Tom, ich glaube, du weißt etwas über das Problem.	Tom, I think you know something about the problem.
Was ist deine Ansicht dazu, Tina?	What are your views on this, Tina?
Herr Kelly, möchten Sie hierzu etwas sagen?	Mr Kelly, would you like to come in here?
Möchtest du vielleicht etwas dazu beitragen, Ron?	I wonder if you would like to comment, Ron?
Frau Gram, möchten Sie etwas dazu sagen?	Ms Gram, would you like to say something about this?
Was ist deine Meinung, Tom?	What's your opinion, Tom?
Hat irgend jemand noch etwas hinzuzufügen, bevor wir zum nächsten Punkt übergehen?	Has anyone anything further they wish to add before we move on to the next item on the agenda?
Ich möchte gerne Herrn Brown das Wort erteilen.	I'd like to give the floor to Mr Brown.
Herrn Brown, ich glaube, Sie sind der Experte auf diesem Gebiet.	Mr Brown, I think you are the expert in this field.

Hat jemand an die rechtliche Seite des Projekts gedacht? Has anybody thought of the legal aspect of the project?

John, ich glaube, du bist der Spezialist in juristischen Dingen. John, I think you are the specialist in legal matters.

Ich glaube, unser Buchhalter möchte dazu Stellung nehmen. I think our accountant would like to make a point.

Ich würde gerne Herrn Direktor Block bitten, uns seine Meinung zu sagen. I would like to invite Director Block to present his views.

The true nature of meetings

The average meeting comprises eight executives, each of whom wishes that at least three of the other seven weren't on it.

Harvard Business Review

P Master your phrases

Task 6: Six ways of asking for contributions

Tom, what's your

v........ r...........n o.........n f.........g p.........n p...... of ......w?

Task 7: Spot the mistakes

1. The purpose of the meeting of today is ...
2. It's my great pleasure of introducing Mr X.
3. We have the honour to be addressed by Mr X.
4. Mr X, we all look forward to your presentation.
5. Let me say how lucky I am to be able to attend this seminar.

Advice from the expert

A breakfast meeting is the most uncivilised idea I've ever heard of. If you're going to have a breakfast meeting, it should be in bed with a beautiful woman.

Gordon White

10. *Fragen weitergeben* – Passing on questions

Vielleicht möchte Frau Child diese Frage beantworten?	Perhaps Mrs Child would care to answer this question?
Ich meine, der Leiter der Produktionsabteilung ist der richtige Mann, um diese Frage zu beantworten.	I think the production manager is the right man to answer this question.
Ich würde gerne meinen Kollegen Tom hinzuziehen, der diese Frage genauer untersucht hat als ich.	I'd like to bring in my colleague Tom, who has studied this question in more detail than I have.
Ich glaube, Dr. Stone kann Ihnen diese Frage besser beantworten als ich.	I think Dr Stone is more qualified than I am to deal with this question.
Wenn Sie gestatten, würde ich unseren Gastredner um eine Antwort bitten.	If I may, I'd like to ask our guest speaker to reply to that.

Time for a smile

A camel is a horse
designed at a meeting.

11. *Disziplin halten* – Maintaining discipline

Darf ich um Ihre Aufmerksamkeit bitten?	Can I have your attention, please?
Versuchen wir, bis fünf Uhr fertig zu werden.	Let's try to finish by five o'clock.
Versuchen wir, diese Besprechung kurz zu halten.	Let's try to keep this meeting short.
Ron, ich fürchte, wir kommen zu weit vom Thema ab.	Ron, I'm afraid we're moving too far away from the subject.
Könntest du bitte beim Thema bleiben.	Could you stick / keep to the point / subject, please?
Wir wollen nicht vom Thema abkommen. Das Problem, das wir diskutieren, ist ...	Let's not get side-tracked. The issue under discussion is ...
Es scheint da ein kleines Mißverständnis zu herrschen.	There seems to be a slight misunderstanding.

Ich muß Sie ermahnen, mein Fräulein.	I shall have to call you to order, young lady.
Wir können nicht alle gleichzeitig sprechen.	We cannot all speak at once.
Ihre Darstellung ist leider nur eine subjektive Interpretation.	I'm afraid your statement is only a subjective interpretation.
Ihr Beitrag ist nicht objektiv und deshalb nicht von Belang.	Your contribution is not objective and therefore of little value here.
Es tut mir leid, dies sagen zu müssen, aber Ihre Bemerkungen tragen nichts zur Sache bei.	I'm sorry to have to say this, but your comments add nothing to the issue at hand.
Das kommt nicht ins Protokoll.	This will not be recorded in the minutes.

Talking at cross purposes

Chairman: "Now, Dobson, this isn't a kindergarten. Order! Order!"
Dobson: "Okay, I'll have a cheese sandwich then."

12. *Die Diskussion lenken* – Conducting the discussion

Sollten wir uns nicht besser der Frage des / der ... zuwenden?	Shouldn't we rather turn to the question of ...?
Ich glaube, es wäre gut, wenn wir uns der wichtigeren Frage ... zuwenden würden.	I think it might be a good idea if we discussed the more important question of ...
Ich fürchte, wir verlieren die Hauptsache aus den Augen. Das Problem ist doch ...	I'm afraid we're losing sight of the main point. The problem is ..., isn't it?
Ich fürchte, dies ist für unsere Diskussion nicht von Bedeutung.	I'm afraid this isn't really relevant to our discussion.
Die Frage ist doch, ob wir ...	The question is whether we ...
Ich meine, wir sollten unsere Aufmerksamkeit dem wichtigeren Problem X zuwenden.	I think we should turn our attention to the more important issue of X.
Was mich betrifft, so glaube ich, der größte Vorteil von ... ist ...	I, for my part, think the main advantage of ... is ...

Ich würde lieber zum nächsten Tagesordnungspunkt übergehen.	I'd rather turn to the next point on the agenda.
Wir können uns mit deinem Problem später befassen.	We may be able to deal with your problem later.
Ich würde lieber mit Punkt zwei weitermachen.	I'd prefer to move on to item two.
Zuerst möchte ich die Frage unseres Gastes beantworten, anschließend komme ich auf Ihren Einwand zurück, Herr Dumbar.	First I would like to reply to our guest Mr Brain and then I'll come back your objection, Mr Dumbar.

Advice from the expert

Having served on various committees I have drawn up a list of rules:

- Never arrive on time: this stamps you as a beginner.
- Don't say anything until the meeting is half over: this stamps you as wise.
- Be as vague as possible: this avoids irritating the others.
- When in doubt, suggest a subcommittee be appointed.

Harry Chapmas

13. *Probleme vertagen* – Putting off problems

Vielleicht sollten wir dies vorläufig beiseite lassen, da Tom krank ist.	Perhaps we should leave this for the time being since Tom is ill.
Schau, Ron, wir können dein Problem später besprechen.	Look, Ron, we may be able to discuss your problem later.
Ich meine, wir sollten später auf dieses Problem zurückkommen.	I think we should come back to this problem later.
Wir können das vielleicht zu einem späteren Zeitpunkt besprechen.	Perhaps we can discuss that at a later date.
Kümmern wir uns später darum. Im Moment haben wir dringendere Probleme.	Let's worry about that later. At the moment we have more urgent problems.

Ich schlage vor, wir heben uns diese Angelegenheit für die nächste Besprechung auf.	I suggest we leave this matter until our next meeting.
Wenn niemand Einwände erhebt, schlage ich vor, wir verschieben diesen Punkt, bis wir die neuesten Zahlen haben.	If nobody has any objections, I propose we postpone this item until we get the latest figures.
Wenn Sie einverstanden sind, verschieben wir diese Sache, bis uns mehr Informationen zur Verfügung stehen.	If you agree, I propose we defer this matter until we have more information at our disposal.
Könnten wir die Besprechung auf Montag vertagen?	Could we adjourn the meeting to Monday?

How to make yourself popular

1. If you want to get along, go along.
2. A motion to adjourn is always in order.
3. Be the first to move for adjournment. This will make you popular – it's what everyone is waiting for.

P Master your phrases

Task 8: Beef up your word power

Add an expression that has the same meaning.

1. Perhaps Mrs Child would *care* / .... to answer this question?
2. Could you *stick* / .... to the point, please?
3. I'd prefer to *move on to* / .... to item two.
4. I propose we *defer* / .... this question until later.

Task 9: Speak your mind

Was sagen Sie wenn

1. Sie die Teilnehmer um ihre Aufmerksamkeit bitten wollen?
2. Tom sich zu weit vom Thema entfernt?
3. Sie lieber zum nächsten Tagesordnungspunkt übergehen möchten?
4. Sie einen Punkt lieber beim nächsten Mal behandeln möchten?

14. *Ergebnisse zusammenfassen* – Summarising results

Um es kurz zu machen, die wichtigsten Punkte / Argumente sind ...	In short, the main points that have been made are ...
Wenn ich kurz die wichtigsten Argumente noch einmal nennen darf ...	If I may just go over the main points which have been raised so far ...
Wenn ich unsere Diskussion zusammenfassen darf ...	Well, if I could just sum up our discussion ...
Ich glaube, ich kann zusammenfassend sagen, daß wir uns über ... einig sind.	To summarise, I think we are in agreement that / on ...
Um es zusammenzufassen, es scheint Einigkeit zu herrschen.	To sum up, it seems that we have a consensus.
Abschließend möchte ich betonen ...	In conclusion I'd like to emphasise ...

Why meetings fail

- ☛ Regardless of the length of the meeting, all important decisions will be made in the last five minutes before lunch or the end of the day.
- ☛ If a problem causes too many meetings, the meetings become more important than the problem.
- ☛ Meetings that you chair are infinitely better than those that you merely attend.
- ☛ The length of a meeting rises with the square of the number of people present.
- ☛ Whoever shouts loudest has the floor.

Arthur Bloch, Murphy's Law

15. *Sonstiges* – Any other business

Sonstiges	Any Other Business (A.O.B.)
Gibt es sonst noch etwas?	Is there any other business?
Noch irgendwelche Punkte?	Any further points?
Gibt es sonst noch etwas zu besprechen?	Is there anything else to discuss?
Hat jemand noch etwas, das wir besprechen sollen?	Has anyone anything further they wish to discuss?

Noch irgendwelche Punkte, bevor wir die Sitzung schließen? — Any further points before we bring this meeting to an end?

Advice from the expert

If you want to kill an idea in the world,
get a meeting working on it.
Charles F. Kettering

16. *Eine Entscheidung blockieren* – Blocking a decision

Ich meine, es wäre klüger, eine Abstimmung zu verschieben, bis alle Fakten auf dem Tisch sind.	I feel that it would be wiser to postpone a vote until all the facts are available.
Ich habe einige Vorbehalte bezüglich / hinsichtlich ...	I've certain reservations about / as to ...
Ich habe einfach das Gefühl, daß wir noch mehr Informationen darüber benötigen.	I can't help feeling that we need some more information on that.
Ich meine, wir sollten uns mehr Zeit gönnen, um alles noch einmal zu überdenken.	I think we should give ourselves more time to think everything over.
Ich fürchte, eine Entscheidung zu diesem Zeitpunkt könnte dazu führen, daß ...	I'm afraid a decision at this stage might lead to ...
Wir sollten auf keinen Fall eine voreilige Entscheidung treffen.	Under no circumstances should we come to a hasty decision.
Ich denke, wir sollten uns nicht zu einer verfrühten Entscheidung drängen lassen.	I think we shouldn't be rushed into making a premature decision.

Experience shows that

if more than one person can be held responsible,
nobody will be found to blame.

17. *Abstimmen lassen* – Putting it to the vote

Stimmen wir darüber ab.	Let's have a vote on this.
Bringen wir es zur Abstimmung.	Let's put it to the vote.
Könnten wir zur Abstimmung übergehen?	Could we move to a vote on this?
Könnten wir darüber abstimmen?	Could we take a vote on it?
Vielleicht sollten wir in aller Form darüber abstimmen.	Perhaps we should take a formal vote on this.
Ich möchte Sie daran erinnern, daß im Falle von Stimmengleichheit meine Stimme den Ausschlag gibt.	In the event of a tie, I would like to remind you that I have the casting vote.
Darf ich um Handzeichen bitten?	Can I ask for a show of hands?
Wer dafür ist, möge die Hand heben.	Those in favour raise their hands.
Wer dafür ist, stimme mit 'ja'.	Those in favour say 'Aye'.
Wer ist dafür?	Those for the motion, please?
Wer ist dagegen?	Those against?
Wer enthält sich der Stimme?	Any abstentions?
Der Antrag ist mit sieben zu vier Stimmen angenommen.	The motion is carried by seven votes to four.
Der Antrag ist mit acht zu drei Stimmen abgelehnt.	The motion is rejected by eight votes to three.
Der Antrag ist einstimmig angenommen.	The motion is carried unanimously.

Time for a smile

Once the chairman of the Board of Directors visited one of his directors in hospital. "Bob", he said, "the Board of Directors wishes you a speedy recovery – and it was a majority decision of seven to five."

18. *Einigkeit betonen* – Emphasising agreement

Sind wir uns alle darüber einig?	Are we all agreed on that?
Darf ich annehmen, daß alle dafür sind?	Can I take it everyone is in favour?
Wir sind uns also weitgehend darüber einig.	Well, we're broadly in agreement on that.
Es scheint so, als hätten wir Übereinstimmung erzielt.	Well, it looks as if we have a consensus.
Ich finde, wir haben eine sehr fruchtbare Diskussion geführt.	I think we have had a most fruitful discussion.
Ich glaube, wir sind zu dem Schluß gekommen, daß ...	I think we've come to the conclusion that ...
Mir scheint, wir haben ein beiderseitiges Einvernehmen erzielt.	We seem to have reached a mutual understanding.
Wir haben offenbar eine sichere Grundlage, auf der wir weiterarbeiten können.	We obviously have a firm basis on which to proceed.
Sehr schön. Es ist also beschlossen worden, daß ...	Fine, it's decided that ...

Last words of a chairman

The great economist Adam Smith's last words were:
"I believe we must adjourn the meeting to some other place."

19. *Die Sitzung beenden* – Closing the meeting

Gut, ich glaube, wir haben alles berücksichtigt.	Well, I think we've covered everything.
Nun, ich glaube, wir haben alles besprochen.	Well, I think we've discussed everything.
Nun, damit haben wir die Tagesordnung abgeschlossen.	Well, I think that completes our agenda.
Damit wäre unser Geschäft für heute erledigt. Vielen Dank.	That concludes our business for today. Thank you.
Wenn niemand mehr etwas zu sagen hat, würde ich die Besprechung gerne schließen.	If nobody has anything to add, I'd like to draw the meeting to an end.

Ich würde die Sitzung gerne mit den Worten schließen: ...	I'd now like to bring this meeting to an end by saying ...
Es bleibt mir nur noch zu sagen, daß ...	It only remains for me to say that ...
Abschließend möchte ich Ihnen allen für Ihre Beiträge danken.	In conclusion I wish to thank you all for your contributions.
Ich möchte allen für ihre konstruktiven Beiträge danken.	I'd like to thank everyone for their constructive contributions.
Ich erkläre die Sitzung für geschlossen.	I declare the meeting closed.
Vielen Dank, meine Damen und Herren.	Thank you Ladies and Gentlemen.
Das ist alles für heute. Vielen Dank.	That's all for today. Thank you.
Ich würde für heute gerne Feierabend machen.	I'd like to call it a day now.

Let's start with a smile

If Moses had held meetings,
the Israelites would still be in Egypt.

C Crossword power

Across

1 Right, shall we get ✎ ? 5 Let's try to ✎ this meeting short. 6 Let's start with the first ✎ on the agenda. 8 Can we take the minutes as ✎ ? 9 And now ✎ to the details. 10 Let's put this problem ✎ until later. 11 Let's ✎ it to the vote. 13 Are you going to ✎ the meeting? 16 What are your ✎ on this, Tom? 18 Is there ✎ other business? 19 Let's have a ✎ on this. 21 I think we've ✎ everything.

Down

1 Could you keep to the ✎, please? 2 Has everyone received a copy of the ✎? 3 Allow me to ✎ a warm welcome to you. 4 I'm happy to ✎ all of you today. 7 This will not be recorded in the ✎ . 11 I have the great ✎ of introducing Mr X. 12 I'd prefer to ✎ on to item two. 14 Could we ✎ item 3 from the agenda? 15 Let's finish ✎ five o'clock. 17 Let's ✎ the formalities. 20 Can I ask for a ✎ of hands?

GEKONNT DISKUTIEREN

DISCUSSING THE CLEVER WAY

It' s difficult to give your opinion without offending others. You have to pick the right phrases to interrupt in a meeting, to disagree with other participants, to get them to listen to your ideas, all these tactics need special vocabulary – and that's what you'll get from this part of the book.

1. *Zu Worte kommen* Catching the chairman's eye

Wenn ich dazu gerade etwas bemerken darf ...	If I can just make a point here ...
Wenn ich dazu etwas sagen dürfte ...	If could I could just come in here ...
Darf ich zu diesem Punkt etwas bemerken?	May I come in at this point?
Wenn ich noch ein weiteres Argument zugunsten von ... beisteuern dürfte ...	If I might just add one more argument in favour of ...
Wenn ich vielleicht ein paar Worte über / zu ... sagen dürfte ...	If I just might say a few words about ...
Wenn niemand etwas dagegen hat, würde ich gerne etwas zu ... sagen.	If nobody objects, I'd like to say a word about ...
Entschuldigen Sie bitte, aber bevor wir fortfahren, dürfte ich darauf hinweisen, daß ...?	Excuse me, but before we go any further, could I point out that ...?
Entschuldigen Sie, aber bevor wir zum nächsten Punkt übergehen, würde ich gerne ergänzend bemerken, daß ...	Excuse me, but before we move on to the next item, I'd like to add that ...
Ich würde gerne etwas dazu bemerken, wenn Sie erlauben.	I'd like to add something here, if I may.
Entschuldigen Sie, aber ich glaube, es ist wichtig hinzuzufügen, daß ...	Excuse me, but I think it's important to add that ...
Dürfte ich wohl etwas zu Ihrem letzten Argument bemerken?	I wonder if I might comment upon your last argument?
Entschuldigen Sie, aber darf ich Ihre Aufmerksamkeit auf die Tatsache lenken, daß ...?	Excuse me, but may I just draw your attention to the fact that ...?

Great lies told at meetings

- This'll be a short meeting.
- I'll only talk for about five minutes.
- To cut a long story short, ...

2. *Das Wort ergreifen*
Taking the floor

Lassen Sie mich eingangs folgendes sagen: ...	To begin with, let me say this: ...
Um die Diskussion in Gang zu bringen, darf ich Ihr Augenmerk auf ... lenken?	I'd like to kick off by drawing your attention to ...
Einleitend möchte ich daran erinnern, daß ...	I'd like to begin by recalling that ...
Vor allem dürfen wir nicht vergessen, daß ...	First of all, we must bear in mind ...
Es gibt eine Reihe von Punkten, die ich ansprechen möchte.	There are a number of points I'd like to raise.
Die Kernfrage ist meiner Ansicht nach ...	In my view the essential issue is ...
Meiner Meinung nach ist die wichtigste Frage doch die: ...	As I see it, the main question is the following: ...
Der Hintergrund zu dieser Problematik ist ...	The background to this issue is ...
Die wichtigste Frage scheint mir ... zu sein.	The most important issue seems to me to be ...
Zwei Dinge müssen wir im Auge behalten.	There are two points to bear in mind.
Ich möchte betonen, daß ...	I'd like to emphasise / underline / underscore that ...

Time for a smile

The difference between a good participant and a bad participant is that a good one sleeps upright and a bad one sleeps horizontally.

3. *Seine Meinung sagen*
Giving your opinion

Sagen, was man denkt – Saying what you think

Wenn Sie mich fragen ...	If you ask me ...
Ich würde sagen, daß ...	I'd say that ...
Ich nehme an, daß ...	I presume ...
Ich schätze, daß ...	I reckon that ...
Wenn Sie meine Meinung wissen wollen, ich würde sagen, daß ...	If you want to know my opinion, I'd say that ...
Ich meine, daß ...	I feel (that) ... / I think (that) ...
Ich glaube, daß ...	I believe that ...
Meiner Meinung nach ...	In my view / In my opinion ...
In meinen Augen ...	In my eyes ...
Wie ich es / die Sache sehe ...	As I see it ...
Was mich anbelangt, so glaube ich, daß ...	As far as I'm concerned, I think that ...
Von meinem Standpunkt sieht das anders aus.	From my point of view things are different.

How to communicate effectively

The director says to one of the participants of the meeting, "I can see, Miller, that you're not yourself today. Enjoy it while you can."

Vorsichtige Meinungsäußerung – Giving your opinion carefully

Ich bin natürlich kein Fachmann für ..., aber ich dachte ...	Well, of course I'm no expert on ... but I thought ...
Nun, was mich angeht, so würde ich sagen ...	I, for my part, would say that ...
Soweit ich dies beurteilen kann ...	As far as I'm able to judge ...
Mir scheint, daß ...	It seems to me that ...

Mir scheint, als ob ...	It appears to me as if ...
Ich würde meinen, daß ...	It would seem to me that ...
Ich neige zu der Ansicht, daß ...	I tend to think that ...
Ich glaube, man könnte sagen, daß ...	I think it would be fair to say ...
Es sieht so aus, als ob ...	It looks as if ...

Gewißheit ausdrücken – Expressing certitude

Ich bin ziemlich sicher, daß ...	I'm quite sure that ...
Ich bin sicher, daß ...	I'm certain that ...
Ich bin überzeugt, daß ...	I'm convinced that ...
Es ist meine Überzeugung, daß ...	It is my conviction, that ...
Ich bin absolut sicher, daß ...	I'm absolutely certain that ...
Es ist völlig klar, daß ...	It's quite /absolutely clear that ...
Es liegt auf der Hand, daß ...	It stands to reason that ...
Es ist meine feste Überzeugung, daß ...	It's my firm belief / conviction that ...
Ich glaube fest, daß ...	I firmly believe that ...
Es ist meine ehrliche Überzeugung, daß ...	I sincerely believe that ...
Es ist meine wohlüberlegte Meinung, daß ...	It's my considered opinion that ..
Ich habe keinerlei Zweifel, daß ...	There is / can be no doubt that ...
Es gibt nicht den geringsten Zweifel, daß ...	There is not a shadow of doubt that ...
Darauf können Sie sich verlassen / wetten!	You can count / bet / rely on that!

Time for a smile

The managing director called a meeting because the company was in serious financial trouble. The secretary came in, tiptoed up to the director and whispered into his ear: "The accountant wants to have a word with you, sir. I think it's urgent" – "Not now!" replied the director angrily. Can't you see that we're in the middle of an important meeting?" – "But he is phoning from the Bahamas, sir."

P Master your phrases

Task 1: It's the verb that counts

If I might just	*c*	in here ...
	a	that ...
	c	upon your argument
	d	your attention to the fact that ...
	p	out that ...

Task 2: What can you do at a discussion?

Repair the words and put them in the third column.

You can raise	*pinots*	....
	susesi	....
	sequintos	....
	bolmerps	....

Task 3: Beef up your word power

Add two more phrases that have almost the same meaning.

I feel	In my view	I'm quite sure	You can count on that!
I	In my	I'm	You can .... on that!
I	In my	I'm	You can .... on that!

Task 4: Spot the mistake

1. I'd like to begin by { A. reminding you of / B. recalling / C. remembering you of } our last meeting.
2. I would like to { A. underscore / B. uplift / C. emphasise / D. highlight } the importance of finding new markets in Asia.
3. As far as I'm { A. able to judge, / B. concerned, / C. convinced, } the main problem is ...

4. *Argumentieren*
Argumentation

Food for thought

There are two sides to every argument – until you take one.

Argumente einführen – Introducing arguments

In diesem Zusammenhang ist es auch wichtig, zu ...	In this context it is also important to ...
Darüber hinaus ...	Moreover, ...
Ferner ...	Furthermore, ...
Hinzu kommt ...	In addition ...
Und, was noch wichtiger ist, ...	And, more importantly, ...
Man könnte an dieser Stelle hinzufügen, daß ...	Here one might add that ...
Und wir dürfen auch ein anderes Problem nicht aus den Augen verlieren.	And we mustn't lose sight of another problem.
Und lassen Sie uns folgendes nicht vergessen: ...	And let us not forget the following: ...
Ferner darf ich betonen, daß ...	Moreover, I'd like to highlight that ...
Des weiteren ist es wichtig zu berücksichtigen, daß ...	Furthermore, it is important to take into account / note that ...
Das führt uns zu dem Problem ...	That leads us to the problem of ...
Das Problem kann man nicht losgelöst von ... behandeln.	This problem cannot be seen / dealt with in isolation from ...
Ich würde gerne hinzufügen, daß ...	I'd like to add that ...
Wenn ich an dieser Stelle noch etwas anmerken dürfte ...	If I might just add something here ...
Lassen Sie mich noch kurz auf die Frage ... eingehen.	Let me now turn briefly to the question / problem of ...
Und es gibt noch einen weiteren Gesichtspunkt, der hier erörtert werden muß.	And there is another aspect which must be considered here.

Dabei kommt mir noch ein anderer Gedanke: ...	There's another thought that occurs to me: ...
Ich möchte dazu noch zwei Sätze sagen.	I wish to add two sentences.
Das erinnert mich an eine andere Sache.	The reminds of another point.

Argumente stützen – Supporting argumentation

Könnten Sie uns ein Beispiel geben, damit wir sehen, was Sie meinen?	Could you help us with an example of what you mean?
Ein typisches Beispiel ist ...	A case in point is ...
Es gibt ausreichend Beweise, die zeigen, daß ...	There is ample evidence to show that ...
Lassen Sie mich Ihnen ein anderes Beispiel geben.	Let me give you another example.
Ein typischer Fall dieser Art ist ...	A typical case of this sort is ...
Was bedeutet das in der Praxis?	What does that mean in practice?
Wie die Ihnen vorliegende Statistik beweist / zeigt ...	As the statistics before you prove / show ...
Gestatten Sie, daß ich Ihnen eine Studie über ... vorlege, die meine Vermutung bestätigt.	Allow / Permit me to present a study on ... which supports my assumption.
Erlauben Sie mir, einen Bericht vorzustellen, der meine Behauptung untermauert.	May I introduce a report that supports my statement.

Siehe auch *Perfect presentations: Introducing examples*, Seite 177.

Some people are hard to argue with

Who will ever forget the words of Noah's wife, who said to Noah, "I don't care what you say. I'm taking an umbrella."

Argumente abwägen – Balancing arguments

Wägen wir einmal das Für und Wider ab.	Let's weigh up the pros and cons.
Wir müssen die Alternativen abwägen, bevor wir eine Entscheidung treffen können.	We have to weigh up the option, before we can take a decision.
Gehen wir die Möglichkeiten durch.	Let's go through the possibilities.
Betrachten wir die Alternativen.	Let's consider the options.
Einerseits ..., andererseits ...	On the one hand ..., but on the other hand ...
Zwar ..., trotzdem	Admittedly ..., nevertheless, ...
Wenn es auch zutrifft, daß ..., so meine ich dennoch ...	Although it is true that ... nevertheless I think ...
Um beiden Seiten gerecht zu werden, muß man zugeben, daß ...	To be fair / to do justice to both sides one should admit that ...
... obwohl wir nicht vergessen dürfen, daß ...	although, we mustn't forget that ...
... wobei wir zugeben müssen, daß ...	whereas we must admit that ...
Trotz des Preises glaube ich doch, daß ...	Inspite of the price I still think that ...
Trotz der Tatsache, daß ..., meine ich ...	Despite the fact that ..., I think ...

Verallgemeinern – Generalising

im allgemeinen ...	in general ...
im großen Ganzen ...	by and large ...
allgemein gesprochen ...	generally speaking / broadly speaking ...
Aus der Distanz betrachtet ...	Looking at it from a distance ...
So stellt sich die Situation insgesamt dar.	This is the overall situation.
Alles in allem glaube ich, daß das neue Projekt ein Erfolg wird.	All in all I think the new project will be a success.
Wenn wir einmal von den Details absehen, so läuft es auf ... hinaus.	Ignoring the details, it boils down to ...

Nach Berücksichtigung aller Aspekte bin ich sicher, daß dies die richtige Entscheidung ist.	All things considered I'm sure this is the right decision.
Insgesamt können wir mit den Ergebnissen zufrieden sein.	On the whole we can be satisfied with the results.

A convincing argument

A lawyer is addressing an all-male jury: "Gentlemen, shall we cast this beautiful young lady into a dark, dim cell, or shall we return her to her lovely apartment on Park Avenue, telephone 555-6969?"

Das Thema wechseln – Changing the subject

Wir wollen wir uns nun dem Problem der Umweltverschmutzung zuwenden.	Let's now turn to the problem of pollution.
Ich möchte nun zu dem Thema ... übergehen.	I'd now like to turn to the subject of ...
Die nächste Frage, auf die ich mich konzentrieren will, ist ...	The next question I would like to focus / concentrate on is ...
Wenden wir uns dem Sicherheitsproblem zu.	Turning to the issue of security ...
Um auf ein anderes Thema zu sprechen zu kommen ...	To turn to another subject ...

Den Beitrag abschließen – Concluding the contribution

Was ich zu sagen versuchte....	The point I've been trying to make ...
Es bleibt mir nur noch hinzuzufügen, daß ...	It only remains for me to add ...
Lassen Sie mich mit den Worten schließen ...	Let me conclude by saying ...
Lassen Sie mich zum Abschluß eines betonen: ...	Let me conclude by emphasising one thing: ...

Lassen Sie mich zum Abschluß eine Tatsache hervorheben.	Let me conclude by stressing one fact.
Ich möchte mit der Feststellung schließen, daß ...	I'd like to conclude by stating that ...
Zum Schluß möchte ich sagen ...	In conclusion, I'd like to say ...
Ich möchte meine Ausführungen mit einem Goethe-Zitat schließen.	I'd like to conclude my comments by quoting Goethe.

Siehe auch *Perfect presentations: Announcing the end*, Seite 187 ff.

How to communicate effectively

Thank you for your contribution, Miller. You're a man of few words, but unfortunately you keep repeating them.

P Master your phrases

Task 5: Add a suitable modal (e. g. *must*)

1. And we .... lose sight of another problem.
2. This problem .... be dealt with in isolation.
3. If I .... just add something.

Task 6: Clear up the mess

The verbs in *italics* have slipped into the wrong sentences.

1. In *connection* one might say that ...
2. Furthermore, it is important to *add* that ...
3. May I *mean* a report that supports my statement?
4. I wish to *note* two sentences.
5. In this *addition* it is also important to consider that ...
6. What does that *introduce* in practice?

Task 7: Guided translation

1. Let's weigh up the (*Alternativen*), before (*treffen*) a decision.
2. And we shouldn't (*aus dem Auge verlieren*) another problem.
3. It is important (*in Betracht zu ziehen*) the political situation.
4. (*Ein typisches Beispiel*) is the success of our Yahoo.
5. Let's weigh up the (*Für und Wider*) of this project.

5. *Vorschläge machen*
Making suggestions

Vorschläge einleiten – Introducing proposals

Ich schlage vor, daß ...	I propose that ...
Ich schlage vor, / rege an, daß ...	I suggest that ...
Ich rate Ihnen ...	I advise you ...
Ich empfehle, daß ...	I recommend that ...
Mein Vorschlag ist ...	My proposal is ...
Mein Vorschlag ist ...	My suggestion is ...
Meine Empfehlung lautet ...	My recommendation is ...
Mein Rat ist ...	My advice is ...

Vorschlagen wie die Briten – Suggesting the British way

Wäre es nicht gut, wenn wir ...?	Might it be an idea to ...?
Wäre es nicht besser, zu / wenn ...?	Wouldn't it be better to / if ...?
Meinen Sie nicht, daß es eine gute Idee wäre, zu ...?	Don't you think it might be a good idea to ...?
Wie wäre es, wenn wir das Patent kaufen?	What about buying this patent?
Wie wäre es, wenn wir die Entscheidung aufschieben würden?	How about postponing the decision?
Warum stimmen wir nicht darüber ab?	Why don't we put it to the vote?

Warum nehmen wir nicht einfach einen frühen Flugtermin?	Why not take an early flight?
Wäre es nicht klüger zu warten?	Wouldn't it be wiser to wait?
Ich würde vorschlagen, daß wir das Angebot annehmen.	I would propose that we accept the offer.
Ich würde empfehlen, das Projekt abzulehnen.	I would recommend rejecting the project.
Ich würde vorschlagen, daß wir die Entscheidung aufschieben.	I would suggest that we put off the decision.
Dürfte ich etwas vorschlagen? Wäre es nicht ratsamer zu warten, bis wir mehr Informationen haben?	I wonder if I might make a suggestion Hadn't we better wait until we have some more information?
Ich würde gerne einen Vorschlag machen. Wir könnten ...	I would like to put forward a proposal. We could ...
Darf ich einen Vorschlag unterbreiten?	May I submit a proposal?
Wenn ich einen Vorschlag machen darf / dürfte, wir könnten ...	If I may / might make a suggestion, we could ...
Wir könnten genausogut versuchen, zu ...	We might just as well try to ...

Vorschläge mit Nachdruck versehen – Emphasising proposals

In meinen Augen ist es höchste Zeit, daß wir etwas unternehmen.	In my eyes it's high time we did something about it.
Ich empfehle dringend ...	I strongly recommend that ...
Ich rate Ihnen dringend, diesen Antrag anzunehmen.	I advise you most strongly to adopt this motion.
Ich bin überzeugt, daß mein Vorschlag der einzig machbare ist.	I'm convinced that my proposal is the only feasible one.
Ich denke, die einzige realistische Alternative ist ...	I think the only realistic alternative is ...
In unseren Augen ist die vielversprechendste Alternative folgende: ...	In our view, the most promising option is the following: ...

Lassen Sie mich nochmals betonen / wiederholen, daß ...	Let me emphasise / repeat once more that ...
Ist es nicht von größter Bedeutung, daß wir ... nicht aus den Augen verlieren?	Isn't it of vital importance that we don't lose sight of ... / we keep in mind that ...?

Advice from the expert

- If you leave the room, you'll be elected.
- If you're early, it'll be cancelled.
- If you knock yourself out to be on time, you will have to wait.
- If you're late, you will be too late.

Arthur Bloch, Murphy's law

Ⓟ Master your phrases

Task 8: Word builder's corner: Suggesting

1. I propose that ...	My .... is ...
2. I suggest that ...	My .... is ...
3. I advise you that ...	My .... is ...
4. I recommend that ...	My .... is ...

Task 9: How to introduce your proposal

1. *W.......................*	take	an early flight?
2. *W.......................*	we take	
3. *W.......................*	taking	
4. *W.......... it ....*	to take	

Task 10: What you can do with a suggestion

How good is your memory? Can you complete these verbs

I'd like to	p_t f_rw_rd s_bm_t m_k_	a proposal
I can I can't I have to	s_pp_rt _cc_pt r_j_ct	this proposal

6. *Klarstellungen* Clarifying

Überprüfen, ob man richtig verstanden hat Checking understanding

Kann ich Ihren Ausführungen entnehmen, daß ...?	Am I to understand from your remarks that ...?
Verstehe ich Sie richtig? Sie glauben, daß ...	Let me see if I understand you correctly: You believe ...
Es kommt ganz darauf an, was Sie darunter verstehen.	It depends what you mean by that.
Was Sie sagen, ist doch im Grunde ...	Basically, what you are saying is ...
Wollen Sie sagen, daß ...?	Are you saying that ...?
Wenn Sie sagen ..., meinen Sie damit ...?	When you say ... do you mean ...?
Wenn ich Sie recht verstanden habe, sagen Sie, daß ...?	If I've understood you correctly, you're saying that ...?
Wäre es richtig, wenn ich sage, daß ...?	Would I be correct in saying that ...?
Gehe ich recht in der Annahme, daß ...?	Am I right in assuming that ...?
Korrigieren Sie mich, wenn ich unrecht habe, aber ...	Correct me if I'm wrong, but ...
Ich glaube nicht, daß das so einfach ist.	I don't think it's quite as simple as that.

Mißverständnisse aufzeigen – Pointing to misunderstandings

Wir scheinen aneinander vorbeizureden.	We seem to be talking at cross purposes.
Ich fürchte, Sie haben mich mißverstanden.	I'm afraid you've misunderstood me.
Ich fürchte, da besteht ein kleines Mißverständnis.	I'm afraid there seems to have been a slight misunderstanding.
Entschuldigen Sie, aber das habe ich nicht gesagt.	With respect, that is not what I said.
Das ist nicht ganz das, was ich meinte.	That isn't quite what I meant.
Das ist nicht genau das, was ich zum Ausdruck bringen wollte.	This isn't exactly what I was trying to get across.

Unklarheiten beseitigen – Clarifying a point

In anderen Worten ...	In other words ...
Um es genauer zu sagen ...	To be more specific ...
Einfacher ausgedrückt ...	In simpler terms ...
Lassen Sie es mich so sagen ...	Let me put it this way ...
Lassen Sie es mich anders formulieren ...	Allow me to rephrase that ...
Legen wir die Karten auf den Tisch.	Let's put our cards on the table.
Um die Sache zu verdeutlichen ...	To shed more light on the matter ...
Gestatten Sie mir ein Wort zu ...	Allow me to add a word about ...
Vielleicht ist es hilfreich, das Diagramm noch einmal zu sehen.	Perhaps it would be helpful to take another look at the diagram.
Vielleicht sollte ich noch mehr ins Detail gehen.	Perhaps I should be more specific.
Ohne in alle Einzelheiten gehen zu wollen, gestatten Sie mir zu erwähnen ...	Without going into too much detail, allow me to mention ...
Ich fürchte, ich habe mich nicht deutlich ausgedrückt. Lassen Sie es mich so sagen.	I'm afraid I didn't express myself clearly. Let me put it this way.

Ich habe mich vielleicht unklar ausgedrückt. Was ich zu sagen versuche, ist folgendes: ... — Perhaps I haven't made myself clear. What I'm trying to say is this: ...

Vielleicht wird es verständlicher, wenn ich es so formuliere ... — Perhaps I should make this clearer by saying ...

Tut mir leid. Ich habe mich vielleicht nicht klar ausgedrückt. Lassen Sie es mich anders sagen. — Sorry, I'm probably not making myself clear. Let me put it another way. ...

Wenn ich vielleicht tiefer in die Einzelheiten gehen dürfte, würde es das Mißverständnis klären. — Perhaps if I might explain in more detail it would clarify the misunderstanding.

Talking one's way to the top

Last night I discovered why my boss had hired me to be his personal assistant rather than all the other candidates. Over a lengthy business dinner he admitted that when he interviewed all the other candidates they seemed to be the cleverest, most dynamic people in the world.

Yet when he interviewed me, I managed to convince him that he was the cleverest, most dynamic person in the world.

C Crossword power

Across

1. May I come in ✎ this point? 2. If I can just make a ✎ here. 4. How ✎ postponing the decision? 7. This problem cannot be ✎ with in isolation. 11. Let me ✎ you another example. 12. I would ✎ that we accept the offer. 14. Be at cross purposes ✎ somebody. 15. Let's ✎ the options. 16. The ✎ question is the following. 18. We seem to be talking at ✎ purposes. 21. It's ✎ time we did something about it. 22. On the ✎ we can be satisfied with the results. 23. Let's weigh up the ✎ and cons.

Down

1. I wish to ✎ two sentences. 2. Let me ✎ it this way. 3. We must ✎ a decision. 5. If nobody ✎, I'd like to show some diagrams. 6. Let's now ✎ to the problem of pollution. 8. I'm afraid I didn't ✎ myself clearly. 9. We mustn't ✎ sight of the problem. 10. To begin ✎, let me say this. 12. What does that mean in ✎? 13. That ✎ us to another problem. 14. Let's ✎ up the pros and cons. 16. There are two points to be borne in ✎. 17. There is not a ✎ of doubt. 19. I'd like to kick ✎ by drawing your attention to ... 20. We mustn't lose ✎ of the problem.

7. *Zustimmung*
Agreement

Food for thought

The boss says, "I tell you what.
I'll admit I'm right, if you admit you're wrong."

Einverständnis ausdrücken – Expressing agreement

Ich kann mich Ihrem Vorschlag anschließen.	I can go along with your proposal.
Ich verstehe, was Sie meinen.	I can see your point.
Ich glaube, Sie haben recht.	I think you are right.
Ich glaube, wir sind uns jetzt einig.	I think we've come to an agreement.
Ich kann mich Ihrem Vorschlag anschließen.	I can go along with your suggestion.
Ich teile Ihre Ansicht, daß ...	I share your view that ...
Darin /damit haben Sie recht.	You have a point there.
Ich denke, wir sind darüber einer Meinung.	I think we are in agreement on that.
Ich glaube, wir können Ihren Standpunkt in diese Sache akzeptieren.	I think we can accept your position on that.
Ich würde diesen Vorschlag gerne unterstützen.	I'd like to support this proposal.

Volle Übereinstimmung – Complete agreement

Ich glaube, ich kann mich Ihnen anschließen.	I think I can go along with you.
Sie haben mich überzeugt.	You've convinced me.
Ich pflichte Ihnen voll und ganz bei.	I completely / quite agree.
Ich bin mit Ihnen völlig einer Meinung.	I totally agree with you.

Ich bin hundertprozentig Ihrer Meinung.	I couldn't agree more.
Ich stimme Ihrem Vorschlag voll und ganz zu.	I'm entirely / fully / completely in agreement with your proposal.
Ich sehe die Dinge genauso wie Sie.	I agree entirely with your point of view.
Ich bin genau der gleichen Meinung.	I'm exactly of the same opinion.
Ich unterstütze Ihren Antrag vorbehaltlos.	I support your motion without reservation.
Wir sind uns völlig einig.	We're in total agreement.
Wir verstehen uns, was diese Angelegenheit betrifft.	We see eye to eye in this affair.

Food for thought

The person who agrees with you will lie about other things too.

Bedingte Zustimmung – Qualified support

Ich stimme mit einigen Vorbehalten zu.	I agree – with reservations.
Grundsätzlich stimme ich Ihnen zu, jedoch ...	Basically / in principle I agree, however ...
Im großen und ganzen teile ich Ihre Auffassung, aber ...	By and large I would accept your ideas, but ...
Ich stimme Ihnen im allgemeinen zu, jedoch könnte man anmerken, daß ...	I agree in general with you, however, it could be said that ...
In diesem Punkt bin ich einverstanden, aber ...	I agree with you on this point, but ...
Bis zu einem gewissen Punkt, teile ich Ihre Meinung, aber ...	I agree up to a point, but ...
Sie mögen ja darin recht haben, aber ...	You may be right in saying that, but ...
Was die Durchführbarkeit von ... angeht, stimme ich Ihnen zu. Jedoch ...	I agree with you about the practicability of ... However ...

Ich kann mich Ihnen teilweise anschließen, jedoch ...	I can go along with you up to a certain point, however ...
Theoretisch haben Sie recht, aber wird das in der Praxis klappen?	In theory you are right, but will it work in practice?
Ich bin Ihrem Vorschlag nicht ganz abgeneigt, aber bitte bedenken Sie ...	I have some sympathy with your suggestion, but please remember ...
In einigen Punkten sind wir einer Meinung, aber ist Ihnen auch bewußt, daß ...?	I don't disagree altogether, but are you aware of the fact that ...?
Schlagen Sie wirklich vor, daß wir von diesem Händler kaufen sollen?	Are you really suggesting we should buy from this retailer?
Ich verstehe Ihren Standpunkt, aber haben Sie auch bedacht ...?	I can see your point of view, but have you considered ...?
Sie haben damit vielleicht recht.	Perhaps you've got a point there.
Gehen wir Ihre Vorschläge Punkt für Punkt durch.	Let's go over your suggestions one by one.

Advice from the expert

If you cannot convince them, confuse them.
Never argue with a fool. People might not know the difference.

8. *Ablehnung*
Disagreement

Ablehnung signalisieren – Signalling rejection

Ich fürchte, ... / Leider ...	I'm afraid ...
Eigentlich ...	Actually, ...
Tatsächlich ... / Eigentlich	In fact, ...
Eigentlich ... / Ehrlich gesagt, ...	As a matter of fact ...
Ehrlich gesagt, ...	Frankly, ...
Um ehrlich zu sein, ...	To be honest, ...
Unter diesen Bedingungen ...	In these circumstances

Nehmen Sie es nicht übel, aber ...	With respect, but ...
Entschuldigen Sie, aber ...	Excuse me, but ...

Advice from the expert

- If you stand up, you'll be seen.
- If you speak up, you'll be heard.
- If you sit down, you'll be appreciated!

Zweifel anmelden – Raising doubt

Ich werde das Gefühl nicht los, daß ...	I can't help feeling that ...
Ich sehe das etwas anders.	I see it a little differently.
Ich bin mir nicht sicher, daß diese Strategie zum Ziel führt.	I'm (still) not sure whether this strategy will achieve its aim.
Das ist leichter gesagt als getan, aber ...	It's all very well to say, but ...
Ich habe immer noch Zweifel.	I still have my doubts.
Es ist zweifelhaft, ob ...	There's room for doubt whether ...
Ich habe Bedenken, ob der Vorschlag realistisch ist.	I'm sceptical about whether the proposal is realistic.
Ich wage zu bezweifeln, daß dies ein guter Plan ist.	I have my doubts whether this is a good plan.
Glauben Sie wirklich? Ich habe da meine Zweifel.	Do you really think so? I have my doubts.
Sie mögen teilweise recht haben. Trotzdem ...	You may be partly right. Even so ...
Ich verstehe, was Sie meinen, aber denken Sie bitte daran, daß ...	I see your point, but please remember that ...
Ich bin noch nicht völlig überzeugt.	I'm afraid I'm not totally convinced yet.
Sie haben nicht ganz unrecht, aber ich fürchte, es ist nicht so leicht, wie Sie denken.	You have a point there, but I'm afraid it's not as easy as you think.
Wäre es nicht besser, dies zu überschlafen?	Wouldn't it be wiser to sleep on it?

Wäre es vernünftig, wenn wir ...?	Would it be reasonable to ...
Ich fürchte, dies ist nicht so leicht, wie es aussieht.	I'm afraid it's not as easy as that.
Ist es nicht ein bißchen gewagt, dieser Firma zu trauen?	Isn't it a bit risky to trust this company?
Ist es sicher, diesem Kunden einen so hohen Kredit zu geben?	Is it safe to give this client such a huge loan?
Sind Sie sicher, daß dieser Vorschlag zu verwirklichen ist?	Are you sure the proposal is feasible?
Gehen wir nicht zu viele Risiken ein, wenn wir ...?	Aren't we taking too many risks if we ...?
Glauben Sie, daß sich das Projekt wirklich lohnt?	Do you think that the project is really worthwhile.
Ich sehe da gewisse Probleme, wenn wir dieser Strategie folgen.	I can see certain problems in adopting this strategy.
Ich sehe da einige Schwierigkeiten vor uns, wenn wir diesen Plan annehmen.	I can see some difficulties lying ahead, if we adopt this plan.
Ich bin nicht völlig überzeugt, daß dies ein realistischer Vorschlag ist.	I'm not entirely convinced that this is a realistic proposal.
Sind Sie wirklich überzeugt, daß dieser Plan durchführbar ist?	Are you really convinced that this plan is going to work?

How to communicate effectively

The chairman said to one of the participants of the meeting, "Miller, I wouldn't say you have told us a bag of lies, but the way you just rearranged the truth in your favour was impressive."

Höfliche Ablehnung – Polite rejection

Ich kann Sie verstehen, obwohl ...	I see what you mean, although ...
Sie scheinen da nicht ganz unrecht zu haben. Trotzdem ...	You seem to have a point there. All the same ...
Ich würde Ihnen gerne zustimmen. Dennoch ...	I'd like to agree. Nevertheless ...

Ich teile nicht ganz Ihre Meinung, daß ...	I don't quite share your view that ...
Ihr Standpunkt ist mir nicht ganz fremd, aber bitte bedenken Sie ...	I have some sympathy with your position, but please remember ...
Auf den ersten Blick scheint dies ein ganz guter Vorschlag zu sein, aber ...	On the face of it, this seems quite a good suggestion, but ...
Ich kann diesen Vorschlag leider nicht ganzen Herzens unterstützen.	I'm afraid I can't give my whole-hearted support to this proposal.
Das ist alles schön und gut, aber ...	That's all very well, but ...
Sie scheinen nicht zu sehen, daß ...	You don't seem to realise that ...
Sie scheinen zu vergessen, daß ...	You seem to forget that ...
Lassen Sie mich versuchen, Ihre Argumente zu entkräften.	Let me try to pick a few holes in your argument.

Neutrale Ablehnung – Neutral rejection

Ich kann dir da nicht ganz zustimmen, Bryan.	I can't quite agree with you, Bryan.
Sie haben ein Recht auf Ihre Meinung. Aber erlauben Sie, daß ich dies anders sehe.	You're entitled to your point of view. But allow me to see it a little differently.
Nehmen Sie es mir nicht übel, aber ich sehe dies anders.	With respect, I see it a little differently.
Ich kann Ihnen leider nicht ganz zustimmen.	I'm afraid I can't quite agree with you.
Ich fürchte, wir sind verschiedener Meinung.	I'm afraid we are in disagreement.
Ich kann leider nicht sagen, daß ich Ihre Meinung teile.	I'm afraid I can't say that I share your view / opinion.
Tut mir leid, aber ich kann Ihre Meinung nicht teilen.	I'm sorry, I can't go along with you.
Ihr Argument hat mich nicht völlig überzeugt.	I'm not totally convinced by your argument.
Ich kann leider nicht anders. Ich bin anderer Meinung.	I can't help feeling that I must disagree.

Ich kann Ihre Meinung zu dem Projekt wirklich nicht teilen.	I really can't share your opinion about this project.
Ich respektiere Ihre Meinung, jedoch ...	I respect your opinion, however ...
Tut mir leid, aber ich verstehe nicht, was Sie meinen.	I'm afraid I can't see your point there.

Entschiedener Widerspruch – Blunt rejection

Ich bin gegen diesen Vorschlag, weil ...	I'm opposed to this proposal because ...
Ich kann diesen Vorschlag leider nicht unterstützen.	I'm afraid I can't support / back the proposal.
Der Plan mag sich auf dem Papier ganz gut ausnehmen, aber in der Praxis ist er nicht durchführbar.	The plan may be good on paper, but it will never work in practice.
So wie die Dinge liegen, könnte ich das Projekt nicht unterstützen.	As it stands, I would not be able to give the project my backing.
Ohne wesentliche Änderungen kann ich dem Vorschlag nicht zustimmen.	Without substantial changes, I cannot give the proposal my support.
Ihre Meinung in Ehren, aber was Sie da sagen, läßt sich unmöglich durchführen.	With all due respect, what you are saying is impossible to implement.
Nehmen Sie es nicht übel, aber ich bin ganz anderer Meinung.	With respect, I disagree entirely.
Um ganz ehrlich zu sein, ich glaube, Sie irren sich.	To be quite frank, I think you're mistaken.
Um es frei heraus zu sagen, Ihre Argumente sind nicht stichhaltig.	To put it bluntly, your arguments don't hold water.
Hier gehen unserer Ansichten über ... auseinander.	I really must take issue with you on ...
Ich kann Ihre Schlußfolgerung einfach nicht akzeptieren.	I simply can't accept your conclusion.
Ich kann Ihren Standpunkt dazu nicht akzeptieren.	I can't accept your position on that.

Ich bin darüber völlig anderer Meinung als Sie.	I totally disagree with you on that.
Es tut mir leid, aber ich kann auf keinen Fall zustimmen.	I'm sorry, but I don't agree at all.
Was diese Zahlen anbetrifft, so muß ich Ihnen widersprechen.	I must take issue with you over these figures.
Ich muß entschieden gegen ... protestieren.	I must strongly protest against ...
Obwohl wir eine Pattsituation genauso sehr vermeiden wollen wie Sie, halten wir Ihren Vorschlag für unannehmbar.	Although we want to avoid a deadlock as much as you do, we find your suggestion unacceptable.
Wir sind nicht völlig davon überzeugt, daß dies eine dauerhafte Lösung ist.	We are not entirely convinced that this is a viable solution.
Ich glaube, es wäre ein Fehler zu ...	I believe it would be a mistake to ...
Ich kann unter keinen Umständen zustimmen.	Under no circumstances could I agree to ...
Es tut mir leid, aber ich habe keine andere Wahl, als das Projekt abzulehnen.	I'm sorry, but I have no alternative but to reject the project.
Hören wir auf, Haare zu spalten.	Let's stop splitting hairs.
Gestatten Sie, daß ich anderer Meinung bin.	I beg to differ.
Wir sind uns einig, daß wir verschiedener Meinung sind.	We'll have to agree to differ.

Time for a smile

The boss wasn't pleased when Dobson came in and asked for the afternoon off as it was the employee's fiftieth wedding anniversary. An angry look on his face, the boss said, "Dobson, don't expect me to put up with this every fifty years!"

Ablehnung begegnen – Responding to rejection

Ist das wirklich Ihre wohlüberlegte Meinung?	Is that really your well-considered opinion?
Es fällt mir ziemlich schwer, Ihren Einwand zu akzeptieren.	I find it rather difficult to accept your objection.
Aber wiegen die Vorteile die Nachteile nicht bei weitem auf?	But don't the advantages by far outweigh the disadvantages?
Man sollte nicht nur immer die negative Seiten sehen.	One shouldn't always look on the black side.
Die vorgebrachten Einwände lassen die Tatsache, daß ..., völlig außer acht.	The objections raised fail to take account of the fact that ...
Entschuldigen Sie, aber Sie scheinen nicht zu berücksichtigen, daß ...	Sorry, but you don't seem to recognise that ...
Ich glaube, Sie machen sich das zu einfach mit Ihrer Ablehnung.	I think you're making it too easy by turning it down.
Diesen Vorschlag kann man nicht so einfach abtun.	This proposal cannot simply be shrugged off.
Die vorliegenden Informationen belegen doch ganz klar, daß ...	The information at hand does clearly demonstrate / prove that ...
Gehen Sie da nicht zu weit, wenn Sie sagen ...?	Aren't you going too far by saying ...?

Enttäuschung ausdrücken – Expressing disappointment

Ehrlich gesagt, Herr Brain, wir hätten mehr erwartet.	Frankly, Mr Brain, we had hoped for more.
Es ist etwas enttäuschend, daß ...	It's a bit disappointing that ...
Ich bin ziemlich enttäuscht von der Leistung dieses Roboters.	I'm rather disappointed with the performance of this robot.
Sie haben uns wirklich im Stich gelassen.	You've really let us down.
Es ist eine Schande, daß ...	It's a disgrace that ...

How to communicate effectively

The director says to one of the participants in the meeting, "Now that we're back on speaking terms, shut up!"

(P) Master your phrases

Task 11: Spot the mistake

There're two mistakes in each sentence. Can you correct them?

1. If I'm understanding you correct, you're saying that ...?
2. Would I be correctly if saying that ...?
3. Perhaps I should make this more clear in saying ...
4. I'm seeing it a little different.

Task 12: Make your phrases more polite

Fit in these words to make your statement less direct.

rather; quite; a slight; a bit; a little

1. I'm afraid there seems to have been .... misunderstanding.
2. That isn't .... what I meant.
3. Isn't it .... risky to trust this company?
4. But allow me to see it .... differently.
5. I'm .... disappointed with the performance of this robot.

Task 13: Guided Translation

1. We seem to (*aneinander vorbeireden*).
2. (*Gehe ich richtig in der Annahme*) that you're suggesting a take-over?
3. That isn't (*ganz das, was ich meinte*).
4. I'm afraid I (*habe mich nicht klar ausgedrückt*).
5. Let (*Sie es mich so sagen*).

How to conduct discussions

Miller, one must have a heart of stone
to listen to your arguments without weeping.

9. *Den Sprecher unterbrechen*
Interrupting the speaker

Unterbrechen, um zu widersprechen – Interrupting to contradict

Entschuldigen Sie, darf ich Ihnen eine Frage stellen?	Excuse me, sir, may I ask a question?
Darf ich Sie für einen Augenblick unterbrechen?	May I interrupt you for a moment?
Entschuldigen Sie, aber könnte ich kurz etwas dazu sagen?	Excuse me, could I just break in a moment here?
Tut mir leid, wenn ich Sie unterbreche, aber ...	Sorry to break in, but ...
Ich möchte Sie nicht unterbrechen, aber ...	I don't want to interrupt you, but ...
Entschuldigen Sie, wenn ich Sie hier unterbreche, aber ...	I'm sorry to interrupt you here, but ...
Wenn ich Sie kurz unterbrechen dürfte.	If I may just interrupt you for a moment.
Ich würde Sie gerne daran erinnern, daß ...	I'd like to remind you that ...
Ich bitte um Entschuldigung, wenn ich Sie unterbreche, aber ist dies wirklich wichtig?	Pardon me for interrupting, but is this really relevant?
Verzeihen Sie, aber darf ich für einen Augenblick des Teufels Advokaten spielen?	Excuse me, but may I play the devil's advocate for a moment?

Unterbrechen, um einen Beitrag zu machen
Interrupting to make a contribution

Wenn ich dazu gerade etwas bemerken darf ...	If I can just make a point here ...
Wenn ich dazu gerade etwas sagen dürfte.	If I could just come in here.

Darf ich zu diesem Punkt etwas bemerken?	May I come in at this point?
Wenn ich noch ein weiteres Argument zugunsten von ... beisteuern dürfte ...	If I might just add one more argument in favour of ...
Wenn ich vielleicht ein paar Worte über / zu ... sagen dürfte ...	If I just might say a few words about ...
Wenn niemand etwas dagegen hat, würde ich gerne etwas zu ... sagen.	If nobody objects, I'd like to say a word about ...
Entschuldigen Sie bitte, aber bevor wir fortfahren, dürfte ich darauf hinweisen, daß ...?	Excuse me, but before we go any further, could I point out that ...?
Ich würde gerne dazu etwas bemerken, wenn Sie erlauben.	I'd like to add something here, if I may.
Entschuldigen Sie, aber ich glaube, es ist wichtig zu berücksichtigen, daß ...	Excuse me, but I think it's important to take into account that ...
Dürfte ich wohl etwas zu Ihrem letzten Argument bemerken?	I wonder if I might comment upon your last argument?
Entschuldigen Sie, aber darf ich Ihre Aufmerksamkeit auf die Tatsache lenken, daß ...	Excuse me, but may I just draw your attention to the fact that ...

Auf Unterbrechung reagieren – Responding to interruption

Vielen Dank für Ihren Beitrag.	Thank you for your comment.
Sie nehmen mir die Worte aus dem Mund.	You took the words right out of my mouth.
Ich verstehe, was Sie meinen, und komme gleich darauf zu sprechen.	I take your point, and I shall be dealing with it in a moment.
Wenn ich fortfahren dürfte. Ich werde Ihre Frage gleich beantworten.	If I could just continue. I'll answer your question in a minute.
Vielen Dank für Ihre Frage, die uns wieder zum Thema zurückführt.	Thank you for your question which leads us back to the subject.

Vielen Dank, daß Sie ein Mißverständnis aufgeklärt haben.	Thank you for having cleared up a misunderstanding.
Das bringt mich zu dem nächsten Punkt.	This brings me to the next point I was going to make.
Wie gesagt, ...	As I was saying ...
Um auf das zurückzukommen, was ich zu erklären versuchte ...	Coming back to what I was trying to explain ...
Zurück zu dem, was ich sagen wollte ...	Going back to what I was saying ... / To go back to what I was saying ...
Um zu meinem Thema zurückzukehren ...	To return to my subject ...
Vielleicht dürfte ich mit meiner Präsentation fortfahren.	Perhaps I could resume my presentation.
Wenn wir zum Thema zurückkehren könnten!	If we could return to the issue.
Wenn ich mein Argument wieder aufnehmen dürfte.	If I might just go back to the point I was making.
Wenn ich mich nun einer anderen Frage zuwenden dürfte.	If I could now turn to another question.

Time for a smile

Call a meeting at 4.30 on Fridays
and you'll get little opposition.

Unterbrechungen ablehnen – Rejecting interruptions

Wenn ich kurz fortfahren dürfte.	If I could just continue.
Wenn ich meinen Satz beenden dürfte.	If I might just finish my sentence.
Wir könnten auf Ihre Frage vielleicht später eingehen.	Perhaps we could return to your question later on.
Entschuldigen Sie, aber ich möchte gerne noch folgendes sagen ...	With respect, I should only like to add this ...
Wenn Sie gestatten, würde ich meine Ausführungen gerne abschließen.	If you would allow me to round off my argumentation.

Wenn Sie so freundlich wären, mich ausreden zu lassen.	If you would be so kind as to let me finish.
Mit Ihrer Erlaubnis würde ich gerne meinen Gedanken zu Ende bringen.	With your permission I'd like to finish the point I was making.

Unterbrechungen vermeiden – Avoiding interruptions

Lassen Sie mich meine Präsentation bitte zu Ende führen. Anschließend werde ich alle Fragen, die Sie dann noch haben, beantworten.	Please let me finish my presentation. Afterwards, I'll answer any questions you might still have.
Wir haben genug Zeit, um alle Ihre Fragen später zu beantworten.	There's enough time to answer all your questions later on.
Ich gebe Ihnen nur noch zwei Beispiele. Dann gehe ich auf Ihre Fragen ein.	I'd just like to give you two examples. Then I'll answer your questions.
Ganz kurz nur noch ein Satz, der Ihre Frage vielleicht beantwortet.	Very briefly, just one more sentence that might answer your questions.
Ich möchte zwei Dinge feststellen, bevor ich Ihre Fragen beantworte.	There are two points I'd like to make before I answer your questions.
Um die Situation voll und ganz zu verstehen, müssen Sie folgendes wissen: ...	In order to fully understand the situation, you should know this: ...
Zuerst möchte ich die Frage unseres Gastes beantworten, anschließend komme ich auf Ihren Einwand zurück.	First I would like to reply to our guest and then I'll come back your objection.

P Master your phrases

Task 14: Beef up your word power

Three phrases for 'unterbrechen'.

1. May I .... you for a moment?
2. Excuse me, could I just .... a moment here?
3. If could I could just .... here.

Task 15: Pesky prepositions

1. May I come .... this point?
2. You took the words right .... of my mouth.
3. I wonder if I might comment .... your last argument?
4. I shall be dealing .... it in a moment.

Task 16: The place of the adverb

Find the right sentence and the right place for these adverbs.

just; only; now

1. If I could turn to another question.
2. If I could continue.
3. With respect, I should like to add this ...

C Crossword power

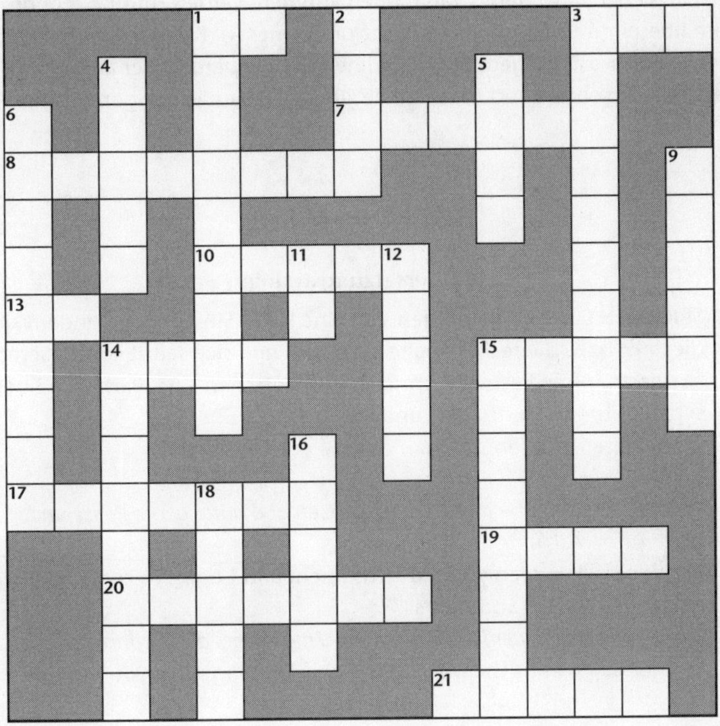

Across

1. I'm afraid it's not ✎ easy as that. 3. We ✎ eye to eye in this affair. 7. Aren't we ✎ too many risks? 8. Don't the advantages ✎ the disadvantages? 10. You took the words right out of my ✎. 13. If I could just come ✎ here. 14. I'm afraid this is easier said than ✎. 15. I can see your ✎. 17. I shall be ✎ with it in a moment. 19. Let's go ✎ your suggestions one by one. 20. With ✎, I see it a little differently. 21. I can go ✎ with your proposal.

Down

1. I think we are in ✎ on that. 2. I'm sorry, I can't go along ✎ you. 3. I can go along with your ✎. 4. Your arguments don't hold ✎. 5. Let me try to ✎ a few holes in your argument. 6. You've ✎ me. 9. I still have my ✎. 11. I can go along with you ✎ to a certain point. 12. Let me try to pick a few ✎ in your argument. 14. I don't ✎ altogether. 15. I cannot give the ✎ my support. 16. I totally ✎ with you. 18. I must take ✎ with you over these figures.

ANREGUNGEN FÜR KURSLEITER

Wie kann man mit *Master your Business Phrases* arbeiten? Hier machen wir Ihnen neun bewährte Vorschläge für Einzel- und Gruppenunterricht, die Sie sicher zu weiteren Variationen anregen werden (mit Einzelschülern übernimmt der Lehrer die Rolle von Partner A). Bevor mit einer Übung begonnen wird, prägen sich die Teilnehmer die *phrases* der ausgewählten Situationen ein und machen die Übungen zum jeweiligen Thema.

I. PARTNERARBEIT

❶ Übersetzungstraining

1. Stillarbeit: Die Partner prägen sich eine kurze Situation ein, indem sie die linke bzw. die rechte Spalte abdecken und sich selbst kontrollieren.
2. Partnertraining: Partner A spricht den deutschen Satz, Partner B übersetzt. Partner A kontrolliert und korrigiert.
3. Anschließend Rollentausch.

Partner A: *Ich habe Ihre Anzeige gelesen und hätte gerne Preise und Zahlungsbedingungen.*
Partner B: I've seen your advertisement and I'd like to know your prices and terms.
Partner A: *Wie teuer ist die neue Druckmaschine, die Sie anbieten*?
Partner B: What's the price of the new printing press you're offering?

❷ Sprachliches Reaktionstraining

Wählen Sie eine Situation, 'Im Reisebüro' oder 'Einen Termin vereinbaren'. Partner A wählt einen Satz aus den Listen; Partner B versucht angemessen zu reagieren.

Partner A: I'd like to book a flight to London.
Partner B: And when is it you'd like to leave?
Partner A korrigiert und bietet Alternativen aus der Liste an.

❸ Schlüsselwort-Training

Die Teilnehmer haben zwei oder drei Abschnitte ausgewählt, z. B. *Telephoning Effectively*. Partner A nennt ein oder zwei Schlüsselwörter, Partner B errät den Satz.

Partner A: *name, please*
Partner B: Could I ask your name, please?/Could I have your name, please?
Partner A: *address*
Partner B: And what's the address, please?
Partner A: *post code*
Partner B: Could you let me have the post code as well, please?

❹ Situationstraining

Die Gruppe bereitet paarweise eine Kette von Situationen vor, die nacheinander durchgespielt werden.

Paar 1: Making an appointment
Paar 2: Arranging the meeting point
Paar 3: Rearranging the appointment
Paar 4: At the Reception desk
Paar 5: Meeting the business partner
Paar 6: Breaking the ice
Paar 7: Introducing colleagues etc.
Paar 8: Negotiating the price

❺ Die On-the-job-Kartei

1. Partner aus der gleichen Abteilung wählen die *phrases* aus, die für ihre Arbeit oder für ihren nächsten Einsatz wichtig sind.
2. Sie stellen eine *On-the-job*-Kartei für ihren Schreibtisch zusammen.
3. Der Kursleiter hilft und ergänzt.
4. Die Karten werden über den Computer ausgedruckt. Die Software und die Karten gibt es im Handel (zum Beispiel Visitenkarten). Die Kartei ist für den Schreibtisch bestimmt.
5. Die Kartei wird für interessierte Kollegen vervielfältigt.

II. GRUPPENARBEIT

❶ Conducting a meeting

Die *phrases* von *Part five*: *Master your meetings* werden vorbereitet. In einer Besprechung werden die folgenden Gruppenthemen besprochen. Chairman und Protokollant werden ernannt und eine Tagesordnung aufgestellt. Gruppenthemen werden vorgeschlagen, angenommen, abgelehnt und zur Abstimmung gebracht.

❷ Presenting the company

Die einzelnen Gruppen bereiten ihr Thema vor. Die Themen werden nacheinander präsentiert. Die Zuhörer machen Notizen und verbessern anschließend.

Gruppe A: Die Firma vorstellen

Our company was founded in 1895.
We're a group that markets soap.
Where's your company's head office? Etc.

Gruppe B: Ein Firmenrundgang

I think I ought to tell you something about the company.
Our production facility is on site.
We have to wear our helmets here. Etc.

Gruppe C, D, E: Produkte und Dienstleistungen präsentieren

I'm glad to have the chance to speak to you on the subject of ...
In my presentation I'll be explaining our new project.

Gruppe F: Show the structure of your company

❸ Diskussion im Plenum

Die *phrases* von *Part six*: *Discussing the clever way* wurden vorbereitet. Hier sind einige Themenvorschläge:

1. Reorganising the European Union.
2. Putting manufacturing outside Germany to reduce costs.
3. The necessity of Berlin to be the capital of Germany.
4. The Year-2000-problem. Will our computers create havoc?
5. The social network in Germany.

❹ Die Business-English-Reihe:

Wollen Sie die Situationen in *Master Your Business Phrases* vertiefen, nehmen Sie den zugehörigen Titel unserer *Business-English*-Reihe. Mit den Bänden zu den einzelnen Teilen von *Master Your Business Phrases* vertiefen Sie Strategie, Taktik, Psychologie und Sprache der jeweiligen Bereiche des Wirtschaftslebens: das Verkaufen in *Sell like Hell*, das Telefonieren in *How to Phone Effectively*, die Pflege von Kontakten in *Small Talk for Big Business*, das Verhandeln und Präsentieren in *Get Through at Meetings*, die Kenntnis interkultureller Unterschiede in *Going International*, die Rhetorik in *Spice up Your Speeches* (erscheint im Januar 2000). Hier finden Sie eine Fülle von weiteren Übungsmöglichkeiten.

SCHLÜSSEL ZU DEN ÜBUNGEN

PART 1: BUSINESS PEOPLE ON THE MOVE

1. Preparing the business trip

Task 1: Complete the dialogue

You	Travel agent
I'd like *to fly* to London.	What *date would you* like to go?
What's *the price* of the flight?	*Economy* or first class?
When *does* the plane *take off*?	*At* 9.40 a.m., sir.
I'd like some *travel* insurance.	Do you want full *cover* sir?

Task 2: Preparing a flight

1. I'm planning to *fly* to Bangkok next month.
2. Do you want to fly first class or *economy*?
3. What *date* would you like to go?
4. I'd like some travel *insurance.*

Task 3: Making a reservation

1. I'd like to *book* a room, please.
2. Single or *double*?
3. With *bath* or shower?
4. How long would you like to *stay*?
5. Could you *confirm* that by fax, please?

Task 4: Making an appointment

1. I was wondering if we could possibly *meet* next week.
2. What day would *suit* you best?
3. *Shall* we *say* Tuesday?
4. Would you like us to arrange *accommodation* for you?

Task 5: Fit in the modals

1. *Can* you make the conference on the 20th?
2. *Should* I take a cab?
3. *Shall* I pick you up at the station?
4. When *would* it be convenient?
5. Ms Child *will* call for you at the hotel at 8.30.

Task 6: Arranging place and time

1. *I'm calling* to check the time of Monday's meeting.
2. How long *do you think* we'll need?
3. So, *we're meeting* at my hotel on the 12th of March.
4. I look forward *to seeing* you on the 12th.

Task 7: What you can do with meetings

I want to { *confirm* / *call off* / *cancel* / *bring forward* / *postpone* / *put off* / *rearrange* } our meeting

Crossword power

		1 H	O	2 W					3 M			4 P	
				5 I	N	S	U	R	A	N	C	E	
6 O	7 F	F		L					K			R	
	L			8 L	9 A	Y	10 O	V	E	R			
	I				I		N					11 C	
	12 G	E	13 T		R			14 O				O	
	H		15 A	P	P	O	I	N	T	16 M	E	N	T
17 A	T		K		O					E		F	
G			E		R					E		I	
R		18 A			T		19 S	20 U	I	T		R	
E		B		21 F				P		I		M	
22 E	C	O	N	O	M	Y				N			
		U		R			23 S	U	G	G	E	S	T
24 P	U	T											

2. On the way

Task 1: At the ticket office

1. Could you tell me the times of a few trains to Glasgow?
2. When's the next train to X?
3. Can I go to Glasgow via Oxford?
4. Can I break the journey there?
5. Where do I have to change?
6. When does the train leave?
7. Which platform does my train leave from?
8. Is the train to Glasgow running late?
9. Will I be able to catch my connection in Luton?
10. A return, please, second class.

Task 2: Complete these questions

1. Excuse me, could you *change my booking*? I'd prefer an earlier flight.	I'm afraid it's not possible to change your booking.
2. How much *luggage can I take*?	Thirty kilos, all in all.
3. Can I take this as *hand luggage*?	I'm afraid it's too big for the rack, sir.
4. When *does* my plane *take off*?	Your plane takes off in 15 minutes, sir.

Task 3: Ask the right questions

1. I feel sick? Please bring me something for air-sickness.
2. What is the estimated time of arrival?
3. What's the local time, please?
4. Excuse me, where's the baggage claim?
5. Is there a shuttle(-service) to the city?

Task 4: Get your terms right

By train	By air	By boat
train	plane	boat
railway	airway	line
journey	flight	cruise / voyage
station	airport	sea port / harbour
platform	gate	quay
engine driver	pilot	captain

Crossword power

1 P	2 L	A	T	F	3 O	R	4 M		5 R			6 B	Y
	O				N		I		U			R	
	7 C	A	8 L	L			9 S	I	N	10 G	L	E	S
	K		E		11 D		S			E		A	
	E		A		E				12 A	T		K	
13 T	R	A	V	E	L		14 Q		I		15 W		
A			E		A		U		16 S	E	A	T	
K					Y		E		L		Y		
E		17 S	C	H	E	D	U	L	E	18 D			
		C			D		E			R			
	19 G	A	T	E						20 O	F	F	
		L								P			
	21 F	E	R	R	Y								
		S											

3. Arrival in a foreign country

Task 1: Give the right answers

What's your nationality?	I'm *German.*
What's the purpose of your visit?	I'm here on *business.*
I'm afraid your passport has expired.	Too bad! Can I *have it renewed at* my consulate?
How long are you planning to stay?	I'll *be staying* for a week.
Have you got anything to declare?	No, I've only articles *for my personal* use.
Where will you be staying?	I'm *going to stay* with a *business* partner in Kiev.

Task 2: At security control

Could I see your flight ticket please?	Here you are.
Is that your *case*?	Yes, it is.
What *is in your* case?	Only presents and souvenirs.
Did you pack it yourself?	Yes, I did.
Did you *leave it unattended* at any time?	No, I stayed with it all the time.
Please *switch on* your laptop.	Where can I plug it in?

Task 3: Let's go *woggling* again

1. I'm afraid I've *lost* my ticket.
2. Could you *issue* me a residence permit?
3. My case hasn't *turned* up.
4. Someone has *switched* suitcases with me.
5. Where can I *report* the loss?

Task 4: Complete these sentences

1. I'm not used to automatic *transmission*. I'd prefer a car with a *gear change.*
2. What does the insurance *cover*?
3. Is fully *comprehensive* insurance *included* in the price?
4. How much is the daily *rental* for a Ford Cortina?
5. Where can I *return* the car in Glasgow?

Task 5: Match problems and phrases

Typical problems ...		and what to say at the garage	
1	you've run out of petrol	K	fill her / it up
2	there isn't enough oil	I	top / fill it up
3	the clutch is slipping	E	adjust it
4	you have a puncture	A	put on / fit the spare
5	the battery is flat	C	recharge it / charge it up
6	the radiator is leaking	B	make it watertight / seal it
7	the car won't start	D	try to bump-start it
8	the fanbelt is slipping	F	tighten it
9	the motor is too loud	G	weld the hole in the exhaust pipe
10	the oil is leaking	H	try to seal the sump
11	the engine sounds rough	J	adjust the ignition / check the plugs

Task 6: Are you a gentleman? Well, then help the young lady.

She is walking on the road.	Give her a *lift.*
Her car got stuck in the mud.	*Tow* it out of it.
And it has got a puncture.	Help her to *put* on the *spare*.
The engine of her car wont start.	Give her a *push* to *bump*-start it.
Hopeless! The car won't start.	Call the *breakdown* service.
The breakdown service is too busy.	Then you have to tow her to the next *repair shop / service garage.*

Task 7: Let's test your memory

1. I've a *reservation in the name of Meier.*
2. Is there a *reduction for* businessmen?
3. Is there a *message for me*?
4. Do you want *full board* or only *breakfast*?
5. I'd like to *see* the manager. I've a *complaint* to make.
6. I'm leaving tomorrow. Could you *get my bill ready*?
7. Could I have a *separate bill* for the calls?
8. Excuse me, but I'm afraid *there is something wrong with my bill.*

Task 8: A mixed bag of questions

1. What do you put into the hotel safe? *your valuables*
2. Another word for booking: *reservation*
3. The document called you have to fill in: *registration form*
4. Three meals at the hotel: *full board*
5. They clean and iron your clothes: *laundry service*
6. Bookings are either *confirmed* or *cancelled*
7. If you are not satisfied, you make a *complaint*
8. You want a detailed bill. Ask for an *itemised* bill

Task 9: Get your prepositions right

1. I've had a room reserved *in* the name of Meier.
2. Could I have a look *at* the room first?
3. Could you have my luggage sent *up* to my room?
4. I want to make a complaint *about* the service at your hotel.

Crossword power

1 E	X	C	E	S	S			2 S			3 P		
X						4 D	U	T	Y		E		
5 P	U	6 R	P	7 O	S	E		A			R		
I		O		N		C		Y			8 M	A	9 P
R		U			10 C	L	A	I	M		I		A
E		N				A		N			T		R
D		D		11 F	O	R		G		12 R			T
				L		E			13 R	E	A	14 D	Y
	15 I	S	S	U	E			16 U		N		E	
	T			S				S		E		P	
	E		17 C	H	A	N	G	E		W		O	
	M		A							E		S	
			18 S	W	I	19 T	C	H	E	D		I	
			H			O						T	

4. All sorts of odd jobs to do

Task 1: Are you fit to have an account?

1. What should you not do with a cheque?	C. lose D. fake
2. What can you not do with an account?	D. commission
3. What does the bank charge you for money transfer?	A. commission

Task 2: Can you match up these phrases?

Customer	Bank clerk
1 I'd like to have money transferred to Germany.	D Please fill in the transfer form.
2 Who do you bank with?	C I have an account with the City Bank.
3 Where do I collect my bank statements?	B Please go to counter 7
4 I'd like to open a savings account.	A Here's your passbook.

Task 3: How did the manager respond?

Customer	Bank manager
1 I'd like to invest a lump sum.	D You'd better spread your investment. It's less risky.
2 What do you advise me to buy?	C Are you thinking of a long term or a short term investment?
3 I prefer a long term investment.	B In that case you should take bonds. Which account may I debit?
4 I was thinking of applying for a loan.	A Have you got any security?

Crossword power

			1 W			2 A	3 P	P	L	Y			
		4 F	I	L	L		L						
			T			5 P	A	S	S	B	O	O	K
			H				C						
			6 D	I	7 S	P	E	N	8 S	E	R		
	9 B	A	R		T				O				
	A		A		A		10 C	U	R	R	E	N	11 T
	L		W		T		U		T				R
	A				E		R		I		12 S		A
	N		13 V		M		14 R	U	N		15 P	I	N
	C		A		E		E		G		R		S
16 R	E	T	U	R	N		N				E		F
	D		L		T		C				A		E
			T				Y				D		R

Task 4: What is it?

Things the postman brings	mail
You put presents into it	parcel
An urgent letter	express letter
A letter for which you get a receipt	registered letter
Money transferred by the post	postal order
The price you pay for a letter	postage
Not a local phone call	long-distance call
You throw postcards into it	letter-box

Task 5: Guess the meaning and match the phrases

Stamps you can find on letters

1 Einschreibebrief	D Recorded Delivery
2 Eilzustellung	C Special Delivery

3 Wertbrief — B Insured letter
4 Luftpost — A By air mail

Task 6: The right words are those in italics

1. *Lift* the receiver.
2. *Insert* your money in the slot.
3. *Listen* for the dialling tone.
4. *Dial* the number required.
5. First dial the *international* code
6. Then the *area* code minus initial '0' ...
7. Then dial the *subscriber's* number.

Task 7: Guided translation

1. Can I make a long-distance call from here?
2. I'd like to make a reversed charge call to New York.
3. I'd like to place a person-to-person call.
4. Could you let me have the yellow pages?

Crossword power

			1 O	R	2 D	E	R		3 T				
			F		O			4 P	A	R	5 C	E	6 L
			F		M				K		U		I
					7 E	X	8 P	R	E	S	S		N
	9 P	A	G	E	S		U				T		E
	O				T		10 B	O	X		O		
	S			11 D	I	A	L				M		
	T		12 D		C		I		13 P	O	S	14 T	E
15 R	A	T	E				C		O			H	
	G		A						S			R	
	E		D		16 C		17 W	I	T	H		O	
					O				A			U	
					18 D	I	A	L	L	I	N	G	
	19 I	S	S	U	E							H	

Task 8: Find a phrase that has the same meaning

Can I help you?	What *can I do for you*?
I think I was next.	I think *it's my turn*.
We need a deposit of 10 %.	We *require* a deposit of 10 %.
When will it be ready?	*How long will it take?*

Task 9: One word for four idioms

1. How long will it *take*?
2. What size do you *take*?
3. I'll *take* this cardigan.
4. Do you *take* German marks?

Task 10: What to say in these situations?

The problem	**What to say**
Your raincoat is dirty.	I'd like to *have this raincoat cleaned*.
The skirt doesn't fit, but you want it afterall.	Could you *alter* this skirt?
The article is a bit too expensive.	*Haven't you got anything cheaper?*
You want to send it as a present.	Could you *gift-wrap* it, please?
It's too heavy and your hotel is far away.	Could you *send these things to the hotel*?

Crossword power

					1 D				2 B	Y		
3 G	L	4 A	S	S	E	S			E		5 T	
L		R			L		6 S		I		A	
A		7 O	P	T	I	C	I	A	N		K	
S		U			V		Z		8 G	9 O	E	10 S
S		N			E		E			N		P
E		D			R			11 M				E
S					Y			A		12 F		C
	13 C							14 P	R	I	N	T
15 B	A	R	16 G	A	I	N				T		A
	N		I						17 W			C
			F		18 F				R			L
			19 T	O	O	T	H	P	A	S	T	E
					R				P			S

Crossword power

		1 E											
2 C		3 V	E	4 R	K	5 E	H	R	6 S	A	7 M	T	
A		E		E		X			I		A		
T		N		C		C			G		P		
A		T		O		8 U	P		H			9 P	
L		S		M		R			T			E	
O				M		S		10 O		11 C		R	
12 G	U	I	D	E		I		F		A		F	
U				N		13 O	F	F		L		O	
E				D		N		I		E		R	
								14 C	I	N	E	M	A
			15 C	O	U	R	16 S	E		D		A	
							O			A		N	
					17 W	A	L	K		R		C	
							D					E	

Task 11: A *woggle* exercise to test your memory

1. May I *introduce* myself? Peter Smith is the *name.*
2. Sorry. I didn't *catch / get* your name.
3. Are you here on *business* or pleasure?
4. I think we've *met* before.
5. It's been nice *meeting* you.
6. *Glad / Pleased* to meet you, too.
7. Do you *happen* to know who the guest *speaker* is?
8. Are you also *staying* at the Hilton?

Task 12: How to say 'Entschuldigen Sie'

1 *Excuse me,* — E do you speak English?
2 *Sorry,* — C was that your foot?
3 *I beg your pardon.* — D I'm afraid I didn't catch your name.
4 *I apologise* — A for being late again. I had a breakdown.
5 *Forgive me* — B for saying so, sir, but I don't like your smoking.

Crossword power

	1 I	N	V	2 I	T	E					3 M	E	T
4 O	N			N			5 G				E		
				6 T	A	K	E	N		7 L	E	T	
		8 F	O	R			T				T		
		R		O							I		
	9 S	O		D					10 L	O	N	G	
		M		U		11 B	Y		I		G		
				C		U			N				
		12 P	L	E	A	S	U	13 R	E				14 W
		A				I		E					A
		R				N		P			15 M	A	Y
		T				E					I		
16 L	O	S	T			17 S	T	A	Y	I	N	G	
						S					D		

5. Visiting fairs and companies

Task 1: Let's go *woggling* again

1. We'd like to take *part* in the exhibition.
2. When is the exhibition to be *held*?
3. Where exactly is the exhibition *site*?
4. The fair will *open / start / begin* on Monday.
5. Do you also *supply / provide* refreshments?

Task 2: Beef up your word power

stand	*booth*
booking	*reservation*
take part in a fair	*participate* in a fair
free tickets	*complimentary* tickets
withdraw an application	*cancel* an application

Task 3: Definition exercise

1. Money you need to rent a stand	*rental*
2. The area the fair is to be held on	*site*
3. Last date for the application	*deadline*
4. Number of square meters for the stand	*exhibition space*
5. Lady who helps the visitors	*hostess*
6. Free gifts for visitors	*freebies / give-aways*
7. He erects the booth for you	*exhibition contractor*

Task 4: Printed material

1 catalogue of	D exhibitors
2 sales	A literature
3 promotional	B material
4 list of	C visitors

Task 5: Scrambled sentences

1. Sorry, but this is a sample and not for sale.
2. What exactly is your product range?
3. How does this product compare with its competitors?
4. Is this tool available in different sizes?

Crossword power

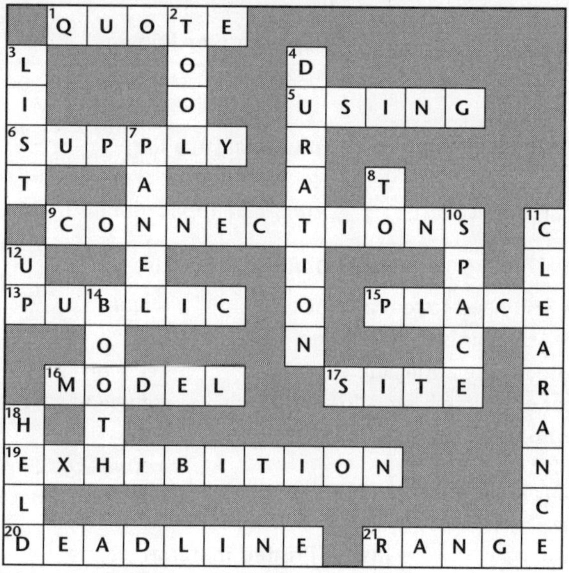

Task 6: At the reception (rec)

You: Could you tell Ms Child that I'm here?
Rec: Is Ms Child expecting you?
You: I've an appointment with her for 10 o'clock.
Rec: Please take a seat. She'll be with you in a moment.

Task 7: Formalities

1. Could you *fill out* this form, please?
2. Here's your *visitor's badge*.
3. *Swipe* your visitor's card through the *slot*.

Task 8: Find the right words

You	Your visitor
I hope *you had a pleasant flight*.	Yes, but I'm still suffering from jet lag.
Did you *find our company straight away*?	*I didn't have any trouble thanks* to your clear instructions.
How *is the family*?	Very well, thanks. And yours?
May I *offer you something to drink*?	Thanks. A coffee would be fine.
Is it alright with you if we get *straight down to business*?	Why not? Business before pleasure is my motto.

Task 9: What to say

1. You enter a British company. The receptionist says
   C. Welcome to Lamy. How can I help you?

2. You are introduced to the purchasing manager. He says 'How do you do?'
   You say: C. How do you do?

3. One of his salesmen arrives. He greets you: 'How are you, Bob?'
   B. Fine, thank you.

Task 10: Presenting the company

1. Our company was *founded* in 1895.
2. We're a *manufacturer* spare parts for cars.
3. Our head office is *located* in France.
4. We *employ* over 300 people

Crossword power

	[1] F	O	[2] R	G	E	T		[3] M	[4] E	E	T			
	L		E				[5] S		L				[6] D	
	O		[7] A	G	R	E	E	M	E	N	[8] T		O	
	O		C				E		V		A		W	
	R		[9] H	E	L	[10] P		[11] T	A	L	K	I	N	[12] G
						L			T		E			L
		[13] B	A	D	G	E		[14] F	O	R				A
						A			R		[15] M	I	N	D
[16] C	U	S	T	O	M	S								
O						A								
M						N								[17] C
I		[18] V	I	[19] S	I	T		[20] S	[21] H	A	L	L		O
N				E					A					A
G				[22] A	P	P	O	I	N	T	M	E	N	T
				T					D					

Task 11: Fill in those nasty little words

1. Would you like to join us *for* dinner this evening?
2. Why don't you bring your colleague *along with* you?
3. I'm looking *forward to* meeting your family.
4. Please, come *on in.*

Task 12: Get your tenses right

1. What *are* you *doing* this evening?
2. My husband *has told* me a lot about you.
3. I'*d love* to join you, but I've got another engagement.
4. My wife *will be* very *disappointed*, if you *turn* us down.

Task 13: Say it in other words

Have you got anything planned for tonight?	What *are you doing* this evening?
Why don't you come for dinner	Would you *like to join* us for dinner

this evening?	this evening?
Would eight o'clock be alright?	Would eight o'clock *suit you*?
I'd love to, but unfortunately I won't be able to.	I'd love to, but *I'm afraid I can't make* it.

Task 14: Get your tenses right

1. When *did* you *arrive*?
2. *Have* you *been* to England before?
3. I'*m enjoying* every single day.
4. How long *have* we *known* each other?
5. *Do* you *remember* the day when we first met?

Task 15: Test your toasts

1. I'd like to *propose* a toast to the conclusion of our contract.
2. Let's *raise* our glasses to the future of Europe.
3. I'd like to *make* a toast to our new colleague.
4. *Here's* to our new director!

Crossword power

[1] M	[2] E	E	[3] T		[4] J	O	[5] I	N					
	N		A				N		[6] R	I	[7] S	E	
	G		L		[8] L	O	V	E			U		
	A		K				I		[9] M		I		
	G				[10] T		[11] T	O	A	S	T		
	E			[12] H	O	M	E		K			[13] C	
	[14] M	O	V	E				[15] L	E	A	V	E	
	E			L			[16] E					L	
	N			[17] P	[18] L	A	N	N	E	D		E	
	T				I		J					B	
		[19] B			F		O					R	
[20] O	V	E	R	S	T	A	Y			[21] G	L	A	D
		E					E					T	
[22] F	A	N	C	Y			D		[23] O	F	F	E	R

Task 16: Cross out the wrong verb

1. They *do* / *serve* / ~~*make*~~ good meals there.
2. What would you *recommend* / ~~*assume*~~ / *suggest*?
3. I think I'll *try* / *take* / ~~*test*~~ the T-bone steak.
4. Could I have the *bill* / *check* / ~~*invoice*~~, please?
5. Do you *take* / ~~*allow*~~ / *accept* credit cards?

Task 17: How are they normally served?

1 duck	F roast
2 salmon	C smoked
3 vegetable	A boiled
4 meat	G minced
5 fruit	E stewed
6 salad	D mixed
7 potatoes	B mashed

Task 18: They mean almost the same

1. Have you *reserved* a table?	Have you *booked* a table?
2. Is this table *taken*?	Is this table *free*?
3. *Separate bills*, please.	We're *going Dutch*.
4. *Let* me *get this.*	*This is on* me.
5. Do you *take* credit cards?	Do you *accept* credit cards?

Crossword

	1 B	O	O	K	E	2 D		3 P	E	A	S		
	O					O		I					
	A					N		N					4 L
5 O	R	6 D	E	R		7 E	8 A	T	I	N	9 G		O
		I					R				A		C
10 K	I	N	D			11 M	E	N	U		M		A
E		E					A			12 V	E	A	L
E						13 V							
14 P	O	15 R	K		16 R	E	C	O	M	M	E	N	17 D
		A		18 J		N							U
19 T		B		O		I							C
20 A	R	B	E	I	T	S	E	S	S	E	N		K
K		I		N		O							
E		T				N							

PART 2: TELEPHONING EFFECTIVELY

Task 1: Answering the phone

Wrong: 1. May I assist you somehow other?

Task 2: Typical German!

1. What can I *do* for you?
2. Who *would* you like to speak to?
3. I'd like to speak to your *husband*, if *I may*.

Task 3: Identifying the caller.

1. Could I ask who *I'm speaking* to?
2. I'm sorry, sir. I *didn't quite catch* your name.
3. *Am I speaking* to ROBOTALOT in Bonn?
4. *Do you spell* Brian with an 'i' or a 'y'?

Task 4: Who do you want to speak to?

1. Could you *put* me *through* to your sales department, please?
2. Could I have *extension* 344, please?
3. Could I have a quick *word* with Mr Brain?
4. I really *need / have* to speak to the director. It's *urgent.*

Task 5: The reason for the call

1. May I ask what it is *concerned* with?
2. And what does it *concern*, please?
3. What's it in *connection* with?

1. I'd like to speak to Dr Brian *on* business.
2. I'm phoning *concerning* the vacancy.
3. I'd like to speak to Dr Brain *about* a private *matter.*

Task 6: Which words fit these requests?

1. Can you *transfer* me to the R&D department, please?
2. Please *connect* me with Fred Niemec.
3. Could you *put* me through to Mr Brain?
4. Could you put me in *contact* with Ms. Child, please?

Task 7: Add an expression with the same meaning.

1. I'm afraid the line is *engaged / busy*.
2. Sorry, I can't *reach / get* this number.
3. I'll be *with you / back to* you in a minute.

Task 8: Why they can't answer the phone:

1. I'm sorry, Dr Brain is *out* of the office *at* the moment.
2. He's *on* another line *at* the moment.
3. He's *in* the middle *of* an interview *for* a job.
4. Could you pass *on* a message *for* me?

Task 9: What can you do with messages?

leave / take / pass on / get / repeat / read back } a message

Task 10: Beef up your word power

Herrn Brain } "erreichen" / reach / get hold of / contact / get in touch with

Task 11: Scrambled sentences

1. When can I reach Dr Brain?
2. How can I get hold of him?
3. Is there a number where I can reach him?
4. When's the best time to ring back?

Task 12: How to be polite

1. I wonder if you could *spare* me a minute.
2. I hope I'm not *disturbing* you.
3. It's *good / nice* to hear from you again.

Task 13: What to say when the connection is bad

1. I can hardly *hear* you.
2. We've got a *crossed* line.
3. The *line* is terrible.
4. There's terrible *interference.*

Task 14: What to say when you are busy

1. I'm hard *pressed* for time.
2. I'm very *short* of time.
3. I'm in a *hurry*.

Task 15: Guided translation

1. Well, I guess *that's all for now.*
2. I'm afraid I'*ll have to cut this short.*
3. I'll *have* to *say goodbye now.*

Task 16: The perfect secretary

1. Will you take the call?
2. Shall I put him through?
3. Mr Brain left strict instructions that he was not to be disturbed.
4. I'm afraid Ms Child is not available.

Task 17: Complete the dialogue

Boss to secretary	**Secretary to caller**
Tell him I'll call back later.	Mr Brain *will call you back* later.
Ask him when he would like me to call back.	When *would be a good time for him* to call you back?
Could you please put him off until tomorrow?	Could you *try again tomorrow*?

Crossword power

			1 A	U	2 T	O	3 M	A	4 T	I	5 C		
6 O			B		O		E		A		O		
U		7 T	O		N		S		K		D		8 R
T			U		E		S		E		E		E
9 S	L	O	T				A			10 L			C
I					11 E	N	G	A	G	E	D		E
12 D	E	13 S	K		M		E			A			I
E		P			E					V			V
		E			R		14 P		15 L	E	A	V	E
16 C	A	L	L		G		U		I				R
A		L		17 B	E	S	T		18 K	E	19 E	P	
T					N				E		L		
C			20 B	A	C	K					S		
H			Y		Y			21 R	E	P	E	A	T

PART 3: PERFECT PRESENTATIONS

Task 1: Tense and aspect

1. Mr X *will* now *speak* to you about marketing on the internet.
2. I *have been* a consultant to IBM for three years.
3. I'*m trying* to give you an overview of our activities.
4. In the handout I'*ll be passing* round, you'*ll find* all the figures.

Task 2: Those tricky little words

1. I'm no more expert *in* this field than you are.
2. This morning I'd like to look back *at* the past fiscal year.
3. *On* behalf of the Board I'd like to welcome you all to ...
4. So much *for* the costs.

Task 3: Spot the mistake

1. I know your problems since I was *a* sales manager like you.
2. I'm no more expert in this field *than* you are.
3. *As* you know, I'm here to present our product range to you.

Task 4: Odd phrase out

1. I'*m glad* is not an expression of gratitude.

Task 5: Beef up your word power

We should not *overlook* the fact that ...	We should not *ignore* the fact that ...
I'd like to *move on* to my next issue.	I'd like to *pass on* to my next item
Can I *continue*?	May I *go on*?
In 1996 profits *reached the lowest point.*	In 1996 profits *hit rock bottom.*

Task 6: Visual aids for presentations

slide	*transparency / OHP sheet*
handout	*chart*
screen	*graphic*

Task 7: Word builder's corner

What's the *explanation* for this? — How can we *explain* this?
What are the *benefits* from this situation? — How can we *benefit* from this situation?
What are the *implications*? — What does this *imply*?

Taks 8: Wrong word order

1. If I understood you correctly you prefer plan C.
2. I can't commit myself yet.
3. Could we leave this issue open until later?
4. I hope you enjoyed it.

Task 9: Scrambled letters

1. I understand your *apprehensions.*
2. We seem to be talking at cross-*purposes.*
3. It's difficult to accept this, but the *evidence* is there.
4. I feel we're losing sight of our *objective.*

Crossword power

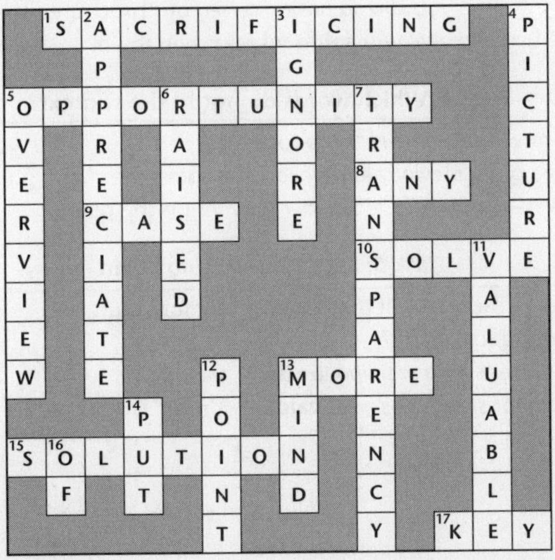

PART 4: SELLING SUCCESSFULLY

Task 1: Guided translation

1. You've come to the *right place*.
2. If I've *understood correctly*, you need something reliable.
3. We've got several products *that would suit you*.
4. *Do you happen to know* who keeps his *schedule*?

Task 2: A question of cleverness

C Mr Brown is expecting me.
A I 'd like to speak to Mr Brown.
B Mr Brown asked me to call at 10 a.m.

A When would be a good time for Mr Brown to call me back?
C When would be a good time to call Mr Brown back?
A Could you please ask Mr Brown to call me back?

Task 3: Get your tenses right

1. I'm not sure whether you remember me. We *met* at the trade fair in Glasgow.
2. In the meantime you *should have received* our brochures about ...
3. You said I *should* give you a ring when I'm in town.

Task 4: Which words do not fit the context?

1. When can we *get* ~~come meet go~~ together?
2. Sorry, I've got a *previous* ~~former~~ *earlier* appointment at 5 p.m.
3. If you ~~memorise~~ *recall / remember* we met on the plane.

Task 5: Let's go *woggling* again

1. I'd prefer to meet you, if that's *convenient* for you.
2. When would it *suit* you?
3. We could meet for a *working* lunch.
4. Thank you for *sparing* us your valuable time.

Task 6: Is it *what, which* or both?

1. *What* sort of lines do you stock?
2. *Which* line is of most interest to you?
3. *What* products would you like to focus on?
4. *Which* do you think is best suited for my needs?
5. *What* discount would you offer on an order for 100 items?
6. You mentioned cameras. *Which* do you intend to offer?

Task 7: Where do these adverbs go?

1. I can *fully* understand your scepticism.
2. Could you *possibly* be a little more precise on this point?
3. Could you please clarify *exactly* what you mean?
4. If I've understood *correctly*, you need something reliable.

Task 8: Fit in these tricky little words

1. I'd like to go *back over* a couple of points you mentioned to me the other day.
2. I've been checking *through* the requirements you described to me last week.
3. We will stick *to* the essential points so as to take *up* a minimum of your time.
4. You will be impressed *by* the information that we have brought *along* for you.

Task 9: Say it the sales way!

1. I *appreciate* that you're a very busy man.
2. I won't *take* up too much of your time.
3. Let's come *straight* to the point.
4. I *assure* you we're exactly *on target* for your needs.
5. If you allow me, sir, I'll just *recap* what we said.

Crossword power

							[1] R							
[2] S	[3] T	A	T	I	[4] O	N	E	R	Y					[5] N
	A				N		M							E
	R		[6] C			[7] R	E	C	[8] A	P		[9] R		U
	G		H				M		B		[10] C	A	L	L
	E		E				[11] B	U	S	Y		N		I
[12] S	T	O	C	K			E		C			G		C
U			K		[13] P	U	R	C	H	A	S	E		H
I					R				I				[14] R	
[15] T	[16] A	K	E		E		[17] P	U	R	P	O	S	E	
	G				F		O		M				C	
	R				E		I		E				A	
	E				R		N		N				L	
	E						T						L	
[18] A	D	V	E	R	T		S							

Task 10: Highlight your USPs (Unique Selling Points)

1. A typical *feature* of this device is reliability.
2. The primary *characteristic* of our service is rapidity.
3. I don't need to tell you the *advantages* of the ABS system.
4. I'd just like to describe the new *functions* of this gadget.

Task 11: Would you buy this product?

1. It has *failed* all the benchmarking tests.
2. It has been *rated* 'unsatisfactory' in a consumer magazine.
3. It hasn't *passed* the 'Elk test'.
4. It doesn't *cover* your requirements.

Task 12: Or would you rather buy this article?

1. It gives your customers a big *incentive* to buy.
2. It is the *latest* generation of our helicopters.
3. It technology is highly *advanced.*
4. It is *state of the art.*

Task 13: Where do these verbs belong?

1. Could you *quote* me a price for this copier?
2. I'd like to *place* an order for 20 copiers.
3. Can you *supply* us with the equipment from stock?
4. The consignment will be *collected* this morning.
5. Can you *dispatch* it at once?
6. How do you want us to *deliver* the goods?
7. I'm afraid I have to *register* a serious complaint.
8. Can we *cancel* the order?

Task 14: Word lover's corner

Verb	Noun	German
neglect	*negligence*	Nachlässigkeit
deliver	*delivery*	Lieferung
package	*packaging*	Verpackung
specify	*specifications*	Lastenheft
complain	*complaint*	Beschwerde

Task 15: Beef up your word power

1. The following *items* are missing.	*articles*
2. Some of the *parts* are defective.	*components*
3. I have to a *make a* serious complaint	*register*
4. You have not *kept* the deadline.	*met*

Task 16: How would you like the delivery to be made?

- by *rail,*
- by *road transport* or
- by *air freight?*

Task 17: Say it the other way round

1. The quality is *unsatisfactory.*
2. This kind of thing is *unacceptable.*
3. The shipment is *incomplete.*
4. The printing press is *unreliable.*
5. I am *dissatisfied* with your customer service.

Crossword power

	[1]C	A	L	L					[2]B				[3]T
	O				[4]W	A	S	T	E		[5]P		A
	[6]V	A	L	U	E				[7]S	T	O	C	K
	E				A				T		I		E
[8]T	R	Y		[9]B	R	I	E	[10]F		[11]O	N		
R				O				A			T		
[12]A	R	[13]T		S		[14]U		I					
D		A		E		[15]P	U	R	[16]P	O	[17]S	E	
E		R		W					R		E		
		G		I			[18]N		O		R		
	[19]F	E	A	T	U	R	E		V		V		[20]D
		T		Z			E		E		I		O
							D		N		C		W
			[21]L	I	N	E	S			[22]M	E	A	N

PART 5: NEGOTIATING PROFESSIONALLY

Task 1: Beef up your word power

1. We can { *allow* / *give* / *grant* / *offer* } a discount of 12% on our catalogue prices.

2. Customers expect { *cash* / *bulk / quantity* / *prompt payment* } discounts.

3. When a company offers a very low price there is often a { *catch* / *snag* / *hitch* } in it.

Task 2: Phrasesmith's workshop

1. *offer* good value for money
2. *strike* a compromise
3. *meet* someone halfway
4. *place* an order

Task 3: Guided translation

1. Why don't we *sort out* the main points first?
2. Then we can *tie up* the loose ends.
3. I thought prices would be *coming down* now.
4. Have you *checked with* our competitors?

Task 4: Word lover's corner

1. We might be able to *get round* this problem.
2. I think I could *go along* with your proposal.
3. I'm sure we can *come to* an agreement on that.
4. Why don't we *sort out* the main points first?

Task 5: Three phrases for „vorausgesetzt, daß"

We are willing to sign { *with the provision* / *provided* / *on the condition* } that you give us a reduction.

Crossword power

		1 I	N	2 S	U	3 R	A	N	4 C	E				5 Q
		M		I		E			A					U
		P		Z		P			6 S	I	7 D	E		A
8 Q	U	O	T	E		E			H		I			N
U		R			9 B	A	C	K			10 S	O	R	T
O		T		11 A		T					C			I
T		12 A	B	L	E				13 P	R	O	M	P	T
A		N		L		14 D					U			Y
T		T		O		E			15 F	I	N	A	L	
I				W		A			R		T			
O			16 B		17 P	L	A	C	E					
N			R		U				I		18 T			
		19 B	E	A	T	E	N		20 G	R	A	N	T	
			A						H		K			
21 B	U	L	K			22 M	E	E	T		E			

PART 6: MASTER YOUR MEETINGS

Task 1: Scrambled letters

1. Ladies and Gentlemen, I *declare* the meeting open.
2. I'm happy to *welcome* all of you today.
3. On behalf of the Board *allow* me to *extend* a warm welcome to you.
4. May I *apologise* for the fact that Director Block is late?
5. I *appreciate* that you are sacrificing a hour of your valuable time.

Task 2: Prepositions

1. I think we should also deal *with* the question of overtime.
2. This question is already covered *under* item 5.
3. Could we delete item 3 *from* the agenda?
4. Let's get *down to* business, shall we?
5. Let's start *with* the first item *on* the agenda.
6. I'd like to begin *by* congratulating Tom *on* his performance.

Task 3: Beef up your word power

1. I suggest we limit / *confine* ourselves to the most important questions.
2. I'd like to suggest / *propose* that we add the following items to the agenda.
3. I think we should also take up / *deal with* the question of whether we ...
4. Could we delete / *remove* item 3 from the agenda?

Task 4: People and functions

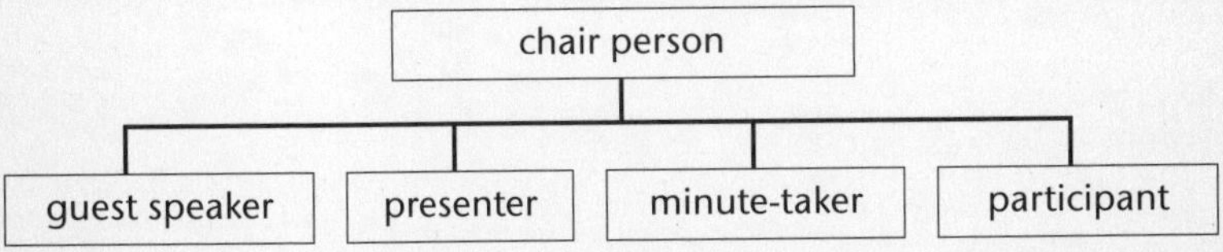

Task 5: Why meetings are held

Meetings should have *objectives* / *purposes* / *reasons* / *results*

Task 6: Six ways of asking for contributions

Tom, what's your

view *reaction* *opinion* *feeling* *position* *point of view?*

Task 7: Spot the mistake

1. The purpose of *today's* meeting is ...
2. I have the great pleasure *of introducing* Mr X.
3. We have the honour *of being addressed* by Mr X.
4. Mr X, We'*re* all *looking* forward to your presentation.
5. Let me say how *happy* I am to be able to attend this seminar.

Task 8: Beef up your word power

Add an expression that has the same meaning.

1. Perhaps Mrs Child would *care / like* to answer this question?
2. Could you *stick / keep* to the *point*, please?
3. I'd prefer to *move on to / turn to* item two.
4. I propose we *defer / postpone* this question until later.

Task 9: Speak your mind

1. Can I have your attention, please?
2. Tom, I'm afraid we're moving too far away from the subject.
3. I'd rather turn to the next point on the agenda.
4. I suggest we leave this matter until our next meeting.

Crossword power

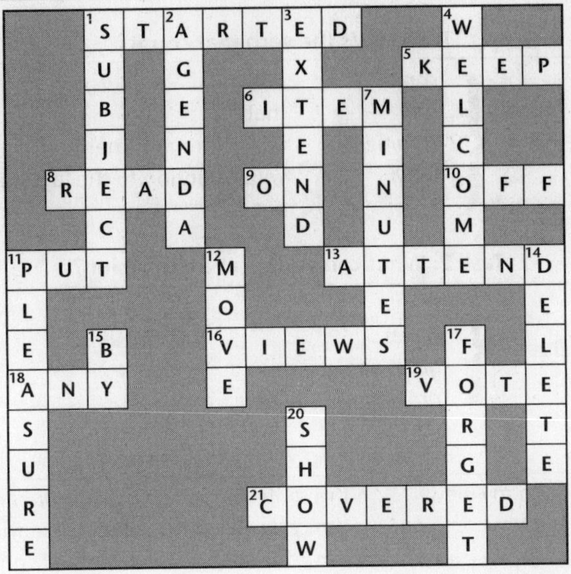

PART 7: DISCUSSING THE CLEVER WAY

Task 1: It's the verb that counts

If I might just	*come*	in here ...
	add	that ...
	comment	upon your argument ...
	draw	your attention to the fact that ...
	point	out that ...

Task 2: What can you do at a discussion?

You can raise	*points*
	issues
	questions
	problems

Task 3: Beef up your word power

I feel	In my view	I'm quite sure	You can *count* on that!
I *think*	In my *opinion*	I'm *certain*	You can *bet* on that!
I *believe*	In my *eyes*	I'm *convinced*	You can *rely* on that!

Task 4: Spot the mistake

1. I'd like to begin by *remembering you of* our last meeting.
2. I would like to *uplift* the importance of finding new markets in Asia.
3. As far as I'm *convinced* the main problem ist ...

Task 5: Add a suitable modal

1. And we *mustn't / shouldn't* lose sight of another problem.
2. This problem *cannot* be dealt with in isolation.
3. If I *might / may* just add something.

Task 6: Clear up the mess

1. In *addition* one might say that ...
2. Furthermore, it is important to *note* that ...
3. May I *introduce* a report that supports my statement?
4. I wish to *add* two sentences.
5. In this *connection* it is also important to consider that ...
6. What does that *mean* in practice?

Task 7: Guided translation

1. Let's weigh up the *options*, before *taking* a decision.
2. And we shouldn't *lose sight* of another problem.
3. It is important *to take into account / consider* the political situation.
4. *A case in point* is the success of our Yahoo.
5. Let's weigh up the *pros and cons* of this project.

Task 8: Word builder's corner: Suggesting

1. I propose that ...	My *proposal* is ...
2. I suggest that ...	My *suggestion* is ...
3. I advise you ...	My *advice* is ...
4. I recommend that ...	My *recommendation* is ...

Task 9: How to introduce your proposal

1. *Why not*	take	an early flight?
2. *Why don't*	we take	
3. *What / How about*	taking	
4. *Wouldn't it be better*	to take	

Task 10: What you can do with a suggestion

I'd like to	*put forward* *submit* *make*	a proposal
I can I can't I have to	*support* *accept* *reject*	this proposal

Crossword power

		1 A	T			2 P	O	I	N	3 T				
		D				U				4 A	B	5 O	U	6 T
		7 D	8 E	A	9 L	T		10 W		K		B		U
			X		O		11 G	I	V	E		J		R
12 P	R	O	P	O	S	E		T				E		N
R			R		E			H				C		
A			E			13 L				14 W	I	T	H	
15 C	O	N	S	I	D	E	R			E		S		
T			S			A		16 M	A	I	N			
I						D		I		G			17 S	
18 C	R	19 O	S	20 S		S		N		21 H	I	G	H	
E		F		I				D					A	
		F		G									D	
			22 W	H	O	L	E				23 P	R	O	S
				T									W	

Task 11: Spot the mistake

1. If I'*ve understood* you *correctly*, you're saying that ...?
2. Would I be *correct in saying* that ...?
3. Perhaps I should make this *clearer by* saying ...
4. I see it a little *differently*.

Task 12: Make your phrases more polite

1. I'm afraid there seems to have been *a slight* misunderstanding.
2. That isn't *quite* what I meant.
3. Isn't it *a bit* risky to trust this company?
4. But allow me to see it *a little* differently.
5. I'm *rather* disappointed with the performance of this robot.

Task 13: Guided Translation

1. We seem to *be talking at cross purposes*.
2. *Am I right in assuming* that you're suggesting a take-over?
3. That isn't *quite what I meant*.

4. I'm afraid I *didn't express myself clearly.*
5. Let *me put it this way.*

Task 14: Beef up your word power

1. May I *interrupt* you for a moment?
2. Excuse me, could I just *break in* a moment here?
3. If could I could just *come in* here.

Task 15: Pesky prepositions

1. May I come *in at* this point?
2. You took the words right *out* of my mouth.
3. I wonder if I might comment *upon* your last argument?
4. I shall be dealing *with* it in a moment.

Task 16: The place of the adverb

1. If I could *now* turn to another question.
2. If I could *just* continue.
3. With respect, I should *only* like to add this ...

Crossword power

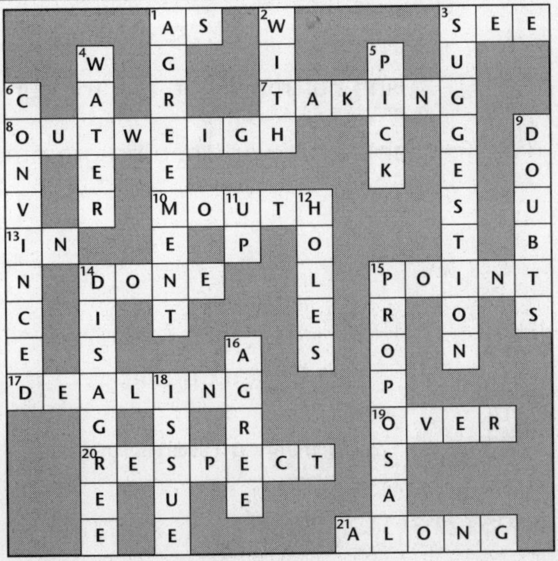